NORTHERN CALIFORNIA

The
CREAKY KNEES
Guide

THE **80** BEST EASY HIKES

NORTHERN CALIFORNIA

The CREAKY KNEES Guide

THE 80 BEST EASY HIKES

Ann Marie Brown

SASQUATCH BOOKS
SEATTLE

Printed in the United States of America
Published by Sasquatch Books
Distributed by PGW/Perseus
17 16 15 14 13 12 11   9 8 7 6 5 4 3 2 1

Cover photograph: © 2011 Radius Images/Inmagine
Cover design: Sarah Plein
Interior design: Rosebud Eustace
Author and interior photos: Ann Marie Brown
Maps: Lisa Brower/GreenEye
Interior composition: Sarah Plein

Library of Congress Cataloging-in-Publication Data is available.

ISBN-13: 978-1-57061-741-6

Important Note: Please use common sense. No guidebook can act as a substitute for
experience, careful planning, the right equipment, and appropriate training. There is
inherent danger in all the activities described in this book, and readers must assume
full responsibility for their own actions and safety. Changing or unfavorable conditions
in weather, roads, trails, snow, waterways, and so forth cannot be anticipated by the
author or publisher, but should be considered by any outdoor participants. The author
and publisher will not be responsible for the safety of users of this guide.

Sasquatch Books
119 South Main Street, Suite 400
Seattle, WA 98104
(206) 467-4300
www.sasquatchbooks.com
custserv@sasquatchbooks.com

SUSTAINABLE FORESTRY INITIATIVE
Certified Fiber Sourcing
Label applies to the text stock   www.sfiprogram.org

Contents

A banquet of peaks and precipices tower over Tuolumne Meadows and the rounded rock of Lembert Dome.

Hikes at a Glance

Stroll in the Park

NO.	HIKE NAME	RATING	BEST SEASON	KIDS	DOGS
77	Mark Twain Scenic Tufa Trail	🚶🚶🚶🚶🚶	Year-round	✔	

Easy Walk

NO.	HIKE NAME	RATING	BEST SEASON	KIDS	DOGS
2	Yurok Loop and Coastal Trail	🚶🚶🚶	Year-round	✔	
3	Fern Canyon Trail	🚶🚶🚶🚶	Year-round	✔	
6	Lady Bird Johnson Grove	🚶🚶🚶	Year-round	✔	
8	Rim Trail: Wedding Rock to Rocky Point	🚶🚶🚶🚶	Year-round	✔	
9	Hookton Slough Trail	🚶🚶🚶	Nov–Apr	✔	
10	Big Tree Area: Bull Creek Flats Trail	🚶🚶🚶🚶	Year-round	✔	
13	Root Creek Trail	🚶🚶🚶	Year-round	✔	
14	Headwaters and Pacific Crest Trails	🚶🚶🚶🚶	Year-round	✔	
15	Hat Creek Trail to Pit River	🚶🚶🚶	Year-round	✔	✔
19	Bumpass Hell Trail	🚶🚶🚶🚶	Jul–Oct	✔	
20	Mill Creek Falls	🚶🚶🚶🚶	Jun–Oct	✔	
21	La Laguna Trail	🚶🚶🚶	Year-round	✔	
24	Big Hendy Grove and Hermit Hut Trails	🚶🚶🚶	Year-round	✔	
26	Bluff Trail	🚶🚶🚶🚶	Year-round	✔	
27	Fort Ross Cove Trail	🚶🚶🚶🚶	Year-round	✔	
33	Wetlands Walking Trail	🚶🚶🚶	Nov–May	✔	
34	Fairy Falls (aka Shingle Falls)	🚶🚶🚶	Dec–May	✔	✔
36	South Yuba Independence Trail	🚶🚶🚶	Dec–Jun	✔	✔
37	Hidden Falls	🚶🚶🚶	Nov–May	✔	✔
38	Codfish Creek Falls	🚶🚶🚶	Dec–May	✔	✔
42	Cosumnes River Walk–Lost Slough Wetlands Walk	🚶🚶🚶	Nov–May	✔	
45	Kehoe Beach	🚶🚶🚶🚶	Year-round	✔	✔
50	Bay View and Red Hill Loop	🚶🚶🚶	Year-round	✔	✔
55	Año Nuevo Point Trail	🚶🚶🚶🚶	Year-round	✔	
60	Cascade Falls Trail	🚶🚶🚶🚶	Jun–Oct	✔	✔
61	Angora Lakes Trail	🚶🚶🚶🚶	Jun–Oct	✔	✔
69	Lukens Lake Trail	🚶🚶🚶🚶	Jun–Oct	✔	
72	Sentinel Dome	🚶🚶🚶🚶	Jun–Oct	✔	

NO.	HIKE NAME	RATING	BEST SEASON	KIDS	DOGS
73	Taft Point Trail	(5 hikers)	Jun–Oct	✔	
76	Bennettville Mine and Mine Creek	(5 hikers)	Jul–Oct	✔	✔

Moderate Workout

NO.	HIKE NAME	RATING	BEST SEASON	KIDS	DOGS
1	Enderts Beach Trail	(4 hikers)	Year-round	✔	✔
4	Brown Creek, Rhododendron, South Fork Loop	(4 hikers)	Year-round	✔	
5	Skunk Cabbage and Coastal Trail	(4 hikers)	Year-round	✔	
7	Tall Trees Grove	(4 hikers)	Year-round	✔	
11	Castle Lake and Heart Lake	(4 hikers)	May–Oct	✔	✔
12	McCloud Falls Trail	(4 hikers)	Year-round	✔	✔
17	Kings Creek Falls	(4 hikers)	Jun–Oct	✔	
18	Terrace, Shadow, and Cliff Lakes	(4 hikers)	Jul–Oct	✔	
22	Ecological Staircase Nature Trail	(4 hikers)	Year-round	✔	
23	Fern Canyon and Falls Loop Trails	(4 hikers)	Dec–May	✔	
25	Chinese Gulch and Phillips Gulch Trails	(3 hikers)	Apr–Jun	✔	
30	Ritchey Canyon and Coyote Peak	(3 hikers)	Year-round	✔	
31	Lake Ilsanjo Loop	(3 hikers)	Year-round	✔	
32	Lake and Fallen Bridge Loop	(3 hikers)	Year-round	✔	
39	Table Mountain	(3 hikers)	Feb–May	✔	✔
40	Hardrock Trail	(3 hikers)	Feb–Jun	✔	✔
43	Tomales Point Trail	(4 hikers)	Year-round	✔	
44	Bear Valley Trail to Arch Rock	(4 hikers)	Year-round	✔	
46	North Ridge and Sunset Trail Loop	(4 hikers)	Year-round	✔	
47	Coastal, Cataract, and Old Mine Loop	(4 hikers)	Year-round	✔	
48	Ocean View, Lost Trail, and Fern Creek Loop	(4 hikers)	Year-round	✔	
49	Huckleberry Path	(3 hikers)	Year-round	✔	
52	Russian Ridge Loop	(4 hikers)	Year-round	✔	
53	Peters Creek and Long Ridge Loop	(4 hikers)	Year-round	✔	
56	Grass Lake Trail	(4 hikers)	Jun–Oct	✔	✔
57	Sardine Lakes Trail	(4 hikers)	Jun–Oct	✔	✔
58	Wild Plum Loop	(4 hikers)	May–Nov	✔	✔
59	Rubicon Point and Lighthouse Loop	(5 hikers)	Jun–Oct	✔	
66	Pyramid Creek Loop	(4 hikers)	May–Oct	✔	✔
68	Merced Grove of Giant Sequoias	(4 hikers)	May–Nov	✔	
70	Lembert Dome Trail	(5 hikers)	Jun–Oct	✔	

71	McGurk Meadow and Dewey Point	🚶🚶🚶🚶	Jun–Oct	✔	
78	Parker Lake Trail	🚶🚶🚶🚶	Jun–Oct	✔	✔
79	Devils Postpile and Rainbow Falls	🚶🚶🚶🚶🚶	Jun–Oct	✔	
80	Heart Lake, Mammoth Consolidated Gold Mine	🚶🚶🚶🚶	Jun–Oct	✔	✔

Prepare to Perspire

NO.	HIKE NAME	RATING	BEST SEASON	KIDS	DOGS
16	Chaos Crags and Crags Lake	🚶🚶🚶🚶	Jun–Aug	✔	
28	Pomo Canyon Trail	🚶🚶🚶	Spring, Fall	✔	
29	Table Rock	🚶🚶🚶	Oct–Apr	✔	
35	Stevens Trail	🚶🚶🚶🚶	Dec–May	✔	✔
41	Feather Falls	🚶🚶🚶🚶🚶	Jan–Jun	✔	✔
51	Purisima Redwoods Loop	🚶🚶🚶🚶	Year-round	✔	
54	Saratoga Gap and Ridge Trail Loop	🚶🚶🚶🚶	Year-round	✔	
62	Glen Alpine Trail to Susie Lake	🚶🚶🚶🚶🚶	Jun–Oct	✔	✔
63	Dardanelles and Round Lakes	🚶🚶🚶🚶	Jun–Oct	✔	✔
64	Emigrant Lake	🚶🚶🚶🚶	Jun–Oct	✔	✔
65	Winnemucca and Round Top Lake Loop	🚶🚶🚶🚶🚶	Jun–Oct	✔	✔
67	Twin and Island Lakes	🚶🚶🚶🚶🚶	Jun–Oct	✔	✔
74	Panorama Trail to Illilouette Fall	🚶🚶🚶🚶	Jun–Oct	✔	
75	Mariposa Grove	🚶🚶🚶🚶	May–Nov	✔	

INTRODUCTION

Twenty years ago, I worked very long hours behind a desk five or six days a week, putting in plenty of overtime and spending way too much time indoors. In my precious free time I tried to get out into nature as much as possible, but with all of life's demands, I rarely had more than a few hours each week to play outdoors. On top of that, I was frequently plagued with injuries to my knees and hips—most likely a result of my chained-to-the-office lifestyle.

But one day I made a decision to commit more of my life to the beauty of the great outdoors, and I began that journey on the trails in this book. These trails are suitable and fun for almost everybody, regardless of your fitness level or how creaky your knees are. When you hike these trails, you can bring along your children, your grandma, or your spouse who thinks the "great outdoors" is nothing but mosquitoes and poison oak. Every trail in this book was chosen because it offers a good payoff—a reason for going besides the exercise. These eighty hikes lead you away from pavement, exhaust fumes, and crowds, to places where you'd rather be: sparkling waterfalls, scenic viewpoints, and peaceful forests.

To choose these hikes, I walked every trail in this book, most of them many times over. I also hiked plenty of other trails that didn't make the cut, often because they were too difficult or too dull to ensure that everybody would have fun. I also made extensive use of "field testers": I brought along my eighty-year-old mom. I forced my not-so-enthusiastic-about-hiking friends to traipse along with me. I even made my friends' kids tag along (and usually they were way out in front).

During my travels, what I found out is that there are plenty of Northern California trails designed for ordinary people, not just Mr. or Ms. Hardcore Outdoors Enthusiast. And when ordinary people hike those trails, they feel happy.

I hope to see you (and your children, grandmas, and spouses) out there . . .

—Ann Marie Brown

USING THIS GUIDE

by Seabury Blair Jr., author of *The Creaky Knees Guide
Washington* and *The Creaky Knees Guide Oregon*

The beginning of each trail description is intended to give you quick information that can help you decide whether the specific day hike is one that interests you. Here's what you'll find:

TRAIL NUMBER AND NAME

Trails are numbered in this guide following the main highway corridors in seven geographic regions in Northern California: North Coast and Redwoods; Shasta and Lassen; Mendocino, Sonoma, and Napa; Sacramento and Gold Country; San Francisco Bay Area; Lake Tahoe and the Northern Sierra; and Yosemite and Mammoth Lakes.

OVERALL RATING

Rating Creaky Knees hikes was difficult for me. "In the first place," I asked the very wise and generous editor, "why would anyone want to take a hike I rate with only one star? A guidebook should only outline hikes that are worth taking, not dung-heap trails you wouldn't recommend to a psycho killer."

He replied: "True, but you must distinguish between the very best trails—with five stars—and the trails that aren't quite so good—with one to four stars." The trails that really suck (and I paraphrase here because editors are much too refined to use that term) won't be outlined here. Some hikes may not be as good as others, but they are all better than the ones that really bite.

Another problem I had was attempting to be objective in rating the trails. I'm a pushover for hikes above timberline, where the wildflowers wave in gentle summer breezes, where mountains claw the clouds, where cooling snowfields linger through summer. So I may have rated these trails higher than you might rate them.

If you're a hiker who loves walking along rattling rivers or past forested lakes, or padding on rain-forest trails softened by mosses, I'd suggest you add one star to every lowland hike and subtract one star from every alpland hike in this guide.

Finally, objective criteria like trail conditions, trail length, and obstacles such as creek crossings can affect the overall rating. On the other hand, you can forget all that junk and just take my word for it.

DISTANCE

The distance listed is round-trip, exclusive of any side trips mentioned along the way. If these excursions off the main trail are longer than 0.2 mile or so, I'll mention it in the description of the hike.

In an effort to prove that trails indeed are getting longer as I grow older, I pushed a bike wheel equipped with a cyclometer around some of the trails in this guide and packed a GPS on others. I learned to my disappointment that trails aren't getting longer—although there are notable exceptions—and that I might have equipped myself better by carrying my own oxygen supply instead of a bloody heavy bike wheel or a GPS unit that is allergic to fir and pine forests.

HIKING TIME

This is an estimate of the time it takes the average hiker to walk the trail round-trip. Since none of us are average hikers, you may feel free to ignore this entry.

For the most part, I calculated the pace on the trail to be about 2 miles per hour. I assumed the pace might slow on trails with significant elevation gain or loss and tried to err on the conservative side. It's my hope that many of you will wonder what sort of trail slug came up with such ridiculously long hiking times.

ELEVATION GAIN

This is a calculation of the total number of feet you'll have to climb on the trail. Don't assume, as one fool early in his hiking days did (I have since learned better), that all of the elevation will be gained on the way to your destination. Some of these trails actually lose elevation on the way and gain it on the return, or alternately gain and lose elevation along the way. It has always been a source of wonder to me that on a round-trip hike, you always gain the same amount of elevation that you lose.

HIGH POINT

This is the highest point above sea level you'll reach on any given hike. In cases like the ocean beach walks, it is always at the trailhead.

EFFORT

This was another tough one for me. I've been hiking for so many years it is a task to remember what it was like to take some of these hikes as a novice. My good friend Grizzly Hemingway once turned back from a hike after encountering a footlog that was too high to cross—a log I had forgotten scared the pee out of me the first time I crossed it, too.

So again, I tried to be conservative in judging the effort it would take to finish each hike. Where previous guides discussed overall difficulty of the trail, I thought the energy expended to hike out and back might be more meaningful. A hike might be difficult, for example, if you had to walk that footlog, but the rest of the trail could be flat as a pancake griddle, requiring no more effort than a stroll in the park. Thus you'll find the following categories:

A **Stroll in the Park** will serve up few, if any, hills to climb and is generally between 1 and 3 miles long round-trip, a hike suitable for families with small children.

On a hike rated as an **Easy Walk**, you might expect to find longer, but still gently graded, hills and trails around 2 to 4 miles long round-trip.

A hike described as a **Moderate Workout** would be one with longer grades and elevation changes greater than about 500 feet from beginning to high point, hikes between 3 and 5 miles long round-trip.

A hike rated **Prepare to Perspire** is one that will make your deodorant fail you, no matter your excellent physical condition. It will have sustained steep climbs of at least 1 mile, with elevation gain and loss greater than 1,000 feet, and is about 4 to 6 miles long round-trip.

A **Knee-Punishing** hike is one that will challenge your physical abilities beyond what you might expect you can accomplish, one that will send you rushing to the anti-inflammatory shelf in your medicine cabinet upon your return. (The good news is there are no Knee-Punishing hikes in this book!)

BEST SEASON
Here is my suggestion for the months I think you'd most enjoy this hike, as well as whether the path will be free of snow throughout the year.

PERMITS/CONTACT
Many of the trails in this book cost nothing to hike, but some—particularly those located in state or national parks—require that you pay a park entrance fee or a trailhead parking fee. Hikers who are fortunate enough to have been on earth 62 years or longer qualify for an America the Beautiful Senior Pass, which, at $10 for life, buys you entrance to most national parks (but not state parks) and gives you half-price camping at National Forest campgrounds. A few trails—particularly those in the Desolation Wilderness and Mokelumne Wilderness near Lake Tahoe—do

not require hikers to pay any fee, but do require that they fill out a free self-serve wilderness permit at the trailhead. This allows the National Forest rangers to keep track of how many people are using the wilderness and for what purpose: day-hiking or backpacking.

MAPS
For every trail in this book, I've listed a map that you might want to carry along on your hike. Some of these are USGS topographic maps, which are available from www.usgs.gov or (888) 275-8747. Others are maps produced by Tom Harrison Cartography, which are available from www.tomharrisonmaps.com or (415) 456-7940. Still others are national or state park maps, which are available from the managing agency of the park you are visiting (and often available by free download from the Internet). Always carry a map with you when you hike; it is your best guarantee of returning safely back to the trailhead.

TRAIL NOTES
Here are some regulations specific to each hike you'll most likely want to know: whether leashed pets can accompany you, whether you'll encounter mountain bikes on the trail, or whether an interpretive brochure for the trail is available at the trailhead. If there are other circumstances about the hike you might need to know, such as whether you'll fry if you hike the trail in summer, we'll mention it here.

THE HIKE
This is an attempt to convey the feel of the trail in a sentence or two, including the type of trail and whether there's a one-way hiking option.

GETTING THERE
Here's where you'll find out how to get to the trailhead. You'll also learn the elevation at the trailhead, so you can get an idea about what sort of terrain and climate you'll likely encounter. All of the hikes are organized according to the major highway corridors you'll follow to get to each trailhead. I've tried to indicate starting points along those corridors, such as cities or towns, or major highway junctions.

THE TRAIL
Here's where you'll get the blow-by-blow, mile-by-mile description of the trail. I've tried to stick to information your feet will find useful and apologize if, every now and then, I look up to recognize an awesome

view or rhapsodize about something absolutely without redeeming social or cultural value.

GOING FARTHER

This is an important category in this guide, because many of you might find some of these hikes too easy, while others will be ready to turn around before they reach my recommended spot. For that reason, I've tried to include a suggestion for extending every hike from the same trailhead—or from a nearby trailhead that can be accessed before your heart rate decreases or your joints stiffen.

BE CAREFUL

(Thanks to Seabury Blair Jr, author of *The Creaky Knees Guide Washington* and *The Creaky Knees Guide Oregon*, for his substantial contributions to this section.)

It is all too easy on a warm, sunny day on the trail to forget all of the stuff you ought to be carrying in your pack. Day hikers especially are likely to leave that extra fleece sweater or that waterproof, breathable outer layer in the trunk. Some folks even forget that First Essential—a hiking partner. Never hike alone.

Virtually all the time, day hikers who forget one or two of the basic rules for safe wilderness travel return to the trailhead smiling and healthy. No trail cop is going to cite you for negligent hiking if you have only nine of the Ten Essentials, or if you hit the trail without registering or telling someone where you're going.

I dislike preaching safety—if you looked in my pack on a good-weather day hike, you might find my extra clothing consists of a spare do-rag and my map clearly shows the hike I took last week. Perhaps the only weighty argument anyone can make to convince another day hiker to follow the rules for safe travel in the out-of-doors is to remind them of the annual, avoidable tragedies that occur because hikers ignore those rules.

First—no matter the distance or difficulty of the hike—please carry the Ten Essentials in your pack. With no apologies to those credit card people: don't leave home without them.

The Ten Essentials include:

🥾 A topographic map of the area.

🥾 A compass, and the ability to use it in conjunction with the map. While excellent aids to navigation, portable GPS units are no substitute for a compass that does not require batteries or satellite reception.

🥾 Extra clothing, which should consist of a top and bottom insulating layer and a waterproof, windproof layer. A hat or cap is absolutely essential: mountaineers will tell you that when your feet are cold, put on your hat. It works. In the high elevations of the Sierra Nevada, even in summer, it's also smart to carry a pair of gloves.

🥾 Food and water. Even if you aren't the least bit hungry or thirsty when you park at the trailhead, you will probably feel completely different after an hour or more on the trail. A small day pack can keep you happily supplied with a couple bottles of water and a few tasty snacks. I like to carry "extra" food for emergencies, too. To avoid needlessly grazing on my extra food, I try to pick something I would only eat if I were starving. Stuff like freeze-dried turnips or breakfast bars that taste like pressed sawdust fire starters. In fact, some of my extra food can be used as emergency fire starters.

⚸ A flashlight with extra batteries and bulbs. I carry a headlamp because it allows me to swat at the moths that fly into the light without dropping the bloody flashlight. Many of these lights have spare bulbs built in. Lithium batteries, though more expensive, make excellent spares because their shelf life is longer than yours.

⚸ A first-aid kit. You can buy these already assembled, and they are excellent. Consider one thing, however: the type of injury that is likely to incapacitate a day hiker will probably be different than that suffered by a backpacker.

If your first-aid kit doesn't include wraps for sprains, add an ankle support, at the very least. Blister treatment for day hikers is another essential. And make sure your kit includes a lightweight space blanket or sleeping bag made of Mylar film, which will keep you warm in any emergency. These weigh next to nothing and come wrapped in a package about the size of a deck of cards.

⚸ Matches in a waterproof case. Although butane lighters are often carried as a substitute, both altitude and temperature can affect their performance.

⚸ A fire starter. Candles work well, along with a variety of lightweight commercial fire starters.

⚸ A pocketknife. In addition to the all-important corkscrew, my Swiss Army knife has 623 blades, including a tiny chain saw.

⚸ Sunglasses and sunscreen, plus high-SPF lip protection.

In addition to these items, most day hikers never hit the trail without toting some toilet paper in a plastic bag and perhaps some type of bug repellent on summer hikes. A loud emergency whistle is a lightweight addition. Binoculars may help you find your route if you become lost and are worth the weight simply for watching wildlife.

WEATHER

No matter where you're hiking, learn to read the clouds and wind and learn the general rules that may keep you safer or more comfortable. Northern California offers a cornucopia of landscapes, terrain, and weather conditions, and reading the weather at the coast is a far different matter than reading the weather above 8,000 feet in the mountains. At the coast, the biggest weather-related danger is usually rogue waves, which can sweep hikers off rocks and blufftop promontories. In the mountains, one of the biggest dangers to day hikers is the possibility of getting caught in a thunderstorm. Always stay off high peaks if clouds are building. Also remember that in the mountains, the weather is extremely variable and it can snow in any month of the year, so carrying extra clothing is more than just a good idea. I like to think of Mother Nature as a schizoid who is most often a friendly, generous old lady who bakes cookies and bread for you, but when you least expect it, puts on a goalie's mask and whacks at you with an icicle or lightning bolt.

So be prepared, Scouts.

WATER

Water is available from natural sources (rivers, streams, lakes, ponds, and springs) in many places in Northern California, but it's never wise to rely solely on finding natural water. In drought years, conditions can vary greatly, and a once-reliable water source can go completely dry. Always carry a couple of quarts of water with you, and if you do obtain water from a natural source, be sure to protect yourself against *Giardia lamblia, cryptosporidium,* and other microorganisms that can make you very, very sick. Protection is easy; simply filter, purify, or otherwise decontaminate your water before drinking it. My favorite way to purify water, whether I'm day-hiking or backpacking, is to use a regular water bottle and an ultraviolet light device (the Steripen is a popular model). Stick the UV lamp in a bottle of water you've filled from a lake or stream, swirl it around for two minutes, and voila—your water is safe to drink. Filter pumps are also very easy to use; the simplest versions are quart-sized water bottles that come equipped with their own filters (Katadyn MyBottle, Exstream, and Aquamira are well-known brands). Simply fill the bottle from any water source (taking extreme care not to contaminate the mouthpiece or drinking cap), drop the filter into place, and screw on the top, and you're ready to drink filtered water. When comparing various filters, always look for an absolute (not minimal) pore size of 0.2 microns, to be sure you are eliminating all the bad stuff.

WILDLIFE

Most animals that share the Northern California wilderness are benign, and seeing wildlife can be a memorable highlight of your hike. Day hikers certainly needn't fear black bears, which are quite common through the Sierra Nevada and parts of Northern California, but they must realize these are wild animals that can cause serious injury if provoked. If you spot a black bear along the trail, it will most likely run away from you, but if you leave your pack lying on the ground, it will most certainly try to garner possession of your peanut butter sandwich. Bears think about little else besides food, as anyone who has ever camped in the Sierra can tell you. Always respect a bear's personal space, and never get between a cub and its mother. If you encounter a black bear on the trail, make certain it knows you're there by addressing it in a calm voice (it will probably run off at this point), give it a wide berth, and count yourself fortunate for seeing it.

A greater potential danger is from mountain lions, which live in almost all areas of Northern California, but are only very rarely seen by humans. You have a much greater chance of being struck by lightning than of getting attacked by a mountain lion in Northern California, but the few lion attacks that do occur are widely publicized and strike fear into the hearts of many hikers. Trailhead signs will tell you how to respond if you are confronted by a mountain lion on the trail. Generally, you must face the animal down. Don't turn your back on it or bend down to get something to throw at it. Maintain eye contact at all times, and make yourself appear as large and threatening as possible. Shouting, opening your jacket and waving your arms wildly, or barking like a dog may send the animal off into the woods.

Perhaps the best way to protect yourself from the possibility of a mountain lion attack is to always hike with a companion or two. When attacking, cougars appear to be so focused on their prey that they completely ignore other people. Even when companions open a big can of whup-ass on that kitty, they are likely to escape a retaliatory attack. Those attacked by cougars can be saved by companions who most likely won't suffer injury from the animal.

Less dangerous but more common hazards to day hikers might include stinging and biting pests, particularly mosquitoes and ticks. Liberal doses of insect repellent can take care of these unwanted companions, and wearing pants and long-sleeved shirts will also help. If you don't like the idea of applying hard-to-pronounce chemicals on your skin, try some of the "natural" bug repellents on the market, which typically contain eucalyptus and lemon oils. They may not work as effectively as 100 percent DEET, but they won't melt your car's dashboard, either.

If you are hiking in a woodsy, grassy area, which is prime tick territory, always check your skin and clothing after your hike to make sure you don't have any ticks crawling on you. Only a very small percentage of Northern California's ticks carry Lyme disease, but even a non-disease-carrying tick has a painful bite. Rid yourself of these critters before they settle into your skin for a meal. If you do get bitten by a tick, watch for flu-like symptoms such as headaches, muscle soreness, neck stiffness, or nausea in the weeks following the bite. If you experience any of these, see a doctor immediately and tell him or her that you suspect Lyme disease. Caught in its early stages, Lyme disease is easily treatable with antibiotics, but left untreated, it can be severely debilitating.

Rattlesnakes are the only poisonous snakes found in Northern California; all other snakes are completely harmless. Rattlesnakes can live almost anywhere below 6,000 feet, but they tend to prefer rocky, warm areas. On warm days, they can sometimes be found sunning themselves on the trail. To enjoy a safe, bite-free hike, simply watch out for them and if you see one, give it a wide berth. Sometimes hikers will hear the snake's rattle before they actually see the snake. If you hear a rattling sound, freeze and look around—you may be just about to place your foot on a rattlesnake. Also, be careful when placing your hands or feet under rocks, where a snake may be lying. Be especially on the lookout for rattlesnakes in the spring, when they leave their winter burrows and come out in the sun. Although rattlesnake bites are very painful, they are rarely fatal. Each year, more than 100 people in California are bitten by rattlesnakes, but there are an average of only one or two fatalities. If you get bitten by a rattlesnake, your car key or cell phone is your best first aid. Call 911 or get yourself to a hospital as soon as possible to be treated.

TROUBLESOME PLANTS

Poison oak grows near the coast and in the lower-elevation foothills, but is easily avoided by learning to identify the plants. Remember the Boy Scout motto: "Leaves of three, let them be." But also remember that poison oak wears different disguises in different seasons. In winter, it loses its leaves completely, but it's still poisonous. If you happen to brush up against poison oak, you can often prevent a rash from developing by washing thoroughly with a product like Tecnu as soon as you return from your hike. Two other products on the market, Zanfel and Biji, are fairly effective for diminishing a poison oak rash after it has developed. If you are hiking above 5,000 feet in elevation, you don't have to worry about brushing up against this meddlesome plant.

Another common plant pest is stinging nettle, which grows along some coastal trails, and is especially prolific in Point Reyes National Seashore. Again, learn to recognize this plant and then simply steer clear of it. Your best protection against plant rashes (and tick bites, too) is to always stay on the trail and avoid venturing off into the brushy, uncleared areas alongside the trail.

Fern Canyon's 30-foot-high walls create a lush riparian corridor.

NORTH COAST AND REDWOODS

Land of the tallest trees, dwelling place of the giants . . . California's northwest coast is home to some of the world's largest remaining stands of old-growth *Sequoia sempervirens*, or coast redwoods. These magnificent trees grow to more than 350 feet tall and live as long as 2,000 years. Nowhere else in California can we gaze upward at such an abundance of the world's tallest living things.

Although a redwood forest is considered to be a monosystem, many other plants thrive alongside the big trees, including ferns of all kinds, vine maples, huckleberry, salmonberry, and redwood sorrel. Per square inch of land surface, redwood forests have the greatest volume of living matter of any ecosystem in the world.

This part of California also features a wealth of wildlife, most notably its herds of giant Roosevelt elk. The adult males can weigh more than 1,000 pounds; their larger-than-life stature and huge antlers are aptly suited to the towering redwood forests. Black bears roam the groves of big trees. Mountain lions and bobcats prefer the high grassland prairies, which are also good birding spots. The rivers and streams of the North Coast, particularly the Smith and Klamath Rivers, are renowned for steelhead and salmon fishing.

No wonder these precious resources are preserved under the umbrella of Redwood National and State Parks, a co-managed park system that extends for 50 miles up the California coast and includes Redwood National Park, Jedediah Smith Redwoods State Park, Prairie Creek Redwoods State Park, and Del Norte Coast Redwoods State Park. Clearly this is land worth protecting.

When you go, don't forget your rain jacket: this is also the wettest climate zone in the state, receiving an average of 75 inches of rain per year. But that's what makes the trees grow to such epic proportions.

NORTH COAST AND REDWOODS

1. Enderts Beach Trail

RATING	🚶 🚶 🚶 🚶 🚶
DISTANCE	1.8 miles round-trip
HIKING TIME	1 hour
ELEVATION GAIN	250 feet
HIGH POINT	250 feet
EFFORT	Moderate Workout
BEST SEASON	Year-round
PERMITS/CONTACT	Redwood National and State Parks, (707) 465-7335, www.nps.gov/redw
MAPS	Redwood National and State Parks (download at www.nps.gov/redw/planyourvisit)
NOTES	Dogs allowed; check a tide table for best tide-pooling times

THE HIKE

Leave the shady redwood forests behind on this windswept hike to one of Crescent City's most scenic beaches, complete with rocky tidepools and brayed, tan sands.

GETTING THERE

From Crescent City, drive three miles south on U.S. 101 and turn right (south) on Enderts Beach Road. Drive 2.2 miles to the end of the road. The trailhead parking lot is just beyond Crescent Beach Overlook.

THE TRAIL

The Enderts Beach Trail leads to a long stretch of rock- and driftwood-strewn beach with rich tide-pooling opportunities. Be sure to check the tide table at the trailhead bulletin board or park visitor center so you can time your trip for low tide, when the most interesting sea creatures will be revealed.

The trip begins where Enderts Beach Road ends near Crescent Beach Overlook, just a few miles south of Crescent City. The trail is an old abandoned road that has partly collapsed into the sea. This was the former Coast Highway used by travelers before the present-day Highway 101 was built. Clearly Mother Nature isn't finished with her demolition

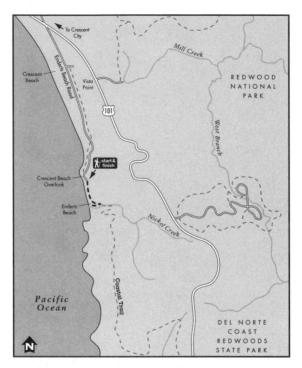

yet: You'll pass by an impressive landslide just a short distance from the parking area.

Most of the route is wide enough for holding hands with your hiking partner, and it's just a simple downhill walk of 0.6 mile to a three-way trail junction. A short nature trail alongside Nickel Creek leads left, straight ahead is the Coastal Trail heading south, and to the right is the path to Nickel Creek Campground and Enderts Beach. Before you make a beeline for Enderts Beach, take a side trip on the 0.25-mile Nickel Creek Nature Trail, which passes by a grove of remarkable fern-covered trees. Licorice ferns grow high off the ground on tree branches and trunks. Alongside Nickel Creek they hang off tree limbs from every possible angle, looking like massive, leafy beehives. This short nature trail ends abruptly at a viewing bench by the creek. Have a seat and remind yourself that you're in the northwest corner of California—judging by your surroundings, you could be in Florida's Everglades.

From Nickel Creek, return to the junction and follow the opposite trail into Nickel Creek Campground. This oh-so-easy-to-reach backpacking camp would make a great overnight trip. Check out its five campsites, make a mental note for a future visit, then take the right fork that leads

A tent site at Nickel Creek Campground provides 24-hour access to spectacular Enderts Beach.

uphill above the restroom. In a matter of minutes you reach a grassy bluff above a long, crescent-shaped beach. Enderts Beach is rocky and driftwood-strewn, but it also has large sandy stretches where you can lay out your towel. If the tide is low and you want to check out the tide-pools, hike along the beach to the south (some tidepools are also found on the beach's north end, but the southern pools are more plentiful). Common sightings include the giant green anemone, black chiton, opal-escent nudibranch, leather sea star, red sea urchin, purple shore crab, and ochre sea star. Remember to leave everything exactly where you found it; no collecting of sea creatures is permitted.

At certain times of the year, park rangers lead visitors on guided tide-pool walks at Enderts Beach. Check with the ranger station in Crescent City for information on current dates and times.

GOING FARTHER
After visiting Enderts Beach, return to the junction before Nickel Creek Campground where the Coastal Trail heads south. Hike south on the Coastal Trail for as far as you like, passing through redwood, spruce, and red alder forests interspersed with open coastal bluffs.

2. Yurok Loop and Coastal Trail

RATING	🚶 🚶 🚶
DISTANCE	2.25 miles round-trip
HIKING TIME	1 hour
ELEVATION GAIN	Negligible
HIGH POINT	50 feet
EFFORT	Easy Walk
BEST SEASON	Year-round
PERMITS/CONTACT	Redwood National and State Parks, (707) 465-7335, www.nps.gov/redw
MAPS	Redwood National and State Parks (download at www.nps.gov/redw/planyourvisit)
NOTES	Dogs prohibited; interpretive brochure available at the trailhead

THE HIKE

Great bird-watching opportunities, dramatic sea stacks, and a scenic beach complete with crashing waves are the highlights of this hike.

GETTING THERE

From Crescent City, drive south on U.S. 101 for approximately 14 miles. Turn right at the sign for Lagoon Creek Fishing Access/Picnic Area. The trail begins on the northwest (ocean) side of the parking lot. (Coming from the south, the trailhead is located 6 miles north of Klamath.)

THE TRAIL

Everybody likes walking along a beach at the end of a day, watching the waves come in and the sun dip into the water. But few enjoy facing the gale-force winds that attack the coast on so many days in Northern California. That's what makes the semiprotected Yurok Loop a great little trail, especially when combined with a short section of the Coastal Trail that leads to spectacular Hidden Beach.

Begin hiking at the northwest end of the Lagoon Creek parking lot. You'll cross a bridge and then head north toward the ocean. The Yurok Loop is an interpretive trail with numbered posts keyed to its brochure, which is usually available from a box at the bridge. Pick up a brochure

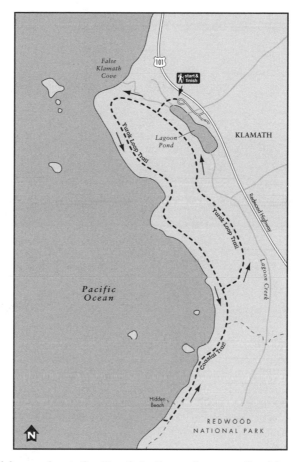

and you'll learn about the Yurok Indians who once lived here. The trail is an ancient Yurok Indian pathway leading south along the sea bluffs, alternating between oak and alder forest and open, grassy areas. Capturing your attention are the views of driftwood-laden False Klamath Cove to the north and massive False Klamath Rock to the west. At 209 feet tall, this huge rocky outcrop dwarfs all the other sea stacks in the area. The Yurok Indians used to dig for the bulbs of brodiaea plants (called "Indian potatoes") by this rock.

Stay to the right when the trail forks at the sign for the Coastal Trail, saving the second part of the Yurok Loop for your return. Ramble along the Coastal Trail, a forested, fern-lined route. In 0.5 mile of mostly level walking, you'll meet up with the spur trail to Hidden Beach. Follow it to the right for 100 yards to reach a classic Northern California stretch

Jagged offshore outcrops add drama to the shoreline at Hidden Beach.

of sand, complete with jagged sea stacks, mighty waves, and drift-wood of all shapes and sizes. Pull out your binoculars; seabirds such as cormorants, pigeon guillemots, brown pelicans, and common murres can often be seen resting on the sea stacks. Hidden Beach is prime for sunset-watching, but you might want to carry a flashlight in case it gets dark sooner than you expect.

For your return from the beach, head back the way you came on the Coastal Trail. This time turn right and walk the other side of the Yurok Loop, descending through a tunnel-like canopy of alders.

When you return to the parking lot, be sure to explore around the freshwater pond on Lagoon Creek. It's covered with big yellow pond lilies and happy waterbirds, including ducks, egrets, and herons. The pond is also popular with trout fishermen.

GOING FARTHER
From Hidden Beach, you can continue south on the Coastal Trail. The path leads another 3 miles to Klamath Overlook.

3. Fern Canyon Trail

RATING	🚶 🚶 🚶 🚶
DISTANCE	0.75 mile round-trip
HIKING TIME	30 minutes
ELEVATION GAIN	Negligible
HIGH POINT	40 feet
EFFORT	Easy Walk
BEST SEASON	Year-round
PERMITS/CONTACT	Prairie Creek Redwoods State Park fee required ($8 per vehicle), (707) 465-7347 or (707) 488-2171, www.parks.ca.gov
MAPS	USGS Fern Canyon
NOTES	Dogs and bikes prohibited; wear sandals or river shoes in the winter months

THE HIKE

Herds of Roosevelt elk, a narrow stream canyon bounded by 30-foot-high walls, and an amazing variety of ferns are the highlights of this walk in Prairie Creek Redwoods State Park.

GETTING THERE

From Eureka, drive north on U.S. 101 for 41 miles to Orick. Continue north for 2.5 more miles to Davison Road, then turn left (west) and drive 6.5 miles to the Fern Canyon trailhead. The access road is gravel and may be rough; no trailers or motor homes are permitted.

THE TRAIL

When you hike the Fern Canyon Loop, the drive to the trailhead is often a big part of the day's adventure. In the winter and spring months, your car may have to cross a few streams—without the aid of bridges. But the dirt and gravel road is suitable for passenger cars, and although it gives some drivers pause when they see those water crossings, most people make it to the trailhead just fine. (In the summer months, the road is usually dry.) Year-round, there's often another kind of surprise awaiting along the trailhead drive. Davison Road cuts through the Elk Prairie section of Prairie Creek Redwoods State Park, home to a large herd of

Photographers take advantage of the murky light that filters through Fern Canyon's high walls..

Roosevelt elk. You'll have a good chance of seeing these enormous creatures, which have the distinction of being California's largest land animals, weighing up to 1,000 pounds. The big elk will frequently stand just a few feet from the road, grazing on grasses. They are extremely docile, although you shouldn't mess with the bulls, especially during mating season.

When you reach the Fern Canyon trailhead, your destination is a secluded fern grotto—a hidden paradise of giant ferns growing on 30-foot-high rock walls on both sides of Home Creek. Park your car, pull on your waterproof hiking boots or your river sandals, and follow the clearly marked trail to the entrance of the canyon. In a few minutes, you'll be heading up Home Creek's rocky streambed. You may, or may not, have to do some delicate rock-hopping to cross the stream. From late spring through fall, the park installs small footbridges, so the going is easy and your feet stay completely dry. In the winter and early spring, the bridges are removed, so be prepared for wet feet.

Make your way up the streambed, observing as the canyon walls grow taller and squeeze tighter. The going may be slow, but nobody minds. Dense ferns line the canyon walls like wallpaper. Home Creek gushes near your feet. Miniature waterfalls pour down the rock walls. Moss grows everywhere, and combined with the multitude of ferns, the canyon feels like a rain forest.

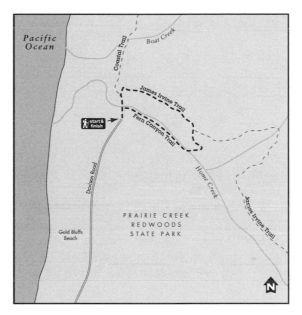

Look for the many frogs, salamanders, and newts that make their home in the canyon, including the rare Pacific giant salamander. If you're very lucky, you might spot the coastal cutthroat trout, which travels from the ocean in spring to lay its eggs in the gravel streambed. Practice your fern identification as you walk. An interpretive sign at the trailhead explains the identifying characteristics of various fern varieties, including sword, lady, five-finger, chain, and bracken ferns—up to eight different species, each waving delicately in the breeze.

Continue up the canyon for 0.5 mile until you reach a signed trail on the left that climbs out of the canyon on wooden stairsteps, then returns through the forest to the parking lot. This is a short section of the James Irvine Trail and the return leg of your loop. Follow it, or do what so many Fern Canyon visitors do: simply turn around and meander back out through the canyon. It's hard to resist seeing this place all over again.

GOING FARTHER
To extend the trip, turn right on the James Irvine Trail after you climb out of Fern Canyon. Hiking a mile or two out and back on this densely forested trail would be a fine addition to your day. Or, from the trailhead parking area, cross the access road and walk down to pristine, windswept Gold Bluffs Beach. Wander on the beach as far as you please.

4. Brown Creek, Rhododendron, and South Fork Loop

RATING	🚶 🚶 🚶 🚶
DISTANCE	3.6 miles round-trip
HIKING TIME	2 hours
ELEVATION GAIN	540 feet
HIGH POINT	800 feet
EFFORT	Moderate Workout
BEST SEASON	Year-round
PERMITS/CONTACT	Prairie Creek Redwoods State Park fee required ($8 per vehicle), (707) 465-7347 or (707) 488-2171, www.parks.ca.gov
MAPS	USGS Fern Canyon
NOTES	Dogs and bikes prohibited

THE HIKE
This loop trail through the redwoods might give you a neck ache. It leads through a colossal old-growth forest in which you can't help walking with your head raised, neck craned, and eyes gazing toward the tops of these massive trees.

GETTING THERE
From Eureka, drive north on U.S. 101 for 41 miles to Orick. Continue north for approximately 5 more miles, then take the Newton B. Drury Scenic Parkway exit and turn left. Drive 2.6 miles to the parking pullout near mileage marker 129. The trail is signed "South Fork Trail."

THE TRAIL
This is a walk for tree huggers. If you don't think that describes you, take this walk anyway and you might become a convert. The redwood-studded loop is a combination of three trails in Prairie Creek Redwoods State Park: Brown Creek, Rhododendron, and South Fork. Start walking from the South Fork trail sign, following the South Fork Trail for 0.2 mile to a left turn on Brown Creek Trail. The path leads through prime redwood forest, complete with virgin groves and lots of old growth. It meanders

Hikers appear as small as Lilliputians next to the giant redwoods on the Brown Creek Trail.

alongside a charming stream, which serves as the lifeblood for the towering trees. Your trail simply follows the creek, crossing it on a footbridge at 0.5 mile out.

The size of these redwoods is truly inspiring. Try as you may, it's impossible to glimpse their tops, which are as much as 300 feet off the ground. Perhaps the strongest impression is made by the fallen giants lying on the ground, toppled by centuries of weather. Their huge root balls look like intricate, sculpted knots, and their horizontal trunks serve as natural planters for entire microcosms of ferns, moss, mushrooms, and sorrel. Some of these trunks make such perfect garden boxes that you'll wonder if Mother Nature hasn't hired elfin landscape architects to do her work.

Brown Creek Trail junctions with Rhododendron Trail at 1.3 miles from the start. Turn right to continue the loop. The path climbs a bit steeply, then curves across the hillside, offering views back down into the canyon. True to the trail's name, in the spring months rhododendrons bloom throughout the forest, adding splashes of vibrant color to the myriad shades of green.

The ascent tops out at 2.5 miles, where you'll meet up with the South Fork Trail. Turn right and finish out the loop with a switchbacking descent. Look for orange leopard lilies in the spring, growing as tall as

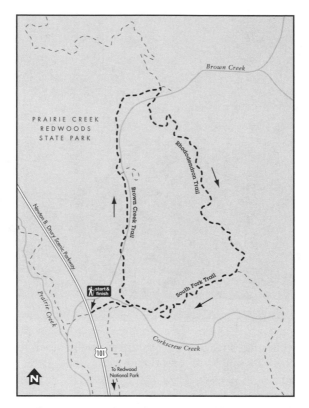

five feet, mixed in among the redwoods, huckleberries, and rhododen-drons. When you reach the Brown Creek Trail again, turn left and follow the South Fork Trail for 0.2 mile back to your car.

GOING FARTHER

At the 2.5-mile mark, where Rhododendron Trail meets up with South Fork Trail, you can remain on Rhododendron Trail heading south for up to 2.5 miles more. Hike out and back, or extend your trip into a much longer loop by following Rhododendron Trail to Cathedral Trees Trail, turning right and then following Cathedral Trees Trail and Foothill Trail back to the Brown Creek Trail/South Fork Trail junction. Make sure you bring along a map.

5. Skunk Cabbage and Coastal Trail

RATING	🚶 🚶 🚶 🚶
DISTANCE	6.0 miles round-trip
HIKING TIME	2.5 hours
ELEVATION GAIN	300 feet
HIGH POINT	300 feet
EFFORT	Moderate Workout
BEST SEASON	March to June, but good year-round
PERMITS/CONTACT	Redwood National and State Parks, (707) 465-7335, www.nps.gov/redw
MAPS	Redwood National and State Parks (download at www.nps.gov/redw/planyourvisit)
NOTES	Dogs prohibited

THE HIKE
The magnificent skunk cabbage, a plant with leaves as long as your arms, is just one of the many oversized species you'll find on this trail through the forest to the coast.

GETTING THERE
From Eureka, drive north on U.S. 101 for 41 miles to Orick, then continue north for 1.1 mile. Just past the right turnoff for Bald Hills Road, take the left turnoff that is signed for the Skunk Cabbage Section of the Coastal Trail. Drive 0.5 mile down the road to the parking area and trailhead.

THE TRAIL
The Skunk Cabbage Trail is a section of the Coastal Trail in Redwood National Park. It leads deep into a lush, jungle-like alder and spruce forest—so dense with foliage that you may think you've walked onto the set of a dinosaur movie. Then, with little or no notice, the trail suddenly opens out to a wide stretch of coast at Gold Bluffs Beach.

The out-and-back trail is 3.0 miles each way, but with very little elevation change. The scenery will capture your imagination, especially beyond the first 0.5 mile, where the trail enters the drainage of Skunk Cabbage Creek. Here, in a vast, swampy bog, you'll find the largest numbers of skunk cabbages growing near the stream. A relative of the corn

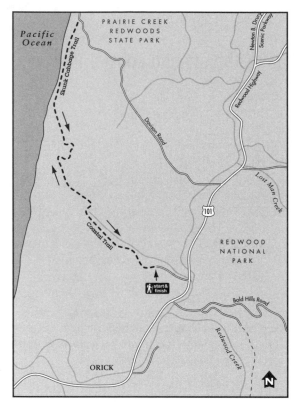

lily, these amazing plants are showstoppers. Vibrant green and as large as 5 feet across, with individual leaves growing a foot wide, they look something like cabbage heads on steroids. If you are lucky enough to visit in early March, their bright yellow flowers will take your breath away, not just for their beauty but also because of their skunk-like odor. (When not in flower, the plants have no scent.) Another name for this plant is swamp lantern, and perhaps that's because of the way its glowing green leaves and bright yellow blooms light up the dark green ambience of the forest.

The skunk cabbages grow in dense clusters under a canopy of bigleaf maples, alders, hemlocks, and Sitka spruce. Your trail weaves among all this foliage, crossing and recrossing Skunk Cabbage Creek on wooden footbridges.

After 2.0 delightful miles, the trail ceases its mostly level meandering and suddenly starts to climb. Leaving the creek behind, you continue up a ridge through a dense alder forest. At 2.7 miles, you round a curve in

The massive skunk cabbage is the namesake plant of Redwood National Park's Skunk Cabbage Trail.

the trail, and—surprise—you're high on a bluff overlooking the ocean. It's quite startling to see this dense, terrarium-like forest end so abruptly at a broad expanse of open coastline.

Here, at a trail junction, you must make a choice: right is the continuation of the Coastal Trail that eventually leads to Gold Bluffs Beach, and left is a spur trail that beckons you to the beach directly below. Just a few yards west of this junction is a fine view of the coast, and perhaps a spot to sit and have lunch. A descent of about 300 feet over steep switchbacks will take you to the dune-like stretch of sand below. Once there, what will you find? Mussel Point, a rocky outcrop, lies about 0.75 mile to the south. Other than that, there's plenty of driftwood, sand verbena, and precious solitude.

GOING FARTHER
If you turn right at the junction at 2.7 miles, you can continue on the Coastal Trail all the way to Gold Bluffs Beach, 2.5 miles away.

6. Lady Bird Johnson Grove

RATING   🚶 🚶 🚶
DISTANCE   1.0 mile round-trip
HIKING TIME   30 minutes
ELEVATION GAIN   Negligible
HIGH POINT   1,300 feet
EFFORT   Easy Walk
BEST SEASON   Year-round
PERMITS/CONTACT   Redwood National and State Parks, (707) 465-7335, www.nps.gov/redw
MAPS   Redwood National and State Parks (download at www.nps.gov/redw/planyourvisit)
NOTES   Dogs and bikes prohibited

THE HIKE

Situated high on a hill, the Lady Bird Johnson Grove surrounds the dedication site of Redwood National Park. Here, as elsewhere in the national park, the size of the trees will amaze and delight you.

GETTING THERE

From Eureka, drive north on U.S. 101 for 41 miles to Orick, then continue north for 1 mile. Turn right on Bald Hills Road and drive 2.7 miles to the trailhead parking area on the right.

THE TRAIL

The Lady Bird Johnson Grove is a place where you can have "The Redwood Experience." In case you've never felt it, it is something like this: You are wandering among ancient redwood trees that are hundreds of feet tall. Perhaps the fog has moved in, casting eerie filtered shadows in the forest. Your footsteps begin to slow. You find yourself noticing minute details, like the dewdrops on the pink petals of a rhododendron, or the bark pattern on one square inch of a 300-foot-tall redwood tree. Your voice drops to a whisper; you walk very softly, almost on tiptoe. Time nearly stops and the world holds its breath, at least for a little while.

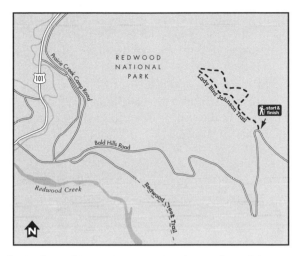

That's "The Redwood Experience." It's what makes visitors return to the old-growth redwood forests year after year. And they can do so thanks to the preservation efforts of forward-thinking souls such as President Lyndon Johnson, who signed the bill that created Redwood National Park in 1968, protecting these trees for generations to come. The 300-acre Lady Bird Johnson Grove was named for the president's wife, who dedicated the park in 1969.

In the words of Lady Bird Johnson: "One of my most unforgettable memories of the past years is walking through the redwoods last November, seeing the lovely shafts of light filtering through the trees so far above, feeling the majesty and silence of that forest, and watching a salmon rise in one of those swift streams. All our problems seemed to fall into perspective and I think every one of us walked out more serene and happier."

From the trailhead parking lot, cross the sturdy bridge over Bald Hills Road to access the trail. The trail through the redwoods is only 1.0 mile round-trip, but you may find it takes you a long time to walk it. You'll want to stop to read the interpretive signs, which explain the history of white men in the redwood region. Jedediah Smith first explored this area in 1828, and Josiah Greg took the first recorded measurements of the redwood trees in 1849.

In the understory of the redwoods, you'll see salmonberry, huckleberry, salal, and rhododendron. Sword ferns and sorrel grace the forest floor. If you picked up an interpretive brochure at the trailhead, you'll learn to identify "goose pens" (hollowed-out redwood trunks that early settlers used for keeping poultry) and "sprout trees" or "cathedral trees" (redwoods that have sprouted additional trunks instead of reproducing by seed). On the return half of the loop, you'll notice more Douglas fir and western hemlock trees in addition to the coast redwoods.

GOING FARTHER

Combine this walk with a hike on the Skunk Cabbage Section of the Coastal Trail (hike #5 in this guide). The trailheads are only 3 miles apart.

7. Tall Trees Grove

RATING	🚶 🚶 🚶 🚶
DISTANCE	3.6 miles round-trip
HIKING TIME	2.0 hours
ELEVATION GAIN	650 feet
HIGH POINT	850 feet
EFFORT	Moderate Workout
BEST SEASON	Year-round
PERMITS/CONTACT	Free permit required (see "Getting There"), Redwood National and State Parks, (707) 465-7335, www.nps.gov/redw
MAPS	Redwood National and State Parks (download at www.nps.gov/redw/planyourvisit)
NOTES	Dogs and bikes prohibited

THE HIKE

In 1963, the world's tallest tree was identified in this alluvial redwood grove. While taller trees have been discovered since then, a walk among these giants is still a humbling and awe-inspiring experience.

GETTING THERE

From Eureka, drive north on U.S. 101 for 40 miles to the Thomas H. Kuchel Visitor Center on the west side of the highway, 2 miles south of Orick. At the visitor center, pick up a Tall Trees Grove permit and the gate combination for the access road. Then drive north on U.S. 101 for 3 miles and turn right on Bald Hills Road. Drive 7 miles to the Tall Trees Access Road on the right (just past Redwood Creek Overlook). Turn right, stop at the gate, use your combination to open it, then drive through. Close and lock the gate behind you. Drive 6 miles on the Tall Trees Access Road (also called C-Line Road) to the trailhead parking lot.

THE TRAIL

It might sound like too much trouble to go to the visitor center, pick up a permit and a gate combination for the Tall Trees Access Road, then drive 16.0 miles to the trailhead just to hike a trail that features big redwoods. After all, there are plenty of other redwood trails in the area that don't

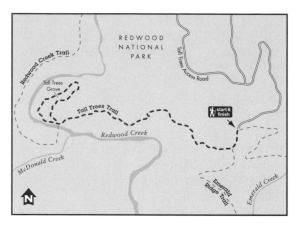

require this much effort. But these aren't your average big redwoods; the Tall Trees Grove includes what was once considered the world's tallest tree at 367 feet high, but in 1999 was downgraded in status after losing about 10 feet of height in a storm. (The honor of being the world's tallest now goes to the Mendocino Tree in Montgomery Woods State Reserve near Mendocino.) Still, a few trees on the top ten list for height are found in the Tall Trees Grove. The fact is, every redwood in this grove is immense. It's impossible to see all the way to their skyscraping summits.

The permit system is necessary because of the narrow, winding Tall Trees Access Road (also called C-Line Road); too many cars would surely result in accidents. But since this also limits the number of hikers in the grove, the trip is made even more special. Only 50 cars are given a permit each day, but that limit is rarely reached except on peak summer weekends. If you are concerned about getting a permit on a particular day, just show up at the visitor center first thing in the morning.

Once at the Tall Trees trailhead, pick up an interpretive brochure at the kiosk and head downhill. You'll pass a junction with the Emerald Ridge Trail in the first 100 yards; stay right. The first stretch of trail leads gently downhill through a mixed forest with myriad rhododendrons—no big redwoods yet. At 1.2 miles, you pass a restroom, which seems oddly out of place in this forest. Just beyond it, the trail bottoms out and you reach the start of the loop through the grove. Follow the trail clockwise (to the left). Take the left spur trail to see Redwood Creek; in summer a bridge spans the creek to connect hikers to the Redwood Creek Trail. The rich soils from the creek's streambed, combined with the coastal climate, cause the redwoods here to grow to their enormous size.

Back on the main loop, in short time you reach the base of what was once the world's tallest tree. But what makes this trail special isn't one specific tree. The entire grove is remarkable. There are so many mammoth trees in such close proximity that humans feel ant-sized in comparison. Even the rhododendrons grow extra large—as tall as 15 feet. They display flashy pink blooms among the dark shadows of the redwoods.

The trail continues past more huge redwoods to the north end of the loop, where you walk through a 0.25-mile stretch of bigleaf maples and California bays—a distinct contrast to the giant redwoods.

This stretch of trail is beautiful in its own way, especially in autumn when the maples turn colors. The loop eventually returns into the big trees and finally rejoins the main trail to head back uphill. Linger a while among the giants before you go.

GOING FARTHER

If the summer bridge is in place across Redwood Creek, cross it and hike for as far as you like on the opposite side of the stream. You'll pass a small backpacker's camp, which makes a good picnic spot.

8. Rim Trail: Wedding Rock to Rocky Point

RATING	🚶 🚶 🚶 🚶
DISTANCE	2.8 miles round-trip
HIKING TIME	1.5 hours
ELEVATION GAIN	100 feet
HIGH POINT	150 feet
EFFORT	Easy Walk
BEST SEASON	Year-round
PERMITS/CONTACT	Patrick's Point State Park fee required
	($8 per vehicle), (707) 677-3570, www.parks.ca.gov
MAPS	Patrick's Point State Park
	(download at www.parks.ca.gov)
NOTES	Dogs and bikes prohibited

THE HIKE
This hike at Patrick's Point State Park gives you a close-up look at the geology of sea stacks and the unparalleled beauty of the Trinidad coast.

GETTING THERE
From Eureka, drive north on U.S. 101 for 25 miles, past the town of Trinidad, and take the Patrick's Point Drive exit. Follow the signs to the entrance station for Patrick's Point State Park, then continue past the Bishop Pine Group Picnic Area. Turn left and park at the paved parking lot near Wedding Rock and Patrick's Point.

THE TRAIL
Thousands of years ago, most of Patrick's Point State Park was submerged in the ocean. When the water receded, dozens of 100-foot-high, cliff-like outcrops were left standing high and dry. The park today shows off numerous examples of these outcrops, known as "sea stacks."

Two of them, dubbed Ceremonial Rock and Lookout Rock, are a part of the landmass of Patrick's Point State Park. Just off the coast, they have many picturesque, isolated cousins, which are continually battered by the ocean waves. On land and in water, the sea stacks create a dramatic scene. See them with a short trek on the park's Rim Trail, which follows the route of an old Yurok Indian pathway across the park's blufftops.

Patrick's Point State Park features a rocky coastline punctuated by large and small sea stacks.

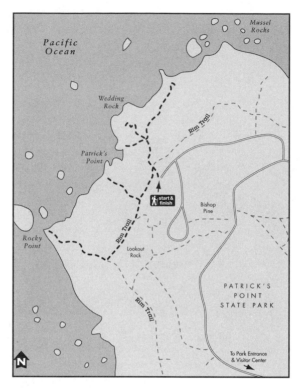

The entire trail is 2.0 miles in length, or 4.0 miles round-trip, which is just fine if you feel ambitious. If you don't, you can sample the park's highlights by hiking only a 1.0-mile section of the Rim Trail and then adding on the short spur trails that connect to three of the park's six coastal promontories—Wedding Rock, Patrick's Point, and Rocky Point. That's the trip described here.

Starting from the parking lot near Wedding Rock, take the connector trail from the Rim Trail to Wedding Rock, a majestic, castle-like rock promontory, with views of Trinidad Head to the south and crashing waves all around. The intricate, carved rock stairs that climb to the top of the 120-foot rock were built by the California Conservation Corps in the 1930s.

Next, head left (southwest) on the Rim Trail and follow a wheelchair-accessible cutoff to Patrick's Point, where you'll have a photo-worthy vista of Wedding Rock and the surrounding coast. The detour to Patrick's Point and back totals 0.25 mile. Back on the Rim Trail, continue farther southwest to your final destination, Rocky Point.

In between these three overlook points, the Rim Trail travels through a mixed forest of Sitka spruce, Douglas fir, red alder, and pine. Wildflowers are abundant in spring, including Douglas iris, trillium, rhododendron, and salal. In spring and fall, be sure to scan the ocean horizon for migrating California gray whales. In summer, humpback whales are sometimes seen feeding fairly close to shore.

While the Rim Trail itself is fairly level, the spur trails to the multiple overlooks require some ups and downs, especially the spur trail to Rocky Point. Even though you won't walk many miles on this trip, you will feel like you are getting a bit of a workout, especially if the wind is howling, which is a common occurrence. But it's so beautiful here, nobody minds.

GOING FARTHER

Drive your car 0.5 mile east to the Agate Campground parking area, then walk the Agate Beach Trail to Agate Beach (1.2 miles round-trip). This is the only large sand beach in the park. Rock collectors flock to Agate Beach for its semiprecious agates, jade, and jasper, which are found right at the surf line.

9. Hookton Slough Trail

RATING	𝕏 𝕏 𝕏
DISTANCE	3.0 miles round-trip
HIKING TIME	1.5 hours
ELEVATION GAIN	Negligible
HIGH POINT	30 feet
EFFORT	Easy Walk
BEST SEASON	November to April
PERMITS/CONTACT	Humboldt Bay National Wildlife Refuge, (707) 733-5406, www.fws.gov/humboldtbay
MAPS	Download at www.fws.gov/humboldtbay/brochure.pdf
NOTES	Dogs and bikes prohibited

THE HIKE

Located on an estuary where fresh water and salt water meet, Humboldt Bay is a critical stop for birds on the Pacific Flyway. This trail along the estuary's edge brings you up close with both the birds and other wildlife.

GETTING THERE

From Eureka, travel 10 miles south on U.S. 101. Take the Hookton Road exit and drive 1.2 miles west on Hookton Road to the Hookton Slough parking area. (The refuge office is located off the same exit but on Ranch Road. It's not necessary to go to the refuge office; you can drive directly to Hookton Slough.)

The Hookton Slough Trail (1.5 miles one-way) starts at the Hookton Slough Unit parking area and follows the west bank of Hookton Slough out and back. The trail is level, gravel-based, and has interpretive panels.

THE TRAIL

The Hookton Slough Trail is a level, wide, and easy trail that practically gives you a guarantee of seeing wildlife as you walk. You want to see birds? No problem. Waterfowl, raptors, shorebirds—the Hookton Slough Trail has them. You want to see harbor seals basking in the mud? Your chances are good if the tide is high; that's when the seals swim up the slough from Humboldt Bay in search of a meal. Sand dabs, leopard sharks, and salmon also migrate through this estuary.

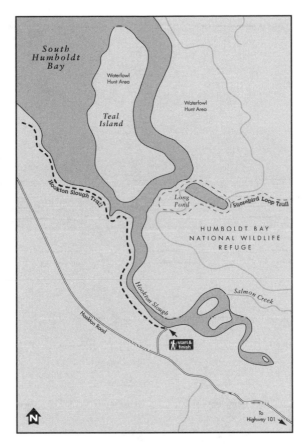

The key to all this wildlife diversity is the eelgrass, mudflats, and wet-lands that provide habitat for thousands of living creatures, from tiny invertebrates to more than 200 species of birds, from migratory fish to mammals like river otters, black-tailed deer, and gray fox. In one spring visit, I saw dozens of white egrets, plus several species of herons, ducks, and gulls. Huge flocks of western sandpipers clustered by the edge of the bay, racing back and forth within inches of the water but never getting wet. Later in summer, I saw terns, cormorants, and pelicans, as well as a grab bag of songbirds.

November through April is the main bird-viewing season, but the most interesting show comes from mid-March to late April, when Pacific black brants (also known as sea geese) pass through on their way from Alaska to Baja. Humboldt Bay is an important resting stop for these weary and hungry birds, because it has the largest beds of eelgrass south of Washington.

Majestic great blue herons are commonly seen at Humboldt Bay National Wildlife Refuge.

More than half of all the Pacific brants traveling the Flyway stop here to fuel up on eelgrass—as many as 20,000 at one time.

The hike is simple: Begin at the parking lot, walk 1.5 miles out to the end of the trail, then turn around and walk back. On the return trip, when I took my eyes off the mudflats and looked ahead to the farms and hillsides in the west, I noticed large white spots in the tops of the trees. The "spots" were actually great egrets, nesting in the tallest treetops.

If you are serious about spotting birds and other wildlife, proper timing is imperative. Not only is the November to April season the most productive (with Pacific brant, Aleutian cackling geese, and migratory shorebird populations peaking in the spring), but time of day matters, too. The best times are usually within one to two hours of either side of high tide.

GOING FARTHER
Add a hike on the 1.7-mile Shorebird Loop Trail, which passes near some of the refuge's best shorebird viewing areas. This trail is located off Ranch Road near the refuge office.

10. Big Tree Area: Bull Creek Flats Trail

RATING	🚶 🚶 🚶 🚶
DISTANCE	2.5 miles round-trip
HIKING TIME	1.5 hours
ELEVATION GAIN	Negligible
HIGH POINT	200 feet
EFFORT	Easy Walk
BEST SEASON	Year-round
PERMITS/CONTACT	Humboldt Redwoods State Park fee required ($8 per vehicle), (707) 946-2409 or (707) 946-2263, www.parks.ca.gov
MAPS	USGS Weott
NOTES	Dogs and bikes prohibited; good family hike; interpretive brochure available at trailhead

THE HIKE

A streamside walk through the Rockefeller Forest takes you past trees taller than 35-story buildings, including the National Champion Coast Redwood.

GETTING THERE

From Garberville, travel north on U.S. 101 for about 20 miles, heading into Humboldt Redwoods State Park. Take the Founder's Grove/Rockefeller Forest exit and drive approximately 4 miles on Bull Creek Flats Road/Mattole Road to the Big Tree Area of Rockefeller Forest. Turn left at the Big Tree Area and park in the lot. The trail begins from the south side of the lot, at the bridge over Bull Creek.

THE TRAIL

Humboldt Redwoods State Park encompasses more than 51,000 acres, making it one of the largest state parks in California. It has seven separate exits off the freeway and an embarrassment of riches in terms of hiking options. First-time visits here can be daunting. The trick, of course, is knowing where to go.

If you're an avid fan of gargantuan *Sequoia sempervirens* and lovely streamside walks, the park's Big Tree Area is your ticket. Just driving

Prepare to be humbled by the immense girth of the Rockefeller Forest's redwoods.

to the trailhead on Bull Creek Flats/Mattole Road is a thrill. The road is winding, shaded, and narrow, with big trees so close that you can touch them by leaning out your car window. All this preserved old growth is largely due to John D. Rockefeller Jr., who donated a couple million dollars to help conservationists purchase 10,000 acres along Bull Creek from the Pacific Lumber Company in 1930. Hence the name "Rockefeller Forest."

From the parking area, walk straight ahead across a long, narrow footbridge, which rises 20 feet above Bull Creek. Turn left on the trail to see the Giant Tree, which is recognized by the American Forestry Association as the National Champion Coast Redwood, a somewhat arbitrary designation that is the sum total of several factors, including the tree's height and trunk diameter. The Giant is a colossal 363 feet tall and 53.2 feet in circumference, so it's no slacker in the size department.

Next, follow the trail signs back to the Flatiron Tree, a huge fallen tree that is flat on one side, looking nearly triangular in shape instead of round.

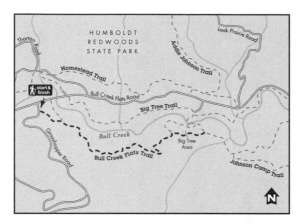

To find more big trees, retrace your steps across the bridge to the parking area, walk across the lot, and locate the trail to the Tall Tree. How tall, you ask? It's a whopping 359.3 feet. A pleasant little loop trail travels around it.

If you've had your fill of trees named every possible synonym for "big," continue from the Tall Tree, heading west on the Bull Creek Flats Trail and paralleling Bull Creek. You can take the trail from the Tall Tree all the way to Albee Creek Campground, a distance of just under 1.0 mile. The trail travels along the creek, where you'll find plenty of horsetail ferns and Douglas irises in the spring. When you come to Bull Creek Flats/Mattole Road and the access road for the camp, turn around and head back to your car.

GOING FARTHER
You can also hike the Bull Creek Flats Trail in the opposite direction, heading east along Bull Creek. From the Big Tree Area it is about 3 miles to the Rockefeller Loop Trail at the Bull Creek Flats Area.

The allure of the North Coast is found in its endless vistas of pocket coves, tree-covered sea stacks, and the surging Pacific.

The Shasta and Lassen region is blessed with an abundance of cascading water, including beautiful Kings Creek Falls at Lassen Volcanic National Park.

SHASTA AND LASSEN

In the northeastern corner of California lies a part of the state where most residents have never set foot. Ranging from the Oregon border south to Redding and from the Nevada border west through the Klamath Mountains, this northern interior is the Golden State's second least populated region—beat out only by sizzling hot Death Valley and the eastern Mojave.

Yet the area is bestowed with some of California's most spectacular scenery: a landscape of rugged mountains, raging rivers in steep canyons, and vast expanses of sagebrush flats and pine- and fir-covered ridges. This is the land where osprey and eagles soar, and remnants of volcanoes sputter and fume.

Lassen Volcanic National Park, California's best example of recent geothermal activity, is found here. In May 1914, Lassen Peak began a seven-year stint of volcanic outbursts. Even today, visitors can witness volcanic action including seething hot springs, steaming volcanic vents, and boiling mud pots (springs filled with hot mud).

Adding to the beauty are 2.1 million acres of Shasta-Trinity National Forest, dominated by mighty Mount Shasta, a dormant volcano whose summit attains the lofty height of 14,162 feet. East of Mount Shasta is McArthur Burney Falls State Park and its showpiece, Burney Falls, which President Theodore Roosevelt called "the eighth wonder of the world."

It probably wouldn't be an overstatement to say that in terms of outdoor recreation, the Shasta and Lassen region has it all. The only thing you won't find in this part of California is a crowd, and that provides another reason to visit here and go for a hike.

SHASTA AND LASSEN

11. Castle Lake and Heart Lake

RATING	🚶 🚶 🚶 🚶
DISTANCE	3.0 miles round-trip
HIKING TIME	1.5 hours
ELEVATION GAIN	600 feet
HIGH POINT	6,050 feet
EFFORT	Moderate Workout
BEST SEASON	May to October
PERMITS/CONTACT	Mount Shasta Ranger District, (530) 926-4511, www.fs.fed.us/r5/shastatrinity
MAPS	USGS Mount Shasta City
NOTES	Dogs allowed

THE HIKE

A great introduction to the natural wonders of the Mount Shasta area, this trail leads from one crystal-clear lake to another.

GETTING THERE

From Interstate 5 in Mount Shasta City, take the Central Mount Shasta exit and drive west on Hatchery Lane. Turn left on South Old Stage Road. In 0.2 mile, bear right and continue on W. A. Barr Road. Drive 2.3 miles on W. A. Barr Road to the dam at Lake Siskiyou. Cross the dam, then turn left on Castle Lake Road and drive 7.1 miles to the parking area for Castle Lake. The trailhead is at the edge of the parking lot to the left of the lake.

THE TRAIL

When you pull into the parking area at Castle Lake's edge, you may gasp in surprise—this lake is a stunner. Set in a glacial bowl at 5,450 feet in elevation, its waters are backed by a high granite cliff and sparkling vistas of huge Mount Shasta. The turquoise lake has a depth of 120 feet against its back granite wall.

An interpretive display by the parking lot explains the unique properties of Castle Lake. Its water is extremely pure, and for many years the University of California at Davis has been studying its clarity in an ongoing comparison with a similar study at Lake Tahoe. The Shasta and

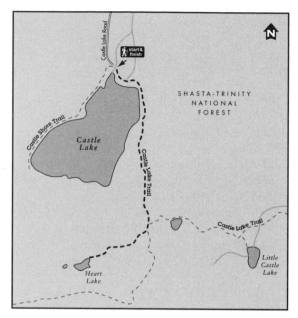

Wintu Indians called Castle Lake "Castle of the Devil." They believed an evil spirit lived in the lake and made the eerie echoing noises frequently heard in winter. The sound is actually just the movement of ice.

In summer, there will likely be lots of people at Castle Lake swimming, fishing, and enjoying the scenery, but by taking this hike, you will quickly leave them behind. Your trail begins at the interpretive signboards. The first 100 feet may be the trickiest: you have to boulder-hop across the lake's outlet stream, which ranges from 2 feet wide in midsummer to 25 feet wide after winter snow and rain.

Once across the outlet, a trail sign points you uphill and the path travels laterally above the lake's east shore, ascending moderately through a sparse forest of red and white firs. Your views of deep blue Castle Lake below keep getting better as you climb. At 0.7 mile, the trail reaches a 5,900-foot saddle on the ridge above the lake, where you can catch your breath, then continue on the trail that leads to the right and southwest (another trail heads straight ahead to Little Castle Lake; see "Going Farther").

Heart Lake is about 0.5 mile away, and yes, it is clearly heart-shaped. More than a few marriage proposals have taken place here. Because the lake is so tiny, it warms up nicely for swimming. Walk around Heart Lake's shoreline and you'll find great views of Mount Shasta and Black Butte.

GOING FARTHER

From the saddle, you can also stay straight on the main trail for Little Castle Lake. Getting there requires a 300-foot elevation drop over 0.5 mile, which you will have to gain back on your return. When you reach a small meadow, leave the main trail and turn right on an unmarked side trail to Little Castle Lake. It isn't as picturesque as Heart Lake, but it displays a mirror-image reflection of Mount Shasta on its surface.

12. McCloud Falls Trail

RATING	🚶 🚶 🚶 🚶
DISTANCE	3.6 miles round-trip
HIKING TIME	2 hours
ELEVATION GAIN	400 feet
HIGH POINT	3,800 feet
EFFORT	Moderate Workout
BEST SEASON	Year-round
PERMITS/CONTACT	McCloud Ranger District, (530) 964-2184, www.fs.fed.us/r5/shastatrinity
MAPS	USGS Lake McCloud
NOTES	Dogs allowed

THE HIKE

Visit the McCloud River's holy trinity of boisterous waterfalls on this scenic hike.

GETTING THERE

From Redding, drive 65 miles north on Interstate 5. Take the Highway 89/ McCloud exit and drive east on Highway 89. Pass the town of McCloud in 9 miles, then continue 4.5 miles farther east to a sign for Fowlers Camp/McCloud Falls/River Access. Turn right and follow the signs to the McCloud River Picnic Area and Lower McCloud Falls. (Bear right when the road forks, driving 0.7 mile past Fowlers Camp.) Park in the day-use parking area at Lower Falls.

THE TRAIL

The McCloud River has three falls within 2.0 river miles of each other, each with its own distinct personality. Lower Falls is a busy family swimming hole, complete with a metal ladder to assist jumpers and divers as they exit the chilly water. Wide, powerful, and commanding, Middle Falls lures photographers and teenage cliff-jumpers. Upper Falls is a narrow funnel of water that drops into a circular turquoise pool. One hiking trail links the three McCloud River falls, so you can visit them all in about an hour.

Middle McCloud Falls plummets with exuberance in early summer.

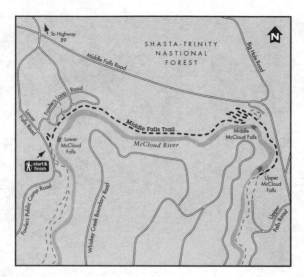

Start hiking at Lower Falls, located just below Fowlers Camp. Lower Falls is the smallest of the three, a 12-foot plunge into a giant pool. In the spring, it's a popular put-in spot for kayakers heading down the McCloud River. In summer, it's crowded with people who want to jump in and cool off. Take a look, then walk the 0.5-mile paved trail along the river that leads through Fowlers Camp. On the camp's east side, near the restrooms, you'll pick up the trail to Middle Falls.

Following the fir-lined route along the McCloud River, in 1.0 mile you'll find yourself face-to-face with Middle McCloud Falls. Tall, wide, and regal-looking, Middle McCloud Falls drops 50 feet over a cliff to form a deep pool at its base. Middle McCloud is at least twice as wide as it is tall, adding breadth to its grandeur. Bold teenagers sometimes jump off the basalt cliffs on the waterfall's left side, or dive headfirst into the chilly waters. The large-leaved plant known as Indian rhubarb or elephant's ear grows in and around the falls, and water ouzels build their homes behind the fall's tremendous flow of water. Watch carefully and you may see them flying in and out.

A series of well-graded switchbacks take you gently to the top of Middle Falls, where the path levels out and heads upriver, clinging to the edge of the canyon wall. Views of the coursing stream below capture and hold your attention. The trail continues with an easy ascent to Upper Falls, and because of its more distant location you'll probably find fewer people here. Upper Falls is more secretive than the two falls downriver; rarely do you get a look at its entire length because it is hidden in a rocky gorge. At an exposed outcrop of basalt boulders across from the fall, you can see its two lowest tiers as they plunge into a rocky bowl. Their circular pools are a remarkable shade of aquamarine. The trail continues to the brink of the falls, but the view is better from here.

You'd think three waterfalls would be about all the excitement you could take on one trail, but another surprise awaits when you turn around and head back: an extraordinary view of Mount Shasta, which was lurking behind you on the way in.

GOING FARTHER

If you'd like to see more of the beautiful McCloud River, pay a visit to the Nature Conservancy's McCloud River Preserve, off Squaw Creek Road near the town of McCloud. Take Squaw Creek Road south from Highway 89, and 2.5 miles after passing the McCloud Reservoir, turn right on Road 38N53, a dirt road. Follow the signs to Ah-Di-Na Campground and you'll reach the preserve parking lot at 18.5 miles from the highway (1 mile beyond the campground). An easy trail leads alongside the river.

13. Root Creek Trail

RATING	🚶 🚶 🚶
DISTANCE	2.0 miles round-trip
HIKING TIME	1 hour
ELEVATION GAIN	200 feet
HIGH POINT	2,600 feet
EFFORT	Easy Walk
BEST SEASON	Year-round
PERMITS/CONTACT	Castle Crags State Park day-use fee required ($8 per vehicle), (530) 235-2684, www.parks.ca.gov
MAPS	USGS Dunsmuir
NOTES	Dogs and bikes prohibited

THE HIKE

Admire the jagged profile of the multiple spires of Castle Crags and walk alongside a babbling brook on this easy jaunt in Castle Crags State Park.

GETTING THERE

From Redding, drive 50 miles north on Interstate 5 and take the Castle Crags State Park exit, 4 miles south of the town of Dunsmuir. Turn west and follow the signs to the park entrance. After paying at the kiosk, turn right and follow the road to its end at the Vista Point parking area. The trail for the vista point is at the parking lot; the Root Creek Trail begins about 40 yards downhill from the parking lot.

THE TRAIL

Have you ever driven north on I-5, gaping at the looming volcanic cone of Mount Shasta, and then suddenly looked over your left shoulder and seen those big, gray, craggy rocks looming over you—the unmistakable jagged outline of Castle Crags' ancient granite spires?

From afar, the Crags look awesome, but getting close to them is even better. The only problem is that the jagged spires of Castle Crags head straight up into the stratosphere. The trails to reach the crags are remarkably steep: The Crags Trail to Castle Dome's base gains 2,300 feet in less than 3.0 miles, a prodigious climb. But here's a more manageable way to get a good look at Castle Crags.

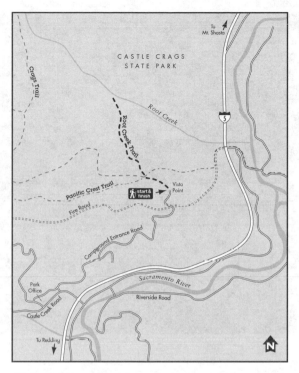

From the Vista Point parking lot, start your trip by allowing plenty of time to admire the view of Castle Crags straight ahead, Mount Shasta to your right, and Grey Rocks to your left. Conical Mount Shasta at 14,162 feet is quite plainly a volcano, but Castle Crags is a completely different type of geological formation, made of granodiorite that was formed below the earth's surface millions of years ago and then slowly forced upward. The formation called Grey Rocks looks vastly different from either Mount Shasta or Castle Crags. It is yet another geologic type, composed of greenstone and slate metamorphic rock that was thrust upward and sideways from the earth and weathered by the centuries.

After taking in all this geologic diversity, head down the access road from the Vista Point parking lot for 40 yards to the trailhead for the Root Creek Trail. This pleasant trail is mostly level and travels through a conifer and hardwood forest to join and then follow the path of Root Creek. Conifer needles cushion your feet and five-finger ferns point the way. Root Creek bubbles over rounded rocks and is framed by an abundance of elephant's ear—giant-leafed water-loving plants, up to 2 feet high—on its banks.

In spring, Root Creek's large-leaved elephant's ear plants begin their growth as delicate flowers.

At trail's end you get a surprising look straight up at Castle Dome—the big, smooth, rounded rock formation that leads the parade of crags. Hang out here for as long as you like (a wooden bench has been installed for that purpose) and then backtrack to the parking area.

GOING FARTHER

The Root Creek Trail connects with both the Crags Trail and the Pacific Crest Trail; you can add an out-and-back hike on either of these trails. Or, if you are in the mood for an adventure, a faint path forks off the Root Creek Trail to Root Creek Falls, which is located outside the state park boundary in national forest land. The distance one-way from the parking lot to the falls is only 2.8 miles, but since this is not a maintained trail, it's very slow going. Plans are in the works to build a "real" trail, but right now this is a path made only by occasional use, so the trip is best saved for tenacious hikers.

14. Headwaters and Pacific Crest Trails

RATING	🚶 🚶 🚶 🚶
DISTANCE	1.0 mile round-trip
HIKING TIME	30 minutes
ELEVATION GAIN	200 feet
HIGH POINT	3,000 feet
EFFORT	Easy Walk
BEST SEASON	Year-round
PERMITS/CONTACT	McArthur–Burney Falls Memorial State Park day-use fee required ($8 per vehicle), (530) 335-2777, www.parks.ca.gov
MAPS	McArthur–Burney Falls Memorial State Park (download at www.burney-falls.com)
NOTES	Dogs and bikes prohibited

THE HIKE

Visit the waterfall that Teddy Roosevelt called "the eighth wonder of the world" on this loop hike in McArthur–Burney Falls Memorial State Park.

GETTING THERE

From Burney, drive approximately 4 miles east on Highway 299 to the intersection of Highways 89 and 299. Turn left and drive north on Highway 89 for approximately 6 miles to the main entrance of the park. Pay at the kiosk, then drive past it and to the left. (The visitor center and main parking area are to the right.) Park in the small parking area a few hundred yards to the left of the kiosk. The trailhead for the Headwaters Trail is on the left side of the parking lot.

THE TRAIL

Plenty of people drive to McArthur–Burney Falls Memorial State Park each spring and summer, park in the main lot, get out of their cars, and look over the railing at the falls. Maybe they even walk 50 yards to get a little closer to the huge surge of plunging water and mist. Then they take a few pictures, jump back in their cars, drive to the nearest Internet café, and tell all their Facebook friends about the great waterfall they just saw.

Year-round, Burney Falls at McArthur-Burney Falls Memorial State Park is a cascading crowd-pleaser.

Sure, Burney Falls is worth the trip, even just for sightseeing and bragging rights. Watching 100 million gallons of water pour over a cliff is far from an everyday experience. But if you want to spend a little more time in this beautiful state park, leave the crowds behind and take this out-of-the-way loop hike first. This trip saves the magnificent falls for last.

Park your car in the small lot to the left of the entrance kiosk (not the main lot to the right), then begin walking on the Headwaters Trail, heading

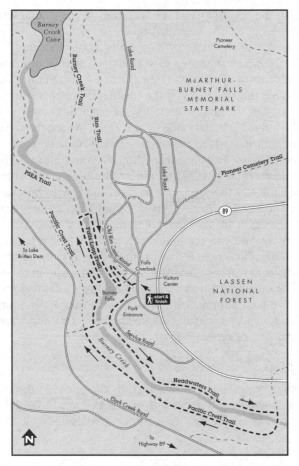

upstream and away from the falls. The woods are filled with conifers, including ponderosa pines (easily identified by their clearly delineated, jigsaw-puzzle bark) and huge Douglas firs, plus hardwoods such as white oaks and black oaks. If you visit in spring or early summer, you may notice the lovely sweet scent of mountain misery, a small shrub with tiny light blue or white flowers.

In 0.5 mile, you'll reach a long footbridge over Burney Creek and an intersection with the Pacific Crest Trail. Cross the bridge and turn right, now following a short section of the Pacific Crest Trail as you loop back downstream. As you hike, keep your eyes on alert for two unusual bird species that frequent this park: migratory black swifts, who build their nests on the sheer cliffs of the waterfall in early summer; and bald eagles, who nest at nearby Lake Britton.

In another 0.5 mile, turn right on Falls Trail near the Fisherman's Bridge. After a couple minutes of walking on gentle downhill switchbacks, you'll come to a placard for the Burney Falls overlook and a small clearing through the woods. Here, the rushing cataract is framed by trees. It could be argued that the waterfall view from this angle is more dramatic than from the opposite side of the creek, where the falls are more often photographed. Certainly there are fewer people here.

At 129 feet, Burney Falls is not the highest waterfall in California, but its flow has remarkable beauty and power. Burney's claim to fame is that it gushes at basically the same rate all year long, with no change in the dry season. The water in Burney Creek comes from underground springs and stored snowmelt in the basalt rock layers that make up the falls. If you look closely, you can see that much of the water actually pours *out* of the face of the cliff, rather than running over the top of the cliff. Due to its underground water source, the water temperature in the pool below the falls, even on warm summer days, is a chilly 42 degrees Fahrenheit.

After you've paid appropriate homage to Burney Falls, simply return to the parking area by backtracking up the Falls Trail for a few hundred yards and then crossing the Fisherman's Bridge.

GOING FARTHER

From the main waterfall overlook, hike in the opposite direction of the loop described above, following Burney Creek Trail to the edge of Lake Britton. Loop back on the Rim Trail for a 4-mile round-trip.

15. Hat Creek Trail to the Pit River

RATING	🚶 🚶 🚶
DISTANCE	3.2 miles round-trip
HIKING TIME	1.5 hours
ELEVATION GAIN	100 feet
HIGH POINT	2,800 feet
EFFORT	Easy Walk
BEST SEASON	Year-round
PERMITS/CONTACT	Shasta County Public Works, (530) 225-5661, www.co.shasta.ca.us
MAPS	USGS Cassel
NOTES	Dogs and bikes allowed

THE HIKE

Anglers, birders, and dog walkers will enjoy this mellow stroll that follows Hat Creek on its course to join the Pit River.

GETTING THERE

From Burney, drive 7.5 miles east on Highway 299, past the intersection of Highways 89 and 299, to just before the highway bridge over Hat Creek. It's 5 miles west of Fall River Mills. Turn left into Hat Creek County Park just before the bridge; park and then walk across the bridge to its east side. The trailhead is a dirt road about 20 feet from the east end of the bridge; head north (left) on this road.

THE TRAIL

There's nothing quite as nice as watching a big stream roll by—unless, of course, you're watching two big streams roll by. That's what you get on this hike along Hat Creek and the Pit River. It's a perfect walk to do with a loved one or ones, because the trail is level, easy, and wide enough so that you can walk side by side.

Start with an easy stroll down an old dirt road, which soon diminishes to a trail. The Pit River flows by on your right and Hat Creek on your left. You walk in between the two waterways for most of the trip, through a meadow filled with wildflowers and bordered by black oaks

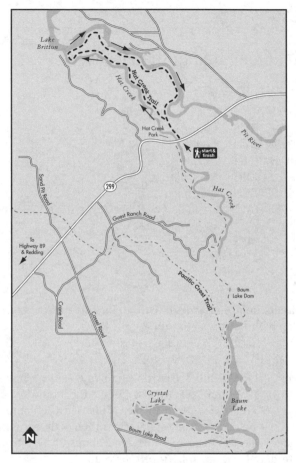

and Oregon white oaks. Note a junction at 0.2 mile; the right fork is the return of your loop.

The faint spur trails you'll see along the way are mostly used by anglers. Hat Creek is famous for its wild trout. Flyfishers travel from all over the country to try their skills at this catch-and-release section of the creek. You won't see any frying pans here. Then again, you're unlikely to see any fish being caught and released here, either. Hat Creek trout are notoriously wily.

Choose to follow any or all of the spur trails without fear of getting lost, because the two waterways always keep you on track. As you wander, keep on the lookout for unusual bird sightings among the usual cabal of Stellar's jays, robins, meadowlarks, blackbirds, red-tailed hawks, and Cooper's hawks. You might get lucky and see a bald eagle; they like to fish in Hat Creek, too. A local birding group has put up nesting boxes along the river in the hope of attracting more songbirds.

After slightly more than 1.0 mile, the trail brings you closer to the Pit River side, and then curves around to the confluence of the Pit River and Hat Creek. Technically, this is the southeast edge of Lake Britton. Just keep following along the edge of this marshy peninsula of land and you'll find yourself starting to loop back, now tracing alongside the Pit River. If you notice your pace slowing, perhaps it is because the broad open fields and oak woodlands that divide the Pit River and Hat Creek seem to naturally encourage good conversation. The peninsula of land where the two waters meet is the perfect place to lay out a blanket and have a picnic. Linger in this special place as long as you can.

GOING FARTHER

Several other trails lead from Hat Creek County Park, and all are worth exploring. For starters, try the path on Hat Creek's west side that leads northwest for 1.6 miles to Lake Britton.

16. Chaos Crags and Crags Lake

RATING	🚶 🚶 🚶 🚶
DISTANCE	3.8 miles round-trip
HIKING TIME	2 hours
ELEVATION GAIN	850 feet
HIGH POINT	6,760 feet
EFFORT	Prepare to Perspire
BEST SEASON	June to August
PERMITS/CONTACT	Lassen Volcanic National Park entrance fee required ($10 per vehicle, valid for seven days), (530) 595-4444, www.nps.gov/lavo
MAPS	Lassen Volcanic National Park (download at www.nps.gov/lavo)
NOTES	Dogs and bikes prohibited

THE HIKE
Time your trip for soon after snowmelt and you'll get to see the ephemeral lake that lies at the base of Chaos Crags, a looming lava formation in Lassen Volcanic National Park.

GETTING THERE
From Redding, drive east on Highway 44 for 46 miles. Turn right on Highway 89 and drive 0.5 mile to the park's northwest entrance station. Continue southeast on Lassen Park Road for 0.5 mile to the right turnoff for Manzanita Lake Campground (just beyond the Loomis Museum). Turn right and drive 100 yards to the trailhead on the left.

THE TRAIL
When most of Lassen Volcanic National Park is still buried in snow, it can feel like summer in the Manzanita Lake area of the park. This early season is an excellent time to hike to Crags Lake and perhaps take a bracing swim before the long days of sunshine dry up the snow-fed lake. Crags Lake is a beauty, and the trail to reach it is an easy ascent of only 1.7 miles, followed by a short but steep drop to the water's edge.

Initially, the path climbs very gently through pine and fir forest. Many of the trees are stunted from the poor volcanic soil; some have a healthy

Crags Lake is an ephemeral body of water that lies at the base of Chaos Crags.

quantity of bright green staghorn lichen coloring their trunks. The forest is situated along the edge of Chaos Jumbles, a two-mile-square rockslide caused by volcanic activity sometime around the year 1700.

The trees hide much of your view of the rockslide, but as you climb, you'll see other evidence of volcanism. A group of six plug domes called

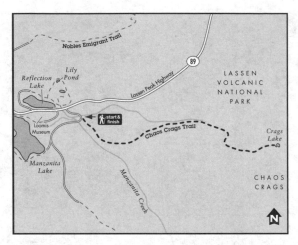

the Chaos Crags rise above the upper reaches of the trail. The Chaos Crags were formed by thick, viscous lava. The lava was so thick that it didn't flow outward; it squeezed upward through vents in the earth and then hardened in place. The Crags are estimated to be about 1,000 years old—much older than the Chaos Jumbles. A depression or small crater at the base of the Crags is what forms the basin for Crags Lake as the snow melts each spring.

As you proceed uphill, the forest cover begins to thin and your views get wider. A few switchbacks take you up to the crest of a ridge, the high point on this trail. You are rewarded with a dramatic view of the Chaos Crags towering hundreds of feet above you. Below you is the steep bowl in which blue-green Crags Lake lies, and far off in the distance are the Chaos Jumbles and forested Hat Creek Valley.

Many people turn around at this point, but it's only a short descent of about 100 yards down to the lake's edge. If you go swimming, you'll find that the water temperature is comfortable near the shore, but it drops dramatically the deeper you go. If you don't want to swim, find a spot along the water's edge and admire this fleeting, ephemeral lake. By late August, its snow-fed waters will have dried up under the Lassen sun.

GOING FARTHER

Another easy hike in the same area of the park is the trail that loops around Manzanita Lake. Start this 1.6-mile loop from the boat ramp and picnic area at Manzanita Lake, which is located just beyond the Manzanita Lake store and off the road to the campground.

17. Kings Creek Falls

RATING	🚶 🚶 🚶 🚶
DISTANCE	3.0 miles round-trip
HIKING TIME	1.5 hours
ELEVATION GAIN	480 feet
HIGH POINT	7,286 feet
EFFORT	Moderate Workout
BEST SEASON	June to October
PERMITS/CONTACT	Lassen Volcanic National Park entrance fee required ($10 per vehicle, valid for seven days), (530) 595-4444, www.nps.gov/lavo
MAPS	Lassen Volcanic National Park (download at www.nps.gov/lavo)
NOTES	Dogs and bikes prohibited

THE HIKE

Hike alongside pristine Kings Creek in the company of mule deer and songbirds to a misty, boisterous waterfall.

GETTING THERE

From Red Bluff on Interstate 5, turn east on Highway 36 and drive 45 miles. Turn north on Highway 89 and drive 4.5 miles to the park's Southwest entrance station. Continue north on Lassen Park Road for 12 miles to the Kings Creek Falls pullouts on both sides of the road. The trail begins on the right side of the road.

THE TRAIL

The waterfall on Kings Creek is pretty, not spectacular, but the beauty of the trail to access it makes Kings Creek Falls one of the most visited attractions in Lassen Volcanic National Park. The hike is a downhill trek along Kings Creek, starting from a nondescript pullout along the park road. On weekdays, a yellow school bus is often parked in this pullout; Kings Creek Falls is a popular destination for visiting school classes.

The first part of the trail meanders under the shade of big fir trees, but at 0.25 mile, the trail leaves the forest for a pleasant traverse along the edge of Lower Meadow. The meadow is dark green and teeming with

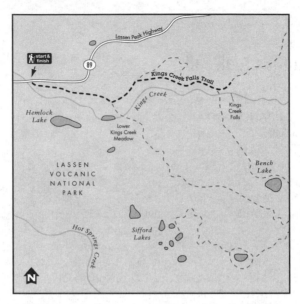

ebullient corn lilies in spring and early summer. It makes a perfect place to rest on the uphill hike back.

Beyond the meadow, you reach a fork and have two options: the Foot Trail or the Horse Trail. If your knees are feeling particularly creaky today, take the Horse Trail, but if you're up for it, the Foot Trail is the more scenic choice. It leads steeply downhill for 0.5 mile on stairsteps cut into the rock, just inches away from a section of Kings Creek called "The Cascades." Hikers who have trekked the world-famous Mist Trail in Yosemite will find a kinship between that trail and the granite walkway to Kings Creek Falls, although the latter has much less of a grade.

Just before you step down the granite staircase, take a look ahead at the far-off valley vista. Once you're on the steps, you'll probably need to keep your eyes on your feet, since you're hiking only a few inches from a rushing cascade of white water. Some hikers mistake these cascades for Kings Creek Falls, and they unknowingly turn around before they reach the real thing. Keep going until you come to a fenced overlook area.

Kings Creek Falls are about 50 feet high and split by a rock outcrop into two main cascades, which make a steep and narrow drop into the canyon. The fence surrounding the waterfall keeps hikers out of trouble on the unstable canyon slopes. If you want to take photographs, plan your trip so you arrive here in the morning when the cataract is evenly lit. Much of the day it is partially shaded.

Boisterous Kings Creek Falls can be seen via an easy, family-friendly hike.

For your return trip, you can retrace your steps on the spectacular Foot Trail back uphill along Kings Creek, or you can take the easier Horse Trail, which connects back with the main trail near Lower Meadow.

GOING FARTHER

You can add on a side trip to Sifford Lakes and then loop back to the trailhead for a total round-trip of 5.2 miles. Look for the right turnoff to Sifford Lakes about 100 yards before the waterfall overlook. Make sure you carry a trail map with you; there are several junctions to negotiate.

18. Terrace, Shadow, and Cliff Lakes

RATING	🚶 🚶 🚶 🚶
DISTANCE	3.8 miles round-trip
HIKING TIME	2 hours
ELEVATION GAIN	700 feet
HIGH POINT	8,060 feet
EFFORT	Moderate Workout
BEST SEASON	July to October
PERMITS/CONTACT	Lassen Volcanic National Park entrance fee required ($10 per vehicle, valid for seven days), (530) 595-4444, www.nps.gov/lavo
MAPS	Lassen Volcanic National Park (download at www.nps.gov/lavo)
NOTES	Dogs and bikes prohibited

THE HIKE

This trail visits three lovely and very different lakes that lie in the shadow of Lassen's Reading Peak.

GETTING THERE

From Red Bluff on Interstate 5, turn east on Highway 36 and drive 45 miles. Turn north on Highway 89 and drive 4.5 miles to the park's Southwest entrance station. Continue north on Lassen Park Road for 8.8 miles to the pullout area on the left. A small trail sign indicates the path to Terrace, Shadow, and Cliff Lakes.

THE TRAIL

There are many lakes in Lassen Volcanic National Park, resulting in a fair amount of debate over which one is the best, the prettiest, and/or the most suitable for swimming. It's hard to make a definitive choice on the matter, but this hike to Terrace, Shadow, and Cliff Lakes takes you to three lakes that should certainly qualify for the park's top ten list. Surprisingly, all three are remarkably different, although they lie only 1.0 mile apart.

Although some hikers trek to the lakes the long way, starting from Hat Lake in the north part of the park, the more common route is a short

Tranquil Shadow Lake warms up nicely for swimming by late summer.

downhill hike from the park road 2.0 miles east of the Lassen Peak trailhead. Following this path, you'll reach Terrace Lake in 0.5 mile, Shadow Lake in 0.8 mile, and Cliff Lake in 1.7 miles. Of the three, Shadow Lake is the largest and is best for swimming, and many hikers choose to cut their trip short here. If you hike only to Shadow Lake, you'll have a mere 1.6-mile round-trip. No matter how far you go, this is an "upside-down" hike: downhill on the way in and uphill on the return.

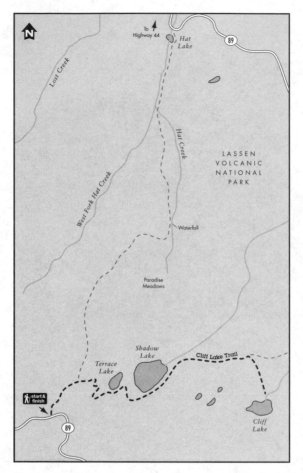

You'll reach the first lake, Terrace, in about 15 minutes of hiking. Terrace Lake is long and narrow, with a cliff forming its back wall and trees and rocks lining much of the rest of its shoreline. The trail leads closely along its south side, where there is a grassy beach area. At the far end of the lake, you can look back and see the pointy tip of Lassen Peak. Hike a few yards farther on the trail and you'll peer down on Shadow Lake, remarkably close by.

The trail drops to Shadow Lake, which is huge and round—at least double the size of Terrace Lake. Like Terrace, it has a rocky shoreline and some trees—a nice hodgepodge of hemlocks, firs, and pines—but its overall appearance is much more exposed. Conveniently, the trail clings to the lake's southeast shore, so at any point, you can kick off your shoes and wade in. It takes about 10 minutes to hike to the far east side of Shadow Lake, and when you get there, look back over your shoulder for a fine view of Lassen Peak in the background.

Shadow Lake makes a fine destination by itself, but it would be a shame to turn around here. The trail descends again, then crosses a stream and passes a small pond in a meadow. Again, look over your shoulder for admirable views of Lassen Peak—the best of the entire trip. The trail then reenters the forest. In less than 0.25 mile, watch for a spur trail leading to the right; this is the path to Cliff Lake. Hike through the trees to the small lake, which does indeed have a cliff, plus an impressive talus rockslide of white rocks on its southwest perimeter. Reading Peak, a volcano of the same type as Lassen Peak and Chaos Crags, rises to the south. The rockslide began on its slopes.

Cliff Lake's waters are shallow, clear, and green. The lake's most intriguing element is a small, tree-lined island on the west end. Walk to your right along the shoreline until you reach the lake's inlet, where you'll find an abundance of wildflowers, including wandering daisies, lupine, heather, and corn lilies.

GOING FARTHER

At the start of this hike, you will have passed a trail fork only 0.2 mile from the road. By taking the left fork at this junction (instead of the right fork to the three lakes), you can hike to lovely Paradise Meadows, about 1.6 miles to the northeast.

19. Bumpass Hell Trail

RATING	🚶 🚶 🚶 🚶
DISTANCE	3.0 miles round-trip
HIKING TIME	1.5 hours
ELEVATION GAIN	300 feet
HIGH POINT	8,000 feet
EFFORT	Easy Walk
BEST SEASON	July to October
PERMITS/CONTACT	Lassen Volcanic National Park entrance fee required ($10 per vehicle, valid for seven days), (530) 595-4444, www.nps.gov/lavo
MAPS	Lassen Volcanic National Park (download at www.nps.gov/lavo)
NOTES	Dogs and bikes prohibited

THE HIKE

Boasting the largest concentration of hydrothermal features in Lassen Volcanic National Park, Bumpass Hell was named after an 1860s settler who lost his leg after falling into a boiling pool.

GETTING THERE

From Red Bluff on Interstate 5, turn east on Highway 36 and drive 45 miles. Turn north on Highway 89 and drive 4.5 miles to the park's Southwest entrance station. Continue north on Lassen Park Road for 5.8 miles to the Bumpass Hell trailhead on the right.

THE TRAIL

If you travel Lassen Volcanic National Park with children, you will quickly learn that Bumpass Hell is their favorite destination because it has the distinction of not one but two foul words in its name. When you explain that "Bumpass" was the name of the man who discovered this strange geologic area, this distinction may be lessened somewhat, but then again, maybe not.

The "Hell" in Bumpass Hell is easy to recognize. Bumpass Hell is an active hydrothermal area, part of the Lassen geothermal system, which encompasses Bumpass Hell, Sulphur Works, Boiling Springs Lake, Little

The steaming, hissing, volcanic landscape of Bumpass Hell can be safely explored by staying on the boardwalks and marked paths.

Hot Springs Valley, Morgan Springs, and Terminal Geyser. Bumpass Hell is geology in action—16 acres of boiling springs, hissing steam vents, noisy fumaroles, and bubbling mud pots.

All this geologic commotion is the result of crack-like fissures in the earth that penetrate deeply enough to tap into volcanic heat (or with a little imagination, into the searing hot landscape of Hades). Surface water from rain and snowmelt seeps into these fissures and travels downward until it touches volcanically heated rock. This creates steam, which rises back up to the surface. As a result, pools of water in the Bumpass Hell area can reach temperatures of 200 degrees Fahrenheit. Kendall Vonhook Bumpass, who discovered Bumpass Hell in the 1860s, lost one of his legs when he stepped into one of these boiling, acidic pools.

Fortunately today we have a trail to follow in Bumpass Hell, and a wealth of signs that remind us to stay on the boardwalk and off the unstable soil. The hike is an easy stroll with a very gradual elevation change. In addition to its fascinating geology, the Bumpass Hell Trail features wide views of surrounding peaks, especially near its start. In 0.5 mile from the trailhead, a spur trail on the right leads to an overlook of Mount Conard, Diamond Peak, Brokeoff Mountain, Mount Diller, and Pilot Pinnacle. These mountains were parts of the ancient volcano Mount Tehama, which stood on this spot in eons past. Long since collapsed and eroded, Mount Tehama once soared to an elevation of 11,500 feet. Lassen Peak may have been formed from lava that flowed from Mount Tehama's side vents.

As you round a curve and reach the highest point in the trail, you find an interpretive sign explaining the wonders of Bumpass Hell, which is

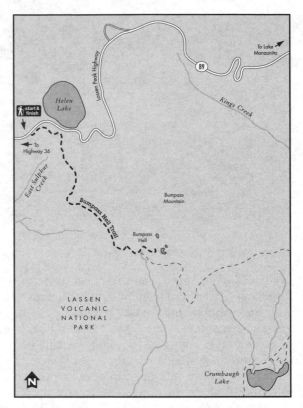

now directly below you. You also hear the strange ruckus caused by all the hydrothermal activity—sounds variously described as steam engines, trucks speeding by, or turbine motors. The smell of sulphur is ubiquitous. A short descent takes you into the hydrothermal area and boardwalks lead you over and around the various hot pools, steam vents, and mud-pots. Most of the hot pools are a striking gray-green to turquoise blue in color. Even the stream that flows through Bumpass Hell is odd looking—its water is milky gray instead of clear.

GOING FARTHER

From Bumpass Hell, you can continue another 1.5 miles to Cold Boiling Lake, then turn around and retrace your steps for a 6-mile round-trip. The "boiling" of this small pond occurs as gases continually bubble up through the surface of the water.

20. Mill Creek Falls

RATING	🚶 🚶 🚶 🚶
DISTANCE	3.2 miles round-trip
HIKING TIME	1 hour, 45 minutes
ELEVATION GAIN	300 feet
HIGH POINT	6,700 feet
EFFORT	Easy Walk
BEST SEASON	June to October
PERMITS/CONTACT	Lassen Volcanic National Park fee required
	($10 per vehicle, valid for seven days), (530) 595-4480
MAPS	Lassen Volcanic National Park
	(download at www.nps.gov/lavo)
NOTES	Dogs and bikes prohibited

THE HIKE

This gentle, meandering trail leads from Southwest Campground at Lassen Volcanic National Park through forest and meadows to an overlook of a 75-foot-high waterfall.

GETTING THERE

From Interstate 5 at Red Bluff, turn east on Highway 36 and drive 47 miles. Turn north on Highway 89 and drive 4.5 miles to the park's southern entrance. Continue 100 yards past the entrance station to the parking area on the right, near the restroom at Southwest Campground. Begin walking on the paved trail by the restroom, heading through the camp to its north side.

THE TRAIL

Mill Creek Falls is not only the highest waterfall in Lassen Volcanic National Park, it's also the loveliest—despite some serious contenders.

The trail to the falls is only 3.2 miles round-trip and undulates so gently up and down that you're never quite sure if you're losing elevation or gaining it. From Southwest Campground, a brief stint on pavement takes you past a few tents and picnic tables to a log bridge over West Sulphur Creek. Cross the bridge and you enter a football-field-sized garden of mule's ears, which dazzle onlookers with large school-bus-yellow flowers

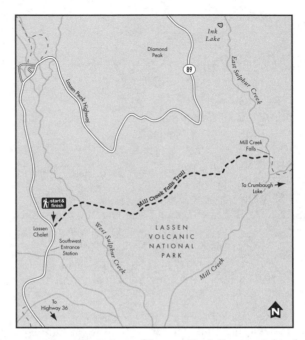

in July. A postcard-perfect view of Lassen Peak lies straight ahead. Many photographs have been snapped here, capturing the stunningly lush, emerald green valley that lies between Sulphur Creek and Lassen's old, snowy volcano.

Exiting the acres of mule's ears, the trail travels under a canopy of red firs, white firs, and pines, many covered with bright green staghorn moss. Occasionally the path skirts by small, open meadows rife with corn lilies and other summer wildflowers.

Heading steadily eastward through the trees, you will suddenly hear the boisterous noise of plummeting water. In a few more footsteps, you are peering across the canyon at Mill Creek Falls.

A 75-foot, plunging freefall, Mill Creek Falls makes a lasting impression. Two creeks, East Sulphur and Bumpass, join together at its lip and spill as one through a very deep and narrow canyon. The pairing and funneling of the two streams results in a tremendous water flow. Perhaps what is most spectacular about the waterfall is the rock face over which it pours—a knobby-looking cliff covered in layers of moss and algae, showing off colors ranging from rust and orange to deep green. Huge old-growth fir trees grow at the waterfall's brink, adding to the majesty. Pull out a sandwich and enjoy this watery view, then return the way you came.

Mill Creek Falls is formed where two creeks, East Sulphur and Bumpass, join together.

GOING FARTHER
The trail continues over the top of the waterfall, then climbs steeply past Crumbaugh Lake and Cold Boiling Lake, and on to the Kings Creek Picnic Area. With a shuttle car waiting at the picnic area, this makes an ideal 4.6-mile one-way hike.

The rocky promontories of Salt Point State Park are framed by graceful Bishop pines.

MENDOCINO, SONOMA, AND NAPA

The Mendocino and Wine Country region encompasses a vast and diverse landscape ranging from wave-swept beaches, rugged cliffs, and rolling sand dunes to vineyard-covered hills and valleys. Despite the technological advances of our modern 21st century, this area has retained its pastoral character more than perhaps anywhere else in California. Highway 1 winds up the rocky Pacific coast past seaside villages with population counts lower than their elevation—which is close to sea level. In the grassland-covered hills east of the Sonoma and Mendocino coast, you're likely to see more sheep and cows than people.

This rural countryside is a marvelous setting for a hiking excursion. Within a few miles of the Mendocino town limits are three state parks with gently graded hiking trails—Russian Gulch, Jug Handle, and MacKerricher. In the redwood forests east of Mendocino lie more public lands, including the intimate beauty of Hendy Woods State Park. And if you're clamoring for a fine meal or a cozy bed-and-breakfast to ease you off the trail at the end of the day, visitors are always welcome at the charming shops and business establishments in downtown Mendocino.

Like the Mendocino coast, the neighboring Sonoma coast is also blessed with unforgettable scenery. Rugged headlands, rocky promontories, and sandy coves offer breathtaking panoramas. Trails at Salt Point State Park and Fort Ross State Historic Park give hikers the opportunity to partake in the seaside drama on gentle paths that traverse the coastal bluffs.

Unforgettable, too, are the inland valleys in and around the Napa and Sonoma Wine Country. The Wine Country's parklands, including redwood-studded Bothe–Napa Valley State Park and the volcanic buttes of Robert Louis Stevenson State Park, offer plentiful hiking trails for visitors seeking a little fresh air and exercise. For a perfect day trip, plan on a morning hike topped off by an afternoon of wine tasting.

MENDOCINO, SONOMA, AND NAPA

21. La Laguna Trail

RATING	🚶 🚶 🚶
DISTANCE	1.3 miles round-trip
HIKING TIME	45 minutes
ELEVATION GAIN	Negligible
HIGH POINT	50 feet (sea level)
EFFORT	Easy Walk
BEST SEASON	Year-round
PERMITS/CONTACT	MacKerricher State Park day-use fee
	($8 per vehicle), (707) 964-9112, www.parks.ca.gov
MAPS	MacKerricher State Park
	(download at www.parks.ca.gov)
NOTES	Wheelchair accessible; dogs and bikes prohibited

THE HIKE

Both wheelchair users and hiking-boot users can enjoy this bird-rich trip around freshwater Lake Cleone.

GETTING THERE

From Mendocino, drive 11.7 miles north on Highway 1 to the signed entrance to MacKerricher State Park on the left (3 miles north of Fort Bragg). Turn left into the park, drive past the ranger kiosk, and turn left again, heading toward the camping areas. In 0.5 mile, you'll see Lake Cleone on your left. Park in the parking lot next to the lake and begin hiking from the trail near the restrooms.

THE TRAIL

MacKerricher State Park is an oceanfront park, but it's also home to a freshwater lake, with a great easy hiking trail around its perimeter. Lake Cleone is a striking circle of deep blue just a short walk from the ocean beach. Except in the wettest months of the year, its trail is usually completely wheelchair accessible, and it's a wonderful place for bird-watching and enjoying some "down time" away from the near-constant frenzy of the wind and waves at the ocean beach.

Start this walk on the ocean side of the Lake Cleone parking lot, where you'll find restrooms and a billboard describing some of the birds you

A boardwalk-lined trail protects the marsh surrounding Lake Cleone and makes the area accessible to wheelchair users.

may see on the lake: mallards, surf scooters, sanderlings, and avocets. More than 90 bird species have been spotted here. Follow the dirt trail parallel to the paved access road for about 75 yards until you reach the La Laguna Trail on your left. The path leads away from the road and into thick vegetation along the lake's southwest side. The only distraction is the faint sound of Highway 1, which soon fades away as you head deeper into this dense thicket. Cutoff trails head to campgrounds and the ranger's residence, but just stay on the main trail as it circles the lake.

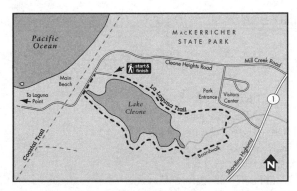

Bird viewing is first-rate, even for novices. From only 10 feet away, we enjoyed watching a great egret catch a small fish and swallow it, leaving a telltale lump in its long neck. The Department of Fish and Game stocks the lake with trout every few weeks in summer, so you may see a few anglers trying their luck from shore or plying the waters in small rafts and kayaks.

At the lake's east end, the trail traverses a marsh on a 0.5-mile-long raised boardwalk, which serves the dual purpose of making this stretch completely wheelchair accessible and also protecting the fragile wetlands.

As you finish out the loop on the north side of Lake Cleone, you'll leave the marsh and come near the lake's edge again, where the shoreline is bordered by Monterey cypress trees, poised to withstand the coastal winds. Picnic tables are located at the end of the trail, near the boat ramp.

GOING FARTHER
Combine this walk with a stroll on the level Old Haul Road, which runs along the beach directly across the parking lot from Lake Cleone. This old railroad trail, also called the Ten Mile Coastal Trail, runs north for 1.2 miles and south for 2.0 miles along the coast, offering nonstop views of sand dunes and crashing ocean waves.

22. Ecological Staircase Nature Trail

RATING	🚶 🚶 🚶 🚶
DISTANCE	5.0 miles round-trip
HIKING TIME	2 hours, 30 minutes
ELEVATION GAIN	250 feet
HIGH POINT	300 feet
EFFORT	Moderate Workout
BEST SEASON	Year-round
PERMITS/CONTACT	Jug Handle State Natural Reserve, (707) 937-5804, www.parks.ca.gov
MAPS	USGS Mendocino
NOTES	Dogs and bikes prohibited

THE HIKE

Learn all about the natural procession of marine terraces on this peaceful nature walk from the coast to the inland hills.

GETTING THERE

From Mendocino, drive 4 miles north on Highway 1 to the entrance to Jug Handle State Natural Reserve on the left. Turn left and park in the parking area. The Ecological Staircase Nature Trail begins on the southwest side of the parking lot.

THE TRAIL

The Ecological Staircase Nature Trail is a 5.0-mile hike featuring a wealth of varied terrain, from rocky ocean coastline to dry grasslands to dense green forest. But the name is a little misleading. The trail is like a staircase only in theory, not in practice—it's not a stairstepped trail. In fact, the trail climbs only 250 feet over its entire distance, and it does so almost imperceptibly.

So why is it called the Ecological Staircase? Jug Handle State Reserve consists of a series of marine terraces, carved by ocean waves and other forces of nature over the course of half a million years or more. Each terrace is 100 feet higher in elevation and 100,000 years older than the one below, with very different soil and plant life. The geological evolution continues to this day, with future terraces still under water. While marine

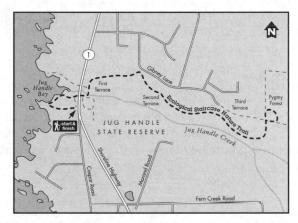

terraces are common along the California coast, they are rarely as well preserved and distinguishable as they are here.

The trail starts off packing a punch with stunning coastal scenery. From the parking lot, it travels 0.5 mile around the Jug Handle Bay headlands, with access to and views of beautiful white sand beaches. April through June are the best wildflower months along this stretch of coast, when the headland bluffs are peppered with colorful golden poppies, Indian paintbrush, coastal lupine, seaside daisies, and wild strawberries. Summer is occasionally blessed with fog-free days, and if that blessing is bestowed, the beach life here is as good as anywhere on the California coast.

After exploring the blufftops, head inland underneath the freeway bridge and along the streambed of Jug Handle Creek. You'll have to tolerate a certain amount of road noise for about 15 minutes while you walk up the creek canyon, but it will soon fade away as you enter the first terrace, a grassland environment dotted with bishop pines.

Another 0.75 mile of hiking brings you to the second terrace, a mixed conifer forest of bishop pine, Douglas fir, Sitka spruce, and western hemlock. The Sitka spruce, which grow along the Pacific coast all the way to Alaska, are at the far southern end of their range here. Farther along the trail on the second terrace is a combination redwood and Douglas fir grove. These tall trees tower over the shade-loving ferns and sorrel that grow at their base.

Watch closely and you can see the warning signs of the approaching third terrace: the tall trees of the conifer forest begin to thin out and diminish in size. This third terrace, nearly 2.0 miles in, is composed of hardpan soil, sand dunes, and pygmy trees. Soil and drainage are so poor here that trees and shrubs grow only in stunted sizes. The soil in the pygmy forest is 300 feet higher in elevation than that at the nearby beach, but 300,000 years older. Contemplate this strange, dwarfed forest and then turn around and head back the way you came.

GOING FARTHER
When you reach the pygmy forest, the trail, which is now a logging road, makes a 1-mile loop around the pygmy forest. At this point you've officially left Jug Handle State Reserve and are within the boundary of Jackson Demonstration State Forest. Walk the loop to add another mile to your trip.

23. Fern Canyon and Falls Loop Trails

RATING	🚶 🚶 🚶 🚶
DISTANCE	4.6 miles round-trip
HIKING TIME	2 hours, 30 minutes
ELEVATION GAIN	220 feet
HIGH POINT	230 feet
EFFORT	Moderate Workout
BEST SEASON	December to May
PERMITS/CONTACT	Russian Gulch State Park fee required ($8 per vehicle), (707) 937-5804, www.parks.ca.gov
MAPS	Russian Gulch State Park (download at www.parks.ca.gov)
NOTES	Dogs prohibited; bikes allowed on paved portion of trail

THE HIKE

An easy trail suitable for hiking or biking takes you through dense forest to a waterfall tucked into a redwood grotto.

GETTING THERE

From Mendocino, drive 2 miles north on Highway 1 to the entrance sign for Russian Gulch State Park on the left. Turn left and then immediately left again to reach the entrance kiosk. After paying, drive past the kiosk and continue straight, crossing back under the highway, to the eastern side of the park. Drive past the recreation hall and all of the campsites to the parking area for the Fern Canyon Trail. Start hiking from the trailhead at the east side of the parking area.

THE TRAIL

There comes a time when you just have to stretch the rules a little. For me, that time was when I hiked the Fern Canyon Trail to the waterfall at Russian Gulch State Park. My cardinal rule was "never hike on pavement," and I was fairly self-righteous about it. But the lure of a waterfall in a fern-filled canyon was too good to pass up, even though it meant walking on an old paved trail for part of the trip.

Russian Gulch Falls is hidden in a redwood-lined grotto a few miles from the coast.

The paved Fern Canyon Trail may not be completely au naturel, but it is pleasantly rutted, cracked, and covered with leaves and fir needles. The route is nearly level and almost always accompanied by the sound of running water from Russian Gulch. A dense riparian forest, filled with second-growth redwoods, hemlocks, Douglas firs, bigleaf maples, alders, and tons of ferns, borders both sides of the trail. In late summer, trailside blackberry bushes provide nourishment for hungry hikers. Stinging nettles and poison oak are also prevalent, so watch where you tread if you stray off the pavement.

The trail directions are simple: Follow Fern Canyon Trail for 1.6 miles to its junction with Falls Loop Trail, where the pavement ends. Here you'll see a few picnic tables and a bike rack, as well as a junction with the North Trail for those who chose to follow an alternate, unpaved route (see "Going Farther," below). The Falls Loop Trail allows you the choice of going left or right; both paths join at the waterfall, but the left trail is much shorter (0.7 mile to the waterfall versus 2.3 miles). For a 4.6-mile round-trip, head left.

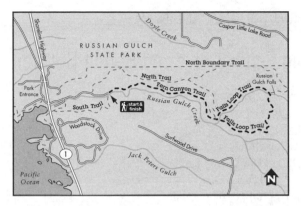

Now on a dirt trail, you'll face a bit of up and down, including some wooden stairsteps. In 0.7 mile, a glimpse of Russian Gulch Falls comes into view just before the trail heads downhill to its base.

The falls at Russian Gulch prove the adage that when it comes to waterfalls, setting counts more than size. At a mere 36 feet, Russian Gulch Falls is no record-setter, but it drops over a vertical slab of rock into a verdant grotto. In winter, the waterfall can be a rushing torrent that spills over the huge boulder at its base, whereas in summer, it is reduced to one main cascade and a smaller, thinner stream that pours down the left side of the rock. Broken tree trunks and branches are jammed around the base of the falls, having fallen and tumbled over its lip. Some have been there so long that plants have taken root on them, creating a lush green frame for the falling water. One tree trunk, leaning vertically against the waterfall's boulder, is completely covered with dense thriving ferns.

It isn't easy to leave this special place. Often you will find hikers picnicking or just hanging out at the footbridge near the base of the falls. Chances are good that you will decide to join them.

GOING FARTHER

Purists can get around the pavement problem by taking the alternate, unpaved North Trail. It starts at the same trailhead as the paved Fern Canyon Trail and then takes a longer, more meandering route to reach the junction with the Waterfall Loop Trail. Taking the North Trail out and back in both directions will add 2 miles to your trip. Another way to extend the hike is to walk the entire 3-mile Falls Loop Trail instead of just the 0.7-mile out and back to the falls.

24. Big Hendy Grove and Hermit Hut Trails

RATING	🚶 🚶 🚶
DISTANCE	2.0 miles round-trip
HIKING TIME	1.0 hour
ELEVATION GAIN	100 feet
HIGH POINT	300 feet
EFFORT	Easy Walk
BEST SEASON	Year-round
PERMITS/CONTACT	Hendy Woods State Park fee required
	($8 per vehicle), (707) 895-3141, www.parks.ca.gov
MAPS	Hendy Woods State Park
	(download at www.parks.ca.gov)
NOTES	Dogs and bikes prohibited

THE HIKE

A hike through big redwoods leads to the homesite of Hendy Woods' hermit.

GETTING THERE

From Mendocino, drive south on Highway 1 for approximately 10 miles to the Highway 128 turnoff. Head east on Highway 128 for 18 miles to the directional sign for Hendy Woods State Park at Greenwood Road. Turn right (south) on Greenwood Road and drive 0.5 mile to the park entrance on the left. Follow the park road to the day-use parking area; the trailhead is on the east (right) side.

THE TRAIL

As you drive on Highway 128 from Cloverdale to Mendocino, watch through your car windows as the landscape changes from dry oak grasslands to dense redwood forest. Would-be hikers may be tempted by the sight of numerous hiking paths leading from the roadside into the redwoods. Who can resist a walk among big trees paralleling the Navarro River?

But if you opt to pull over, you may be disappointed. None of these trails go farther than a few hundred yards, ending at swimming and fishing holes. For a more lengthy hike in these woods, head to Hendy Woods

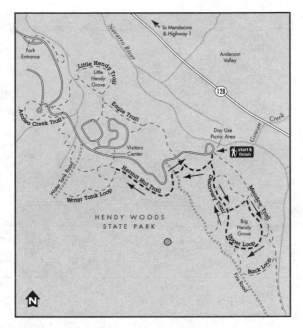

State Park, where you'll find beautiful redwood groves, plus a story that will add an unexpected dimension to your trip.

From the park's day-use parking area, start hiking on the wheelchair-accessible All-Access Trail, turning left and following the trail signs for the Discovery Trail and Big Hendy Grove. You'll pass tall standing redwoods as well as several downed trees. Children love to play on their huge horizontal trunks and gnarled root balls. The farther you go from the parking area, the more peaceful and quiet this old forest becomes. Patches of sorrel form soft green clouds on the ground. Black-tailed deer munch on the greenery. Sunlight filters through the tall trees, softly illuminating the scene.

After looping around the Big Hendy Grove, walk a little farther south on the All-Access Trail (away from the parking area) until you reach the Hermit Hut Trail on your left. This trail climbs steadily up from the redwood-lined valley floor through a drier forest of oaks and madrones. You'll feel the temperature rise as you climb out of the redwoods' dense shade. After crossing a fire road, you'll climb another 100 yards until you reach an unmarked intersection. Continue straight to a billboard displaying newspaper clippings about the Hermit Hut Trail's hermit, a Russian immigrant named Petrov, who died in the early 1980s.

The height of the Big Hendy Grove's redwoods make this six-foot-tall man appear diminutive.

Petrov lived for 18 years in these woods, building huts out of branches and tree stumps. He ate food he gathered from the forest and neighboring gardens, and wore patched-together, discarded clothing from campers and park visitors. One of the huts that he built is located right behind the billboard. A ramshackle batch of branches serves as a roof over a large, hollowed-out tree stump. Another of Petrov's huts is found a few yards away near the unmarked junction you just passed.

Not surprisingly, children are mesmerized by Petrov's story. Maybe it's the magical ambience of the redwoods, or maybe it's the way the light filters through the forest, but it isn't hard to picture him here, living a simple life in the woods.

GOING FARTHER

Park your car near the ranger station and visitor center and hike to the Little Hendy Grove of redwoods, which is smaller in size but no less impressive than the Big Hendy Grove.

25. Chinese Gulch and Phillips Gulch Trails

RATING	🚶 🚶 🚶
DISTANCE	2.8 miles round-trip
HIKING TIME	1 hour, 15 minutes
ELEVATION GAIN	250 feet
HIGH POINT	500 feet
EFFORT	Moderate Workout
BEST SEASON	April to June
PERMITS/CONTACT	Kruse Rhododendron State Reserve, (707) 847-3221, www.parks.ca.gov
MAPS	Salt Point State Park/Kruse Rhododendron State Reserve (download at www.parks.ca.gov)
NOTES	Dogs and bikes prohibited

THE HIKE

Witness an extravagant, hot-pink flower display when the rhododendrons bloom at this coastal park.

GETTING THERE

From Jenner, drive north on Highway 1 for 24 miles, passing several Salt Point State Park entrances. Turn right on Kruse Ranch Road, 100 yards north of the Fisk Mill Cove parking area. Drive 0.5 mile on Kruse Ranch Road to the small dirt parking area at the trailhead. Begin hiking on the north side of the parking lot at the wooden steps on the left that lead to Chinese Gulch.

THE TRAIL

You've made the long trip to the Sonoma coast on Memorial Day weekend and the sun hasn't shown itself for days, so you're not exactly enjoying clear views of the coast. Well, take heart, because this is a coastal hike that's enjoyable even in the densest fog.

The Chinese Gulch and Phillips Gulch Trails in Kruse Rhododendron State Reserve combine to make a pleasant woodland loop hike that shows off the park's featured species, the coast rhododendron (*rhododendron macrophyllum*). You have to show up in the right season, though. From April to June, these tree-like shrubs display large clusters of pinkish-purple

Wooden stairsteps lead hikers up and down the canyons of Chinese and Phillips gulches.

flowers, each about the size of a small bouquet. But in the non-blooming months, the rhododendrons blend so well into the forest backdrop that you might not even notice them.

The rhododendrons thrive because of a fire that burned through this area many years ago, causing a succession of plant regeneration that will eventually lead to a completely reforested second-growth redwood and fir grove. The showy shrubs are slowly losing their hold in the forest as the trees grow up and around them, blocking out their light.

Even if the flowers aren't blooming when you visit, a loop trip on the Chinese Gulch and Phillips Gulch Trails offers myriad charms, including plentiful ferns and a dense redwood and fir forest. Both Chinese and Phillips gulches are good-sized streams flowing under rustic wooden bridges, whimsically built of rough-hewn logs with branches for railings. Large mushrooms grow on some of the bridges.

The loop route is well marked. At several points, the trail junctions with paths that lead to "County Road" (the dirt and gravel road you drove in on), but stay on the gulch trails unless you want to take a short-cut back to the parking lot. At about 1.5 miles, you'll cross the road to transfer from Chinese Gulch Trail to Phillips Gulch Trail. The hiking is generally easier on the Phillips Gulch Trail, the second half of your loop.

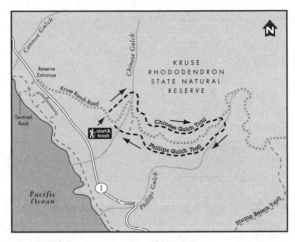

Redwood logs along the way make comfortable benches. This is a path for taking your time and stopping to enjoy the forest as you go.

Your final stream crossing is at Chinese Gulch, which flows all the way to the Pacific Ocean. From here you begin a short but steep climb back up to the parking lot; it's just enough of an ascent to make you feel like you got a workout right at the end of the trip.

GOING FARTHER

If it's the regal rhododendron you've come to see, take a walk on the 0.25-mile Rhododendron Trail Loop that starts at the same parking lot. Neighboring Salt Point State Park has many excellent hiking trails; see the description for the Bluff Trail (hike #26 in this guide).

26. Bluff Trail

RATING	🚶 🚶 🚶 🚶
DISTANCE	2.0 miles round-trip
HIKING TIME	1 hour
ELEVATION GAIN	Negligible
HIGH POINT	100 feet
EFFORT	Easy Walk
BEST SEASON	Year-round
PERMITS/CONTACT	Salt Point State Park fee required ($8 per vehicle), (707) 847-3221, www.parks.ca.gov
MAPS	Salt Point State Park/Kruse Rhododendron State Reserve (download at www.parks.ca.gov)
NOTES	Dogs and bikes prohibited

THE HIKE

Wander along the Salt Point State Park's wooded blufftops, enjoying peekaboo views of the crashing shoreline.

GETTING THERE

From Jenner, drive north on Highway 1 for approximately 24 miles. Bypass the main Salt Point State Park entrance at Gerstle Cove and turn left at the Fisk Mill Cove parking area, located 2.6 miles north of Gerstle Cove. Park in the parking lot on the left, then find the trailhead on the ocean side of the lot, near the picnic tables and fire grills.

THE TRAIL

Salt Point State Park is blessed with a long stretch of pristine Sonoma coastline, rich tidepools and kelp beds teeming with sea life, and plentiful hiking trails. One of the easiest and most rewarding is the Bluff Trail that begins at Fisk Mill Cove, a few miles north of the main park entrance and campground.

The trail is good from the get-go. As you start down the dirt path, a trail marker points you to the left to South Cove (0.1 mile away), or to the right to Sentinel Rock and Fisk Mill Cove. If you're visiting in winter or early spring, this signpost is a good place to get a view of a seasonal waterfall that plunges from the bluffs down to the sea. Head left to South

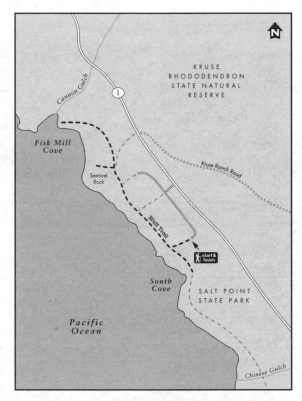

Cove, ending up right on top of this small waterfall. Then continue a short distance to the bluffs beyond the cove, gaining more coastal views before the path dissipates in the coastal scrub. When you've seen enough, simply turn around and hike back, keeping the ocean on your left. When you reach the trail sign again, continue past it toward Sentinel Rock and Fisk Mill Cove.

This is not a hike in which you'll mind retracing your steps. While wandering on the Bluff Trail, you're never more than 50 feet from the ocean's crashing shoreline, and often you are tantalizingly closer. Your level path meanders through a forest of ferns, rhododendrons, cypress, and bishop pines. Even while enveloped in the shade of this peaceful woodland, you have peekaboo views of rocky pocket beaches with crashing waves, playful seals swimming in the surf, and abalone divers plying their trade.

The trail crosses three wooden footbridges, spanning streams that carry runoff from the hills down to the ocean. A highlight is a large sandstone formation with tiny hollowed caves. Perhaps most enticing is a lovely

From the Bluff Trail's high perch, Salt Point State Park's dramatic coastline is revealed below.

trailside meadow, protected from the wind on three sides. During mid- to late April, this meadow is completely covered with purple Douglas irises.

Branching off the Bluff Trail are short spurs leading to vistas of the ocean and coves below. The spurs either dead-end or rejoin the main trail, so it's impossible to stray too far. The trail's only major ascent occurs on the stairstepped path to the viewing platform atop Sentinel Rock, a dramatic coastal overlook. A bench on top of the rock invites you to stay a while.

After descending from Sentinel Rock, finish out your trip by following the short path that leads down to rocky Fisk Mill Cove, a picturesque beach and popular spot for abalone diving. Then make the 1.0-mile return walk to your car. Picnic tables and fire grills are situated right at the trailhead, so you might cap off your hike with a spot of lunch.

GOING FARTHER

Proceed to the main park entrance and turn into the inland side of the park, which is signed for Woodside Campground. From the parking area just beyond the kiosk you can take a steep 1-mile hike to see the park's pygmy forest of stunted cypress and pine trees.

27. Fort Ross Cove Trail

RATING	🚶 🚶 🚶 🚶
DISTANCE	2.0 miles round-trip
HIKING TIME	1 hour
ELEVATION GAIN	50 feet
HIGH POINT	100 feet
EFFORT	Easy Walk
BEST SEASON	Year-round
PERMITS/CONTACT	Fort Ross State Historic Park fee required ($8 per vehicle), (707) 847-3286 or (707) 847-3437, www.parks.ca.gov
MAPS	Fort Ross State Historic Park (download at www.parks.ca.gov)
NOTES	Dogs and bikes prohibited

THE HIKE

Visit a well-preserved relic of the Sonoma coast's past, then hike an adjacent trail along the coastal bluffs to Fort Ross Cove and the beach beyond.

GETTING THERE

From Jenner, drive north on Highway 1 for approximately 15 miles to the entrance to Fort Ross State Historic Park on the left.

THE TRAIL

On this hike at Fort Ross State Historic Park, you'll have the chance to learn a little history, explore an old Russian colonial fort, and stroll along the scenic Sonoma coastline.

The Fort Ross Cove Trail is a wander-as-you-please meander through Fort Ross's stockade walls and along the top of steep bluffs that drop 100 feet into the sea. You can choose your own route, stopping to enjoy the history or the scenery as you wish.

The old Russian fort, with its huge barracks and two-story blockhouses complete with cannons, is an intriguing sight. Built in 1812 in only a few weeks by Russian colonists who were eager for eastern expansion, the fort was occupied until 1841. The smell of the old wooden buildings

The well-preserved buildings of an early 1800s Russian fort are found along a scenic stretch of the Sonoma Coast.

evokes images of those earlier times, when colonists tried to develop an economy at first based on sea otter pelts and later on agriculture. Neither led to substantial profits.

When you've seen enough of the fort's buildings, follow the gravel road that leads out the main gate toward the ocean. The road circles down into Fort Ross Cove, which was the first shipyard in California, established by the Russians for their pelt-trading business. A few picnic tables are located there.

Explore the tiny cove, which is covered with odd-shaped driftwood and wave-smoothed rocks. A small, shallow stream must be crossed in springtime—a little strategic foot placement on rocks should work, although some hikers prefer the leap-and-pray method of stream crossing. On the cove's far side, a trail leads up the bluffs; follow it. In spring, you'll see the usual cabal of coastal wildflowers—lupine, paintbrush, and Douglas irises. Year-round, raptors and seabirds soar overhead.

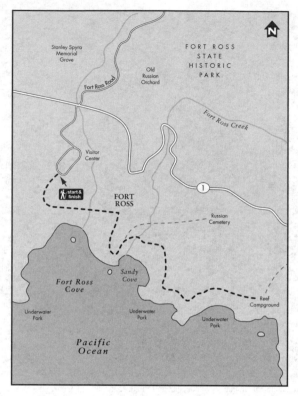

The trail soon descends to a gravel road where you'll find restrooms and a 20-site campground. A path leads off to the right, down to the beach. Two tiny streams join together here on their way to the ocean, with horsetail ferns growing along their banks. Pick your way among the rocks down to the beach.

GOING FARTHER
Just 1.5 miles north on Highway 1 is another park worth exploring. Drive to Stillwater Cove Regional Park and park in the day-use area. The Stockoff Creek Loop Trail starts here and makes a 1.25-mile loop through a secluded redwood forest; take the spur trail to visit the historic one-room schoolhouse.

28. Pomo Canyon Trail

RATING	🚶 🚶 🚶
DISTANCE	6.0 miles round-trip
HIKING TIME	3 hours
ELEVATION GAIN	800 feet
HIGH POINT	900 feet
EFFORT	Prepare to Perspire
BEST SEASON	Spring, fall
PERMITS/CONTACT	(707) 875-3483 or (707) 865-2391, www.parks.ca.gov
MAPS	Sonoma Coast State Park (download at www.parks.ca.gov)
NOTES	Dogs and bikes prohibited

THE HIKE

From April to June, this trail is one of the best places on the Sonoma coast to enjoy spring wildflowers. The rest of the year, the trail's redwood grove and views of the Russian River and Sonoma coast will inspire you.

GETTING THERE

From Highway 1 in Bodega Bay, drive north for 7 miles to the Shell Beach parking lot on the west side of the road. Park in the lot, then walk across Highway 1 to access the trail on its east side, signed as Dr. David Joseph Memorial Pomo Canyon Trail.

THE TRAIL

If the wind is howling on the Sonoma coast or the fog has smothered the beaches in a cool, white-gray blanket, you don't have to pack up and head inland. A first-rate hike can still be had on the Pomo Canyon Trail from Shell Beach, where wind and fog can't ruin the trip.

Pomo Canyon Trail meanders over coastal grasslands covered with spring wildflowers, then visits a secluded grove of second-growth redwoods in a wind-protected canyon. Clear weather will provide great views of the ocean and the Russian River, but if the skies are fickle, no worries: Hiking through Pomo Canyon's redwood grove in dense fog or light rain can still be a delightful experience.

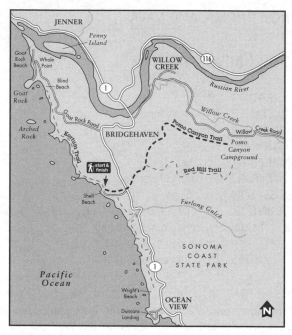

Wildflower lovers take note: The coastal hills and grasslands along Pomo Canyon Trail are well known for erupting in spring blooms. More than 100 different species may flower at one time. This great diversity draws flower worshippers here every year.

Start your trip at the Shell Beach parking lot north of Bodega Bay. Carefully walk across Highway 1 to access the Pomo Canyon trailhead. The trail begins on an old paved road that has eroded into part gravel, part pavement, and part grasses, and heads uphill away from the coast.

At a junction at 0.7 mile, where the path ascends to a grassy plateau punctuated by a few large rock formations, bear right, then bear left shortly afterward. You'll leave the worn pavement behind and follow grassy double-track, which soon narrows to single-track. Bright blue and pale white Douglas iris dot the grasslands in early spring; blue gentian and tarweed follow later in summer.

The path rolls along the ridgetop, traveling generally downhill toward Willow Creek's canyon. Heading north, you'll gain fine views of the Russian River's graceful curves and Goat Rock Beach beyond. Watch for a short spur trail on the left, about 1.0 mile from the start, which leads to a grassy knoll topped with a picnic table. There you gain a wider view of the 110-mile-long river at its junction with the sea.

Pomo Canyon Trail leads hikers inland from the Sonoma Coast across flower-filled hills.

From here, the trail begins to descend in earnest. It crosses several seeps and springs that provide year-round water for the lichen-covered Douglas firs and Monterey pines, passes a signed turnoff for the Red Hill Trail (see "Going Farther," below), then at about 2.0 miles, enters the first grove of redwoods. Their trunks are covered with a gray-green lichen, giving the trees a ghostlike appearance. You might expect that any moment a leprechaun will pop out of this mysterious forest.

Pomo Canyon Trail wanders along the edge of the grove, then opens out into the grasslands with wide views of the lush Willow Creek drainage and Russian River canyon. In another 0.5 mile, it enters a second stand of redwoods and then drops steeply to its end at Pomo Canyon Campground, a secluded walk-in camp. If the sites are empty, you might select a picnic table for a rest stop. Otherwise, just turn around and head back over the ridge. The beauty of this trail is worth seeing all over again.

GOING FARTHER

Make a semi-loop out of this trail by connecting to the Red Hill Trail at Pomo Canyon Campground. Follow the Red Hill Trail for 1.25 miles until it reconnects with Pomo Canyon Trail. Along the way, climb the summit of Red Hill via a short spur trail; the tip-top is marked by a circle of rocks. You'll finish out the trip by heading back to the Shell Beach parking lot on Pomo Canyon Trail.

29. Table Rock

RATING	🚶 🚶 🚶
DISTANCE	4.4 miles round-trip
HIKING TIME	2.5 hours
ELEVATION GAIN	1,100 feet
HIGH POINT	2,465 feet
EFFORT	Prepare to Perspire
BEST SEASON	October to April
PERMITS/CONTACT	Robert Louis Stevenson State Park, (707) 942-4575, www.parks.ca.gov
MAPS	USGS Mount St. Helena
NOTES	Dogs and bikes prohibited

THE HIKE

Take a walk on the "other side" of Robert Louis Stevenson State Park, where a single-track trail leads to a rock outcrop with a superlative view.

GETTING THERE

From Highway 29/128 in Calistoga, turn north on Highway 29 and drive 8 miles (through the town of Calistoga) to the signed trailhead. Park in the pullouts on either side of the road. The trail begins on the right side of the road.

THE TRAIL

Hikers not feeling ambitious enough to tackle the 10.0-mile round-trip to the top of mighty Mount St. Helena have another reason to drive winding Highway 29 from Calistoga to Robert Louis Stevenson State Park. It's the Table Rock Trail, a much easier hike that offers some of the Wine Country's best views. A mere 4.4 miles round-trip with only a moderate amount of up and down leads you to the craggy summit of Table Rock, a large block of igneous rock with sheer drop-offs on three sides. This moonscape-like outcrop with its crags, gullies, and pockmarks is fascinating enough from a geological perspective, but it's the view from the top that you will long remember: a postcard panorama of the Napa Valley.

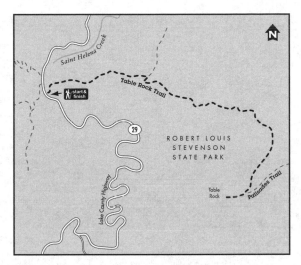

The trailhead is directly across the highway from the trailhead for Mount St. Helena. If at all possible, park on the Table Rock trailhead side of the road (southeast or right side), and not the Mount St. Helena side, so you don't have to cross Highway 29 on foot. Drivers speed up this mountain road as if it was the autobahn, so be extra cautious.

The hike begins with a climb up a small hill through a canopy of tan oaks, madrones, and Douglas firs, topping out at a boulder-studded vista point looking north, at 0.7 mile from the trailhead. From here and other points along the trail, Mount St. Helena is visible to the west, looming 2,000 feet higher, as well as the green hills and vineyard-lined valley below. Snow Mountain to the north is usually snow-covered in winter and easy to spot.

This brief climb is followed by a rocky descent to a small valley, where someone has gone to the effort to build a small labyrinth of stones suitable for a short walking meditation. In another few minutes of easy strolling you reach a signpost for Table Rock Overlook; bear right and you'll arrive in less than 100 yards. The rock, perched at 2,465 feet in elevation, offers outstanding views of Calistoga and its environs, plus Mount St. Helena and Snow Mountain.

Table Rock's sheer cliffs attract a nesting pair of peregrine falcons; you can often hear them squawking and you might get lucky enough to see one in flight. Peregrines, with their blue-gray backs and white undersides, are famous for being able to reach speeds of 200 miles per hour.

A hiker stands atop the igneous block of Table Rock and surveys the wildlands of Napa Valley.

GOING FARTHER

To the east of Table Rock are the magnificent Palisades, a massive band of volcanic rock. To see the Palisades close-up, continue east on the obvious trail from Table Rock, now on the Palisades Trail. You'll descend about 300 feet to Garrett Creek, cross it, and then continue onward to Lasky Point. Soon the trail rounds a shoulder and you get your first view of the sheer volcanic cliffs of the Palisades. Continuing onward, the trail passes right along the base of the Palisades cliffs. The trip from the Table Rock trailhead at Highway 29 to the Palisades is about 5 miles one-way.

30. Ritchey Canyon and Coyote Peak

RATING	🚶 🚶 🚶
DISTANCE	4.6 miles round-trip
HIKING TIME	2 hours, 30 minutes
ELEVATION GAIN	850 feet
HIGH POINT	1,170 feet
EFFORT	Moderate Workout
BEST SEASON	Year-round
PERMITS/CONTACT	Bothe-Napa Valley State Park fee required ($8 per vehicle), (707) 942-4575, www.parks.ca.gov
MAPS	USGS Calistoga
NOTES	Dogs and bikes prohibited

THE HIKE

In the midst of the sunbaked Napa Valley, this trail follows a perennial stream and visits one of the easternmost groves of coastal redwoods in California.

GETTING THERE

From Highway 29/128 in St. Helena, drive north on Highway 29/128 for 5 miles to the entrance of Bothe-Napa Valley State Park on the left side of the highway. (It's 3.5 miles south of Calistoga.) Turn left and drive 0.25 mile to the entrance kiosk, then continue past the visitor center to the horse trailer parking lot on the right. The trail begins on the right side of the horse trailer parking lot.

THE TRAIL

Even the most devoted and enthusiastic Napa Valley wine tasters eventually tire of their task. If it's a hot summer day, perhaps they start to day-dream of a shady redwood forest where they could walk for a while or sit by a stream. Such musing might seem preposterous: Where in the midst of the sunbaked vineyards could a redwood tree possibly grow?

At Bothe-Napa Valley State Park, that's where. Ritchey Canyon and Redwood Trails take you through a delightful stand of them, one of the easternmost groves of coastal redwoods in California. Joining the redwoods are plenty of Douglas firs, buckeyes, and bigleaf maples, plus

The redwoods of Ritchey Canyon are a cool, welcoming sight in the arid Napa Valley.

ferns galore. Look carefully among the branches of the trees: Five different kinds of woodpeckers dwell within the park's borders. We spotted the largest of these, the pileated woodpecker, on a tree right by the picnic area. He was working his way up and down a big Douglas fir like a telephone lineman on triple overtime.

Start your hike by heading up Ritchey Canyon Trail from the horse trailer parking lot. (You can also start by the small bridge near the visitor

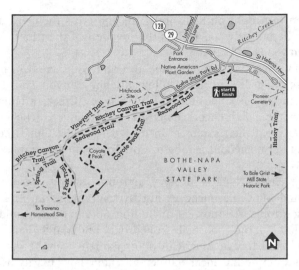

center, or campers can access the trail from the park campground.) The first 0.5 mile is somewhat noisy due to the proximity of the highway and campground, but soon you leave those distractions behind. Ferns, wild grape, and spicebush line the path. Second-growth redwoods are mixed in with Douglas firs. Black oaks and bigleaf maples form a canopy over the trail and Ritchey Creek, which runs dependably year-round. Keep the creek on your right; the trail narrows and meets up with Redwood Trail, which you join and follow. Ritchey Canyon Trail crosses to the north side of the stream.

You'll reach a junction with Coyote Peak Trail 0.75 mile from the start and bear left to begin climbing. Here you'll quickly leave the conifers and enter drier slopes and a bay and live oak forest. In short order the oaks give way to low-growing chaparral and scattered rock outcrops. Wide views open up on your right of conifer-covered Ritchey Canyon below.

Near the top of the climb you reach a junction; the right fork will be your return. Bear left and make a short but steep ascent to a knoll just below Coyote Peak's summit. You're rewarded with a pastoral view of the vineyards and valley far below. The summit is a short distance farther, but its vista is somewhat obstructed by trees. You should be able to make out Mount St. Helena to the northwest.

Return to the junction with the western leg of Coyote Peak Trail and follow it steeply down the opposite side of the mountain. You'll leave the toyon, chamise, and ceanothus in favor of shady redwoods. At a junction with South Fork Trail, turn right. Follow a concrete apron across Ritchey

Creek, then turn right on Redwood Trail and cross the creek again. The next 0.5 mile on Redwood Trail is the loveliest of the trip, featuring the densest redwoods and ferns.

If Ritchey Creek isn't running too full and wide, cross it at an obvious (but unbridged) spur, then follow Ritchey Canyon Trail for part of your return. On the opposite bank of Ritchey Creek, Ritchey Canyon Trail passes the old Hitchcock homesite, where Lillie Hitchcock Coit and her parents spent their summers in the 1870s. Lillie Coit is best known for lending her name and money to Coit Tower on Telegraph Hill in San Francisco.

Although Bothe–Napa is lovely year-round, spring is especially nice. In April and May, the buckeyes are in fragrant bloom and the creek is running strong. Wildflowers, including Solomon's seal and redwood orchids, bloom in the cool shade in February and March. Park volunteers manage a small Native American plant garden near the visitor center, with signs interpreting local native flora and how it was used by the people who once lived here.

GOING FARTHER

Another rewarding path at Bothe–Napa Valley State Park is the History Trail, which leads from the picnic area beyond the group campground. This trail runs 1.2 miles to neighboring Bale Grist Mill State Park, where you can see the 36-foot waterwheel, still in operating condition, which ran Edward Bale's flour mill in the 1840s and 1850s.

31. Lake Ilsanjo Loop

RATING	🚶 🚶 🚶
DISTANCE	5.3 miles round-trip
HIKING TIME	3 hours
ELEVATION GAIN	500 feet
HIGH POINT	900 feet
EFFORT	Moderate Workout
BEST SEASON	Year-round
PERMITS/CONTACT	Annadel State Park fee required ($6 per vehicle), (707) 539-3911, www.parks.sonoma.net or www.parks.ca.gov
MAPS	Annadel State Park (download at www.parks.ca.gov)
NOTES	Dogs prohibited; bikes allowed on some trails

THE HIKE

A casual meander through Santa Rosa's favorite park is the ideal outing for wildflower admirers and hikers who like to fish.

GETTING THERE

From U.S. 101 in Santa Rosa, take the Fairgrounds/Highway 12 exit. Highway 12 becomes Farmers Lane. Turn right on Montgomery Drive and follow it for 2.7 miles (veering to the right), then turn right on Channel Drive. Follow Channel Drive into the park and continue 2.2 miles to the end of the road and the trailhead.

THE TRAIL

Annadel State Park is a horsey kind of place. If you count the horse trailers in the parking lot, the hoofprints all over the place, and the horse droppings along the trail, you might think more horses visit here than people.

Then again, Annadel is also a mountain biker's kind of place. Almost all of the trails at Annadel are open to bikes, and not just the usual wide fire roads. Mountain bikers and equestrians share the trails with great equanimity, and trail conflicts are rare to nonexistent.

Considering all this, it's surprising that Annadel is also a hiker's kind of place. But it is. Annadel's 5,000 acres are filled with woodlands, meadows,

The well-signed trails of Annadel State Park welcome hikers, horses, and mountain bikers, and all users seem to get along just fine.

seasonal creeks, wildflowers, and even a 26-acre lake, all of which are worth seeing on foot. One particularly pleasant trail, Steve's S, is designated for hikers only. If you are a flower aficionado, don't miss a visit to Annadel in April or May. Among many other species, lupine, poppies, mule's ears, redwood orchids, sticky monkey flower, checkerbloom, and scarlet fritillary make an appearance here.

With dozens of trail junctions in this large park, a good map is essential. Pick one up at the ranger station when you drive in, or download one from the park website before you come. Start your trip at the Warren Richardson trailhead at the end of Channel Drive. Take the hikers-only trail from the far end of the parking lot or the wide fire road from its center; both meet up in a few hundred feet. At that junction, head uphill on narrow Steve's S Trail, leaving the road to the cyclists and horses. The

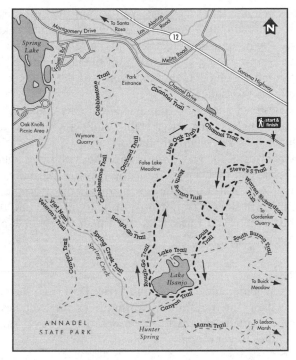

trail makes a good climb over nearly 1.0 mile with just enough of a pitch to get your heart rate up. It weaves through a dense and shady Douglas fir forest interspersed with occasional bay laurel and coast redwood trees. The woodland floor is lined with sword ferns. In early spring, look for rare redwood orchids among them.

If you are wondering what the "S" in Steve's S Trail stands for, it's a secret. Literally. This was one of the "secret" trails built by Steve Hutchison, the grandson of the family who once owned this land.

After gaining a ridge, Steve's S Trail meets back up with Warren Richardson Trail. Go right (south) and then in 0.4 mile, go right again on North Burma Trail. In 0.3 mile, turn left on Louis Trail. You'll walk through an open meadow peppered with wildflowers in the spring. Bordering the meadow is a variety of oaks—coast live, black, and Oregon, which attract a wealth of birds, especially woodpeckers. Many birders come to Annadel specifically in hopes of spotting the pileated woodpecker, a resident in this park. Continue on Louis Trail through a forest of black oaks and madrones for 0.7 mile to the northern edge of Lake Ilsanjo.

Go left to circle the lake clockwise. You'll gain the best views of blue water, tules, and paddling waterbirds as you walk across Lake Ilsanjo's earthen dam. The natural-looking reservoir is a refreshing contrast to the xeric chaparral surrounding it. The origin of the lake's name, "Ilsanjo," is a combination of Ilsa and Joe, the first names of the land's former owners, who built the lake's dam.

Ilsanjo's tule-lined shores are popular with bikers, hikers, picnickers, swimmers, and anglers. The latter stalk Ilsanjo's shoreline to cast for large-size black bass and plentiful bluegill.

About two-thirds of the way around the lake, you'll see a left fork for Rough Go Trail. Follow it away from the lake for 0.5 mile, then bear right on Live Oak Trail. Continue north for almost 1.0 mile until you connect with North Burma Trail. North Burma will lead you 0.7 mile to Channel Trail, where you turn right and finish out your loop back at the parking lot.

GOING FARTHER

To add on a few more miles, take Spring Creek Trail from the west end of Lake Ilsanjo's dam. The trail follows Spring Creek for 1.7 miles to Rough Go Trail and eventually rejoins the loop described above. This will add just under 3 miles to your loop.

32. Lake and Fallen Bridge Loop

RATING	🚶 🚶 🚶
DISTANCE	4.2 miles round-trip
HIKING TIME	2 hours
ELEVATION GAIN	500 feet
HIGH POINT	1,100 feet
EFFORT	Moderate Workout
BEST SEASON	Year-round
PERMITS/CONTACT	Jack London State Historic Park fee required ($8 per vehicle), (707) 938-5216, www.jacklondonpark.com or www.parks.ca.gov
MAPS	Jack London State Historic Park (download at www.parks.ca.gov)
NOTES	Dogs are allowed at the ranch but not on most trails; bikes are allowed on fire roads only

THE HIKE

Tour novelist Jack London's beloved ranch, vineyard, and swimming lake in the scenic Valley of the Moon.

GETTING THERE

From Sonoma on Highway 12, drive north for 4.5 miles to Madrone Road and turn left. At the end of Madrone Road, turn right on Arnold Drive and follow it for 3 miles into Glen Ellen, then turn left on London Ranch Road. Follow London Ranch Road for 1 mile to the park entrance kiosk. Park in the day-use area on the right. The trail leads from the parking area.

THE TRAIL

Author Jack London wanted beauty, and so he "bought beauty, and was content with beauty for awhile." That's how he described his love affair with his Sonoma ranch and its surrounding hills, which are now part of Jack London State Historic Park.

London, famous for his novels *The Call of the Wild* and *The Sea Wolf*, which made him one of the most popular and highest-paid fiction writers of the early 1900s, wanted to build his home in Glen Ellen to escape

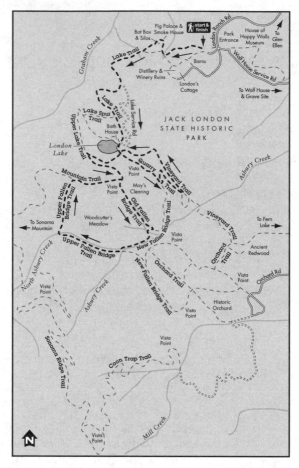

city life. After two years of construction, his ranch dream house caught fire and burned to the ground just days before he and his wife were scheduled to move in. It was a devastating loss, both personally and financially, for the Londons. The couple lived on the ranch in a small wood-frame house until Jack London's death in 1916.

London's vision of beauty is the setting for this moderately easy loop hike that begins at the ranch vineyards, then leads to a small lake and high vistas. Be sure to begin or end your trip with a visit to the Jack London Museum, which features interesting exhibits and photographs from the author's adventurous life.

Take the paved trail from the parking lot to the picnic area, then pick up the dirt road signed as Lake Trail. Head right, past the barns and

Acres of grapevines surround Jack London's ranch in the foothills above Glen Ellen.

winery buildings. Turn right at the sign for Pig Palace—the extravagant sty enjoyed by London's beloved pigs. Check out this elaborate stone structure, then return to the main path. Skirting past carefully tended vineyards, the road forks at a gate; hikers take the right turnoff on single-track Lake Trail. You'll climb for 0.5 mile through mixed hardwoods and Douglas firs to the lake's edge.

London's prized lake is more of a pond nowadays. With sediment continually encroaching upon it, it has shrunk to half its original size. A redwood log cabin that was used as a bathhouse still stands. The Londons swam, fished, and entertained guests at the lake.

Beyond lies the park's "real" hiking trails, which consist of two separate loops. From the ranch road on the southeast edge of the lake, take single-track Quarry Trail east. A 0.25-mile walk leads you to a bench and a vista point that overlooks the bucolic Valley of the Moon. Enjoy this spot, then continue on Quarry Trail, turn left, and loop back on Vineyard Trail and Vineyard Road.

Back near the lake again, follow the wide ranch road uphill through a few switchbacks. (The road is now called Mountain Trail.) At a large clearing and second vista point, you gain another wide view of the Sonoma Valley. This is also the intersection with Fallen Bridge Trail, where you'll make a 1.3-mile loop. Take the left fork first, crunching through the leaves lining the path. The route tunnels through madrones and oaks, then meets up with Asbury Creek and parallels it. Bear right to loop back on Upper Fallen Bridge Trail, now climbing steeply through the redwood-lined creek canyon. At a junction with Mountain Trail, turn right and follow the dirt road back to the clearing, then continue downhill through the switchbacks to the lake.

GOING FARTHER

If you're feeling more ambitious, you can hike to a ridgetop overlook just below the summit of 2,463-foot Sonoma Mountain (the summit itself is on private property). This vantage point provides broad views of Mount St. Helena, San Pablo Bay, and Mount Tamalpais. To get there, simply stay on Mountain Trail, a wide fire road, and follow it all the way to the park border (a 6.6-mile round-trip). A short spur trail at its end leads to the overlook. The lovely Sonoma Ridge Trail also goes to the overlook. It has a much easier grade, but it's an 11-mile round-trip.

Lovers of literature and scenic beauty will enjoy a stroll past the lush vineyards and stone buildings of author Jack London's estate in Glen Ellen.

Rush Creek Falls drops below an old wooden flume in the Auburn foothills.

SACRAMENTO AND GOLD COUNTRY

The Sierra Nevada foothills region surrounding the north-south corridor of Highway 49 is known as the Gold Country or the Mother Lode. It's the place where James Marshall discovered gold in January 1848, sparking a huge and frenzied migration westward. When it became known that a rich vein of gold ran underground from Mariposa to Downieville, the history of California was forever changed.

Evidence of the area's mining past is obvious, from historic brick and wooden buildings to old bridges, mines, water ditches, and an abundance of antique shops. Many of the region's towns have barely changed since their heydays: streets are just wide enough for two stagecoaches to pass, buildings are constructed of stone from local rivers and streams, and storefronts look like they are right out of a movie set. You can travel for many miles in the Gold Country without ever seeing a traffic light. There's a whole lot of California here just waiting to be rediscovered.

The landscape of the Gold Country is composed of low-elevation foothills studded with oaks and pines, and deeply carved, roaring river canyons. Hot weather is the norm in summer, which means the area's hiking trails are best explored in the autumn, winter, and spring months.

Also a part of this region is the Central Valley, with its endless acres of cotton, orchards, and grazing lands, and its famous rivers: the Sacramento, American, and Feather, among others. Extending for hundreds of miles from these rivers are marshy wetlands that attract migrating birds and waterfowl. The Central Valley, which may seem like an empty wasteland to hurried drivers on Interstate 5, is a place of critical refuge for millions of birds on the Pacific Flyway. By getting out of your car and into your hiking boots here, you may develop a new appreciation for this vast landscape of grasslands and waterways. After all, that many birds just can't be wrong.

SACRAMENTO AND GOLD COUNTRY

33. Wetlands Walking Trail

RATING	🚶 🚶 🚶 🚶 🚶
DISTANCE	2.0 miles round-trip
HIKING TIME	1 hour
ELEVATION GAIN	Negligible
HIGH POINT	5 feet (sea level)
EFFORT	Easy Walk
BEST SEASON	November to May
PERMITS/CONTACT	Sacramento National Wildlife Refuge day-use fee required ($3 per vehicle), (530) 934-2801, www.fws.gov/sacramentovalleyrefuges
MAPS	Available at trailhead
NOTES	Dogs and bikes prohibited

THE HIKE

Bring your binoculars and your bird identification books for this level walk through a federal wildlife refuge, where farmlands and wetlands are "for the birds."

GETTING THERE

Traveling north on Interstate 5 from Sacramento, take the Norman Road/Princeton exit, 18 miles north of Williams. (It is signed for the Sacramento National Wildlife Refuge. If you're driving south on I-5, the exit is 7 miles south of Willows.) At the first intersection, turn left on County Road 99W and drive 1 mile, then turn right into the refuge. The trail begins at the parking area.

THE TRAIL

This trail may require a leap of faith to get you hiking on it. Not because it's steep or patrolled by a pack of hungry wolves, but because this peaceful little path in the Sacramento National Wildlife Refuge is situated only a mile from the endless noise and exhaust of Interstate 5. This area could win the award for "Least Likely Place for a Nature Preserve."

But don't let the proximity of the highway fool you. The region surrounding this part of I-5 is prime farmland, mostly for rice and other grains. But long before modern farmers moved to the area, the Central

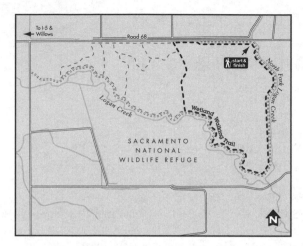

Valley was a key stop for birds on the Pacific Flyway. Even today, an estimated 60 percent of all ducks, geese, swans, and other birds on the Flyway spend part of each year in the Central Valley.

The birds and the farmers all want the same thing—the valley's huge expanses of marshes and wetlands, which are created by seasonal flooding of the Sacramento River. That's why as early as the 1950s the federal government protected this and other wildlife refuges in the Central Valley, allowing the farmers to use the dry land in the spring and summer months, and the birds to use the flooded land in the fall and winter months. This particular refuge, comprising more than 10,000 acres, has been designated as a Globally Important Bird Area by the Audubon Society.

So even though minutes ago you were passing trucks on the freeway at 70 miles per hour, now you are walking through peaceful seasonal marshes, gazing at placid ponds and vernal pools, and seeing an incredible amount of wildlife. I saw more jackrabbits along the refuge's 2.0-mile loop trail than I saw collectively in a year of hiking. You may also see raccoons, deer, squirrels, frogs, lizards, and of course, birds galore. The list is longer than can be described here, but expect to see migrating waterfowl, great blue herons, great egrets, pheasants, hawks, harriers, coots, avocets, sandpipers, owls, woodpeckers, and songbirds.

The trail is a breeze to follow, completely level and well signed. From the parking area, the path crosses the entrance road, then makes two connected loops, forming a figure eight. Late fall and early winter is the prime season to see wildlife, particularly migratory waterfowl. But even as late as May, there is much life in these marshes. Time your trip so that

A black-crowned night heron watches for a fishy snack in the wetlands of the Sacramento National Wildlife Refuge.

you arrive early in the morning or late in the afternoon, the best times for wildlife watching. And if by chance this trail wasn't "birdy" enough for you, try driving the refuge's designated Auto Tour and you'll probably add a few more species to your life list.

GOING FARTHER

There are four other wildlife refuges that make up the entire Sacramento Wildlife Refuge Complex. If you've enjoyed your visit here, check out the Colusa Wildlife Refuge to the south, where you can walk a 1-mile trail along a lush riparian slough. To get there from Interstate 5, head south to Williams and then take Highway 20 east to Colusa.

34. Fairy Falls (aka Shingle Falls)

RATING	🚶 🚶 🚶
DISTANCE	5.4 miles round-trip
HIKING TIME	2.5 hours
ELEVATION GAIN	300 feet
HIGH POINT	650 feet
EFFORT	Easy Walk
BEST SEASON	December to May
PERMITS/CONTACT	California Department of Fish and Game, (530) 538-2236, www.dfg.ca.gov
MAPS	USGS Camp Far West
NOTES	Dogs and bikes allowed

THE HIKE

Sadly misnamed Dry Creek flows year-round, and with great velocity soon after winter rains. See its waterfall, Fairy Falls, on this pleasant tromp through the foothill grasslands.

GETTING THERE

From Marysville, drive east on Highway 20 for approximately 14 miles, then turn right (south) on Smartville Road. Drive 0.9 mile and bear left at the fork to stay on Smartville Road. Continue another 3.8 miles to Waldo Road and bear left on the gravel road. Follow Waldo Road 1.9 miles to the Waldo Bridge. Cross it and turn left on Spenceville Road, then drive 2.2 miles to the end of the road at an old, blocked-off bridge. Park by the bridge and walk across.

THE TRAIL

From the first autumn rain until midsummer, Dry Creek is anything but dry. Because the creek is located in the middle of arid oak-and-grassland country, it's surprising that Dry Creek maintains a steady flow of water year-round, but it does. The creek is fed by perennial springs and forms a lovely waterfall known by two names: Fairy Falls and Shingle Falls. The waterfall and this trail are at their best soon after winter rains, when the surrounding grasslands are deep green and peppered with wildflowers.

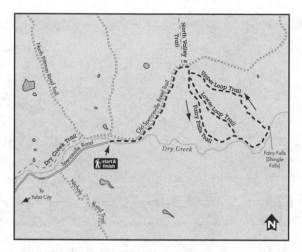

Access to Fairy Falls/Shingle Falls is through Spenceville Wildlife Area, an 11,000-acre preserve. Don't be put off by the trailhead, which is a blocked-off, old concrete bridge at the end of Spenceville Road. The scenery improves quickly. Turn right on the dirt road immediately following the bridge (Old Spenceville Road Trail) and hike eastward. Dry Creek is on your right, gurgling over rounded rocks. The route is wide and level, winding through open grasslands and stands of white, valley, and canyon oaks. When the white oaks' leaves drop in winter, their branches are completely shrouded with lime-colored lichens. Spring wildflowers can be fantastic in these oak grasslands. April and early May are usually the best months to see California poppies, blue gilias, Chinese houses, many species of brodiaea, and other colorful blooms.

Keep on the lookout for wild turkeys. We saw a large flock of them, as well as a couple of handsome ring-necked pheasants, scurrying across the trail. The plentiful turkeys invite plentiful hunters during turkey season; you might want to avoid this trail during the Saturdays and Sundays of late March and April.

Stay on this main road, ignoring any side trails, for just shy of 1.0 mile, then turn right and hike south where the left fork is gated off. Shortly beyond a cattleguard, two trails take off on your left, the Upper and Lower Loop Trails, open to hikers only. Either of these will take you to the falls, but a better choice is to stay on the main path, which becomes Fairy Falls Trail. This trail brings you alongside Dry Creek, then heads upstream to Fairy Falls/Shingle Falls. The first waterfall you reach is about 30 feet tall, pouring through a notch in the rounded rock. A more impressive fall awaits about 100 yards upstream, this one dropping

123

Fairy Falls, also called Shingle Falls, cascades over a volcanic cliff in Spenceville Wildlife Area.

50 feet into an immense pool. A sign warns against diving off the cliffs but it's hard to believe that anyone would try it. It's a long, scary drop to the pool.

The story behind the name "Fairy Falls" is a bit of a mystery, but it may be related to the wildflowers commonly called fairy lanterns that bloom in the grasslands near the falls. Locals call this waterfall by the name of "Shingle Falls." Shingle was the name of a retired military officer from nearby Beale Air Force Base.

From the upper fall, you can choose to simply backtrack for your homeward trip, or follow the Upper or Lower Loop Trails back to the cattleguard and Old Spenceville Road Trail.

GOING FARTHER

There are many more trails to explore in Spenceville Wildlife Area. A favorite is the Dry Creek–Waldo Bridge Trail, which is accessed by following the Old Spenceville Road Trail (as described above) west or downstream from the old concrete bridge for 0.4 mile to the South Pittman trailhead.

35. Stevens Trail

RATING	🚶 🚶 🚶 🚶
DISTANCE	7.0 miles round-trip
HIKING TIME	3.5 hours
ELEVATION GAIN	1,150 feet
HIGH POINT	2,380 feet
EFFORT	Prepare to Perspire
BEST SEASON	December to May
PERMITS/CONTACT	Bureau of Land Management Mother Lode Field Office, (916) 941-3101, www.blm.gov/ca
MAPS	USGS Colfax
NOTES	Dogs and bikes allowed

THE HIKE

The Stevens Trail, part of a historic Gold Rush–era livery trail, travels downhill to the blue-green pools and cascades of the North Fork of the American River.

GETTING THERE

From Sacramento, drive east on Interstate 80 for 45 miles to Colfax. Take the Colfax/North Canyon Way exit and turn left at the stop sign. Drive east on the frontage road (North Canyon Way) for 0.7 mile, past the Colfax cemetery, to the trailhead parking area. On weekends, this parking lot can fill up, so if you can't fit your car into the lot, be sure to park legally alongside the road without blocking any driveways.

THE TRAIL

Most people need a darn good reason to get out of their air-conditioned cars when driving east of Sacramento on I-80. The Stevens Trail is an excellent one. But keep in mind that this is an "upside-down" hike, meaning downhill on the way in and uphill on the way back. You need to save your energy, and lots of water, for the trip back, although the slope is so gentle that even novice hikers can make the trek. Still, don't hike here in the middle of the day—unless it's a very cold day—and time your trip for sometime between December and May. By midsummer, it can be uncomfortably hot.

Hikers can cool off their toes in the pools and cascades found alongside the Stevens Trail.

At the trailhead, you can hear the near-deafening roar of cars whizzing by on the freeway, but don't be discouraged. In 10 minutes of walking, you will be completely free of any noise except the enchanting sounds of nature. The Stevens Trail cuts through a tranquil oak, pine, fir, and

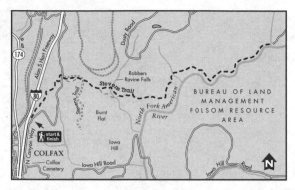

dogwood woodland on its 3.5-mile descent to the confluence of Secret Ravine and the North Fork of the American River. In 2002, this trail was listed on the National Register of Historic Places, as it was originally part of a major livery trail that ran from Colfax to Iowa Hill. The latter city was a bustling metropolis during the Gold Rush. The bridge that crossed the North Fork to connect the two towns is long gone, but from 1870 to 1895, this was a heavily trafficked route.

But during the spring months, you won't be thinking about history, because you'll be too focused on the wildflowers. In April and May, you'll see dogwoods and redbuds busting out all over, and colorful clouds of baby blue eyes, shooting stars, and lupine at your feet. Later in the spring, poppies and monkey flower seem to be everywhere you look.

The trail is well signed the entire way, which is fortunate because you need to negotiate a few turns. After an initial right turn, the remaining turns are all lefts. Besides the beauty of these woods, a major highlight of this trail is spotting the railroad bed of the First Continental Railroad, which was cut into the steep canyon wall by Chinese laborers who were dangled in rope-strung baskets from the cliffs above. Trains still run on this section of the original railroad bed.

Equally as fascinating are the long-distance views of the American River Canyon, and in the final mile of trail, the close-up views of the river itself. This last stretch travels upriver, passing occasional indications of mining activity and the foundation of an old suspension bridge. The river's pools and cascades tempt swimmers in the summer season, but if you are visiting in spring when the river runs dangerously fast, don't put more than your big toe in the water.

36. South Yuba Independence Trail

RATING	🚶 🚶 🚶
DISTANCE	4.0 miles round-trip
HIKING TIME	2 hours
ELEVATION GAIN	Negligible
HIGH POINT	1,450 feet
EFFORT	Easy Walk
BEST SEASON	December to June
PERMITS/CONTACT	South Yuba River State Park Bridgeport Visitor Center, (530) 432-2546, www.southyubariverstatepark.org
MAPS	South Yuba River Park (download at www.parks.ca.gov)
NOTES	Wheelchair accessible; dogs allowed

THE HIKE

The first "wheelchair wilderness trail" in the United States, this historic flume trail allows wheelchair users the chance to ride off-pavement.

GETTING THERE

From Interstate 80 at Auburn, drive north on Highway 49 for 27 miles to Nevada City. Continue on Highway 49 for 8 miles past Nevada City to the trailhead on the right side of the highway, shortly before the South Yuba River bridge. Park at the pullout at the trailhead, or if there are no spaces available, at one of several pullouts farther north.

THE TRAIL

Most wheelchair-accessible trails have one major drawback: they are paved. Although this may seem like a necessity, wheelchair riders often say that paving the ground takes away from the nature experience. After all, most people go outdoors to get away from man-made materials like pavement.

That makes the unpaved South Yuba Independence Trail a stroke of genius and a blessing. It's the first identified "wheelchair wilderness trail" in the United States, and it leads a total of 6.0 miles on hard-packed dirt and over wooden flumes along the Yuba River canyon.

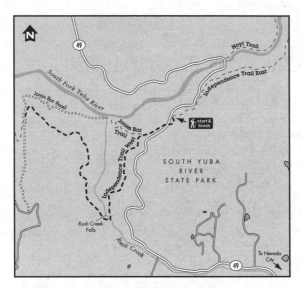

Everything about this trail has been done right. For much of its length, two paths run parallel, one designed for wheelchairs and one for hiking boots. Outhouses built for wheelchair riders are positioned along the trail, as well as accessible platforms for picnicking and fishing on Rush Creek. A nonprofit group called Sequoya Challenge maintains the trail in partnership with California State Parks.

The trail was originally built in 1859, not as a hiking trail but as a canal to carry water from the South Yuba River to a hydraulic mining site in Smartsville, 25 miles downstream. Consisting of rock-lined ditches with adjacent paths for ditch tenders, plus wooden flumes (similar to bridges) allowing passage over creeks, the canal followed a nearly level contour along the steep hillsides above the South Yuba River.

At the trailhead, you have a choice of hiking east or west. (The trail does not loop; if you want to walk the whole route, you must go out and back in both directions.) The trip described here heads west, or right. In the first 50 yards from the trailhead sign, you must duck your head and pass through a tunnel under Highway 49. The noise of highway traffic is overbearing at first, but soon dissipates. The path travels through a densely wooded forest of oaks and pines. In the first 0.25 mile, you'll pass by a roofed platform that provides a scenic overlook of the South Yuba River canyon. In the next 0.5 mile, you'll cross over a few wooden flumes or bridges. Admire the handiwork of those who built this trail, and also those who maintain it.

Wooden flumes remaining from the mid-1800s Gold Rush curve around the canyons above the South Yuba River.

At 1.0 mile out, you emerge from the forest at an amazing cliff-hanging flume, its wooden boards making a horseshoe-shaped turn around the back of a canyon. Above and below it, Rush Creek Falls flows over polished granite in a multitiered cascade. This area is known as the Rush Creek Ramp at Flume 28. Here, volunteers built an intricate wooden ramp spiraling 520 feet down from the flume to the swirling edge of Rush Creek. It's a fine place for all trail users to picnic, fish, or just admire the flow of water.

From here, the "west" segment of the South Yuba Independence Trail continues for another 1.0 mile to Jones Bar Road, through more forest and across more flumes. There you must turn around and hike back, making a 4.0-mile round-trip.

GOING FARTHER

You can also hike the eastern section of trail from the parking area, a 5-mile round-trip that includes more flumes, views of the river and foothills, and springtime wildflowers.

37. Hidden Falls

RATING	🚶 🚶 🚶
DISTANCE	3.0 miles round-trip
HIKING TIME	1 hour, 30 minutes
ELEVATION GAIN	350 feet
HIGH POINT	1,000 feet
EFFORT	Easy Walk
BEST SEASON	November to May
PERMITS/CONTACT	Hidden Falls Regional Park,
	(530) 886-4901, www.placer.ca.gov
MAPS	Hidden Falls Regional Park
	(download at www.placer.ca.gov)
NOTES	Dogs and bikes allowed

THE HIKE

A hike through the Auburn foothills leads through oak woodlands to a 30-foot waterfall and a series of rocky cascades.

GETTING THERE

From Sacramento, drive east on Interstate 80 for 30 miles to Auburn. Take the Highway 49 North exit and drive 2.7 miles to Atwood Road. Turn left (west) on Atwood Road and follow it for 1.7 miles until it turns into Mount Vernon Road. Continue straight on Mount Vernon Road for 2.7 miles to Mears Road. Turn right on Mears Road and drive 0.5 mile. Turn right on Mears Place and drive 0.2 mile to the trailhead parking area.

THE TRAIL

There's a brand-new waterfall in the foothills between Auburn and Lincoln, and Gold Country hikers are thronging to see it. Well, OK, it's not really a new waterfall—the 30-foot cascade has been around for a substantial amount of geologic time—but the park that contains it is new as of 2006, and it's a beautiful, well-managed chunk of public land.

Hidden Falls Regional Park is tucked into the foothill country, accessible by driving a series of winding back roads through the oak woodlands. This land was previously known as the Didion Ranch before its owners donated

Hidden Falls Regional Park offers shady trails leading through oak and bay laurel forests.

the land to Placer County. As of 2011, 221 acres of the ranch are open to the public, but the long-term plan is to increase that to 1,200 acres. Criss-crossed by two creeks, Coon and Deadman, the park is a lush, shady oasis in a region that is notoriously hot and dry in the summer months. The pre-dominant tree species is the blue oak, but you'll also notice canyon oaks, foothill pines, bay laurel, and even a few ponderosa pines.

The park's large parking lot has two separate trailheads. For this trip, head for the trailhead next to the restrooms, where three separate trails begin. Walk just a few feet past the signboard and then immediately turn right and step down a few stairs to the lower (right-hand) trail, which is Poppy Trail. (The upper trail is a wheelchair-accessible path that circles back to the parking lot; the middle trail is a wide gravel road called Pond Turtle Road, which will eventually join up with your path.)

Once on Poppy Trail, you'll switchback gently downhill to roughly parallel the babbling course of the Whiskey Diggins Canal. In 1.0 mile, Poppy Trail meets up with Pond Turtle Road at a sturdy footbridge; turn right and cross the bridge. On the far side, a few more footsteps bring you to another junction of trails. Bear left on Blue Oaks Loop, and then almost immediately head left again on Hidden Falls Access Trail. Yes, there are a ton of trail junctions in this park, but each one is so well signed it is virtually impossible to get lost.

Walking for 0.5 mile on the Hidden Falls Access Trail under a shady canopy brings you to a final switchback leading down to an overlook

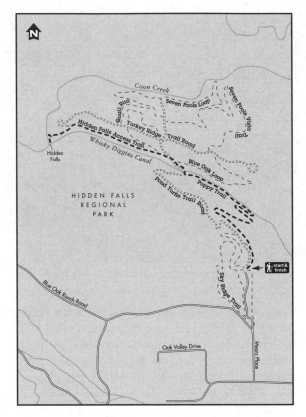

platform across from the 30-foot falls. During the rainy season, this waterfall can put out some serious hydropower, and the large wooden platform is the safest place to view it. Enjoy this special spot, then head back the way you came, or continue onward to explore more of this lovely park (see "Going Farther," below).

GOING FARTHER
Next to Hidden Falls, my second favorite trail in this park is the Seven Pools Loop. To get there from Hidden Falls, backtrack for about 0.25 mile and then turn left to connect to Turkey Ridge Road. Turn right on this road and follow it for 0.5 mile to Quail Run Trail. Head left (north) on Quail Run to connect to the Seven Pools Loop. Go left to loop around and hike alongside lovely Coon Creek, then climb above it and reconnect with Pond Turtle Road, which you can follow back to your car for a 5-mile round-trip.

38. Codfish Creek Falls

RATING	🚶 🚶 🚶
DISTANCE	3.4 miles round-trip
HIKING TIME	1 hour, 30 minutes
ELEVATION GAIN	70 feet
HIGH POINT	950 feet
EFFORT	Easy Walk
BEST SEASON	December to May
PERMITS/CONTACT	Auburn State Recreation Area, (530) 885-4527, www.parks.ca.gov
MAPS	Auburn State Recreation Area (download at www.parks.ca.gov)
NOTES	Dogs and bikes allowed

THE HIKE

Codfish Creek Falls is a lovely sight, but the main reason to hike this trail is to enjoy the beautiful scenery of the North Fork American River.

GETTING THERE

From Sacramento, drive east on Interstate 80 for 40 miles to Weimar. Take the Weimar/Cross Road exit, then turn south on Ponderosa Way. In 3 miles, Ponderosa Way turns to dirt. Continue for 2.5 additional miles (this dirt stretch can be very rough and rutted after winter rains; a high-clearance vehicle may be required and the going is slow) until you reach a bridge over the American River, a total of 5.5 miles from Weimar/Cross Road. Don't cross the bridge, but park along the road near it. Begin hiking on the trail on the north side of the bridge, heading west (downstream).

THE TRAIL

It's unlikely that you'll see any codfish swimming in Codfish Creek, but you will have a chance at some private time by a pretty waterfall along the North Fork of the American River.

Nobody could tell me where this creek got its name, but everyone said that I had to see its waterfall in springtime. So off we went on a fair Saturday in May, following Ponderosa Way from the little town of

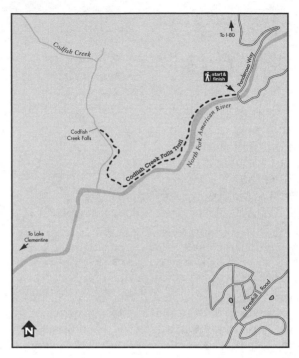

Weimar down to the American River canyon. The final 2.5-mile stretch of this dirt road can be a white-knuckled ride or a mellow country drive, depending on what recent storms have done to the roadbed. Know in advance that there are very few pullouts along this very narrow thoroughfare, and that you will be driving quite slowly. A high-clearance vehicle is a very good idea, but plenty of passenger cars make the trip later in the season when the mud has dried.

Park your vehicle along the road just before the river bridge and start hiking on the trail on the north side of the river. You'll head west, paralleling the river for about 1.0 mile. You may spot occasional fortune hunters looking for gold by the river and sun lovers floating on their backs in the blue-green pools.

At 1.3 miles, the trail turns right and leads upstream along Codfish Creek, heading away from the river. We passed a hand-painted plaque naming the Codfish Creek Trail, with a dedication to a certain someone "and all others who love nature." It was put there by a group of wonderful people called PARC, which stands for Protect the American River Canyon, an Auburn-based conservation group. Before you start off on this trip, it's a good idea to download their "Codfish Creek Falls

Discovery Trail" brochure from their website (www.parc-auburn.org). If you aren't familiar with the wildflowers and shrubs of this foothill country, this brochure will educate you as you hike.

Although the trail along the river is very exposed, Codfish's canyon is shaded by big manzanitas and deciduous trees. After just a few minutes of walking under the forest canopy, you'll discern the sound of falling water. The trail brings you smack-dab to the middle of the waterfall, which is a big cascade totaling about 80 feet.

The fall's lower reaches are gentle cascades, while the top is more vertical and dramatic. A few clumps of Indian rhubarb grow with great enthusiasm by the water's edge. We climbed up the side of the fall and lay around on the colorful black, gray, and rust-colored rocks.

GOING FARTHER

For a similarly pleasant ramble along the North Fork American River, take the Colfax/Grass Valley exit off Interstate 80. Take the first right onto Canyon Way, and drive 2.2 miles to Yankee Jim's Road. Turn left and drive 4.7 miles to the river bridge (the road turns to dirt but is passable for passenger cars). Park on the side of the road. You must cross over Shirttail Creek to begin the hike, and this may be difficult or impossible during peak runoff in early spring. After that crossing, the rest of the hike is an easy walk alongside the river.

39. Table Mountain

RATING	🚶 🚶 🚶
DISTANCE	3.0 miles round-trip
HIKING TIME	1.5 hours
ELEVATION GAIN	500 feet
HIGH POINT	1,800 feet
EFFORT	Moderate Workout
BEST SEASON	February to May
PERMITS/CONTACT	New Melones Reservoir, (209) 536-9543 or (209) 536-9094
MAPS	Download at www.usbr.gov/mp/ccao/newmelones/maps
NOTES	Dogs allowed

THE HIKE
Pay a springtime visit to Tuolumne County's geologic oddity: Table Mountain, a long, flat-topped volcanic ridge with an extraordinary display of wildflowers.

GETTING THERE
From Highway 49 in Sonora, drive south for 3 miles to Jamestown, then turn right (north) on Rawhide Road. Drive 2 miles and turn left on Shell Road; follow Shell Road 1.8 miles (take the left fork) to the end of the pavement at a yellow gate across the road. The trail starts to the right of the gate.

THE TRAIL
Wildflower lovers, this is your trail. The only trick is timing your visit for the exact period when Table Mountain is at its most colorful splendor. The peak of the bloom varies from year to year, so your best bet is to start calling the New Melones visitor center in late February to see how the Table Mountain flowers are coming along. When they say it's "go time," don't wait too long. The mountain's flowers put on a fleeting show that must be seen at exactly the right time to fully savor their splendor. Some years it's all over by the middle of May, although Table Mountain's lovely high vistas are there for the taking at any time of year.

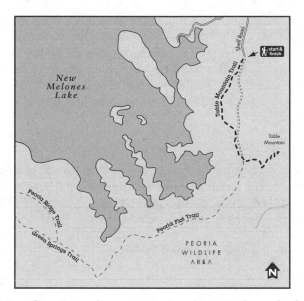

The driving directions above suggest parking at the end of the pavement on Shell Road and hiking from there, although you may see some people who continue driving another mile on the dirt road, which shortens their hike. A high-clearance vehicle may be needed to negotiate this last stretch on dirt, and if you drive, you will miss some of the grassland wildflowers. It's much better to walk, both for your car and you. Most of Table Mountain is private property, so it's important that you use this one public trail to access it.

From the pavement's end, the road/trail crosses through a grassy oak woodland dotted with basalt rocks. Straight ahead is Table Mountain, a flat-topped plateau that juts upward from the surrounding lowlands. The plateau was formed by a lava flow about 10 million years ago, when a volcano erupted east of Sonora Pass. The mountain is a source of pride for local geologists, as it is one of America's best examples of an "inverted stream," a feature formed by a riverbed filling with lava.

Table Mountain's craggy rock is favored by rock climbers year-round, but in the spring months it is amateur botanists and native plant lovers who flock here. In February and March, Table Mountain's volcanic soil creates ideal conditions for vernal pools—multicolored rings of flowers that surround small pools of water. Fairy shrimp can often be seen in the pools. A bit later in spring, the mountaintop hosts a colorful array of wildflowers including sky lupine, Indian paintbrush, blue dicks, owl's clover, harvest brodiaea, and goldfields.

Before you start out on this trip, note that although this trail's distance is short, the going can be slow, as the volcanic rock is rather rough, and the last 0.25 mile to the top is steep, narrow, and rocky in places. (Hiking boots are a very good idea here.) Besides, you'll be staring at the ground trying not to miss a single wildflower species. If you can take your eyes off the flowers, the top of Table Mountain provides a wide vista of New Melones Reservoir.

GOING FARTHER
Another nearby trail that is equally fascinating from a geologic standpoint is the Natural Bridges Trail, also managed by New Melones Reservoir. The signed trailhead is located off Parrotts Ferry Road between Columbia and Murphys. The 1.5-mile trail leads you down to Coyote Creek's amazing swimming holes. You can actually swim through limestone canyons and under a natural bridge.

40. Hardrock Trail

RATING	🚶 🚶 🚶
DISTANCE	4.5 miles round-trip
HIKING TIME	2.0 hours
ELEVATION GAIN	450 feet
HIGH POINT	2,900 feet
EFFORT	Moderate Workout
BEST SEASON	February to June
PERMITS/CONTACT	Empire Mine State Historic Park, (530) 273-8522, www.empiremine.org
MAPS	Available at park visitor center
NOTES	Dogs and bikes allowed

THE HIKE

This figure-eight loop in Empire Mine State Historic Park tours the landscape above the largest and richest gold mine in California.

GETTING THERE

From Auburn, drive north on Highway 49 for 24 miles to the Empire Street exit in Grass Valley. Drive east (right) on Empire Street 0.6 mile to the Penn Gate trailhead. The visitor center is 0.75 mile down the road. (Parking is free at the Penn Gate trailhead, but $5 per person if you park at the visitor center.)

THE TRAIL

It's a toss-up whether the best reason to come to Empire Mine State Historic Park is to immerse yourself in its fascinating hardrock mining history or to hike on its smooth and scenic trails. When you visit, be sure to do both. Check out the mine museum, take the mine tours, and learn all about the history of this gold-rich land, then go for a walk on the Hardrock Trail.

This land contained one of the oldest, largest, deepest, longest, and richest gold mines in California. It operated from 1850 to 1956, with more than 360 miles of underground tunnels and shafts. Sadly, the mine owners completely destroyed the landscape—environmentalism hadn't been invented yet—but Mother Nature has done an amazing job of healing

Tall pines frame the trails surrounding the old mine buildings in Empire Mine State Park.

herself. Today you'll find a profusion of pines, white and black oaks, big manzanita bushes, and a few scattered remains of rusting mining equipment and decaying buildings.

The starting point for your hike is the Hardrock trailhead, known as the Penn Gate ("Penn" is short for the Pennsylvania Mine, which you'll pass almost immediately). It's located 0.75 mile down the road from the main park entrance and visitor center. The wide dirt road is popular with local dog walkers, joggers, and hiking clubs for good reason—it's centrally located in the middle of Grass Valley and makes a perfect path for either quick strolling or longer excursions. Even in the heat of summer, there's shade to be found here. The only negative is the sound of Highway 49, which seems to follow you almost everywhere you go.

Take a map with you (they are usually available at the trailhead if you didn't bring one). Although it's difficult to stray too far off the path, this park has numerous junctions, and not all are signed. The Hardrock Trail passes by several old mines, including the W.Y.O.D. mine—an acronym that stood for "Work Your Own Diggins." Here, the wealthy mine owner allowed the peon miners to lease sections of the mine and try to dig up their own fortunes. Not surprisingly, no one got rich this way, except the mine owner.

Past the W.Y.O.D. mine, turn left at the fork (0.5 mile from the start) on a path that is unimaginatively named Short Loop Trail. After a brief climb, the trail brings you to an overlook above the mineyard buildings. Head

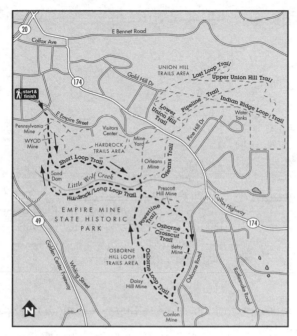

right, past the Orleans mine and stamp mill, and cross Little Wolf Creek on a wooden bridge. On the far side of the bridge, head left and uphill on Osborne Loop Trail, now joining the second part of your figure-eight loop. This ascent will bring you to the top of Osborne Hill, passing several abandoned mine sites along the way. From the hilltop, you have a partially obstructed view over the park.

Continuing on Osborne Loop brings you around to Long Loop Trail, on which you walk west along the ridge and then back downhill. Long Loop Trail heads through a lovely grove of oaks, which "bloom" in hues of gold and yellow during October and November. Stay on this trail as you pass a cutoff for Short Loop Trail and the W.Y.O.D. mine and you'll wind up back at Penn Gate and your car.

GOING FARTHER

You can also head to the "other" trailhead at Empire Mine State Historic Park and hike from there. The Union Hill trailhead is located at the end of Gold Hill Drive, which intersects Silver Way off Highway 174 near Empire Cross Road. A hike on dirt roads shows off the old pipeline that brought water to the mines.

41. Feather Falls

RATING	🚶 🚶 🚶 🚶 🚶
DISTANCE	8.8 miles round-trip
HIKING TIME	5.0 hours
ELEVATION GAIN	1,100 feet
HIGH POINT	2,400 feet
EFFORT	Prepare to Perspire
BEST SEASON	January to June
PERMITS/CONTACT	Plumas National Forest, Feather River Ranger District, (530) 534-6500, www.fs.fed.us/r5/plumas
MAPS	USGS Brush Creek
NOTES	Dogs and bikes allowed

THE HIKE

Visit California's fourth-highest freefalling waterfall on this woodsy, scenic hike near Oroville.

GETTING THERE

From Highway 70 in Oroville, take the Oroville Dam Boulevard exit (Highway 162) and drive east 1.6 miles to Olive Highway/Highway 162. Turn right and drive 6.5 miles on Highway 162. Turn right on Forbestown Road and drive 6 miles. Turn left on Lumpkin Road and drive 10.8 miles. Turn left at the sign for Feather Falls and drive 1.6 miles to the trailhead.

THE TRAIL

The Feather Falls National Recreation Trail is one of the finest loop hikes in all of Northern California, and it leads to a destination that is tough to beat: Feather Falls, the sixth-highest freefalling waterfall in the continental United States and the fourth-highest in California.

The 640-foot waterfall is nothing short of spectacular, and so is the trail that reaches it. Built as a loop, one leg is shorter (3.3 miles) and steeper; the other leg is longer (4.5 miles) and more gradual. If you hike one leg in and the other leg back, you'll complete an 8.8-mile trip, including the short sections where the trails join as one. But you can always shorten (or lengthen) the trip by hiking the shorter (or longer)

Feather Falls is the fourth highest freefalling waterfall in California.

leg in both directions. Have it your way. It may help to know that both trails are mostly downhill on the way to the falls, which means you face a mostly uphill climb on the way back. If you don't like steep ascents at the end of your hiking day, take the longer leg for your return; it is so gently graded that you'll hardly even notice you are climbing. Because it's a designated National Recreation Trail, both legs of the loop are frequently maintained and have posted trail markers every 0.5 mile.

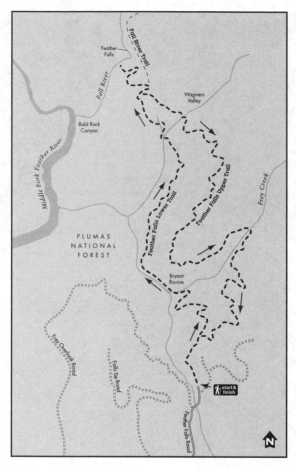

This is not a trail for hurrying. The northern Sierra foothills terrain shows off an incredible variety of plant life, including 17 species of trees: ponderosa pine, incense cedar, Douglas fir, black oak, white alder, dogwood, and more. They are joined by 20 kinds of shrubs and 10 varieties of ferns. Wildflower lovers should visit from March to May, when more than 180 species have been identified. That's also when the waterfall is at its peak flow.

Start hiking from the parking lot trailhead and reach the start of the loop in an easy 0.25 mile. I recommend you opt for the shorter leg on the way in, so take the left fork (the short way), and prepare to drop elevation for the first 2.0 miles, crossing a bridge over Frey Creek at about 1.1 mile. Be sure to look for ladybugs here, which huddle up on shrubs and branches near the creek in the winter before traveling back to the Central Valley in the spring. The trail then parallels the creek until it breaks out to a stunning view of the steep-walled Middle Fork Feather canyon and Bald Rock Dome. The granite dome rises 2,000 feet above the river canyon. It's a sacred meditation place for Maidu Native Americans.

Soon after the dome vista, the trail starts to climb, and it continues to do so fairly steadily between the 2.0- and 3.0-mile markers. At 3.2 miles, you reach a wooden bench and a junction where the two legs of the loop connect. They become one for the final 0.5-mile ascent to the falls overlook. A couple of easy switchbacks bring you to a fenced viewpoint above the Middle Fork Feather River. After a few more minutes of walking, you're at the left turnoff for the falls overlook.

In its final stretch, the route follows an elaborate series of short walkways, which lead to the top of a granite outcrop jutting out into space high above the canyon. The overlook, perched atop this outcrop, provides a brink-to-base view of the billowing waterfall and the Feather River canyon. It's guaranteed to take your breath away.

42. Cosumnes River Walk and Lost Slough Wetlands Walk

RATING	🚶 🚶 🚶
DISTANCE	3.0 miles round-trip
HIKING TIME	1.5 hours
ELEVATION GAIN	Negligible
HIGH POINT	5 feet (sea level)
EFFORT	Easy Walk
BEST SEASON	November to May
PERMITS/CONTACT	Cosumnes River Preserve, (916) 684-2816, www.cosumnes.org
MAPS	Available at visitor center
NOTES	Dogs and bikes prohibited; Lost Slough Wetlands Walk is wheelchair accessible

THE HIKE

The Cosumnes River is the only remaining undammed river in the Central Valley and a prime spot for wildflife-watching.

GETTING THERE

From Stockton, take Interstate 5 north to the Thornton–Walnut Grove Road exit. Go east to Thornton Road, where you turn left and drive 2 miles. The road becomes Franklin Boulevard. Continue over the Thornton–Franklin Bridge to the Cosumnes Preserve visitor center on your right. Or, if you are heading south on I-5, take the Twin Cities Road exit and head east for 1 mile to Franklin Boulevard. Turn right on Franklin and drive 1.7 miles to the Cosumnes Preserve visitor center on your left.

THE TRAIL

When I heard about a fantastic nature trail located in Galt, I had my reservations. To my mind, that part of the Delta suburbs was the home of 18-wheelers heading up I-5 and a dizzying selection of big-box stores. But in only one visit, it became obvious I had misjudged this region. Galt's Cosumnes River Preserve is a special place and the Cosumnes River Walk and Lost Slough Wetlands Walk are two very special trails.

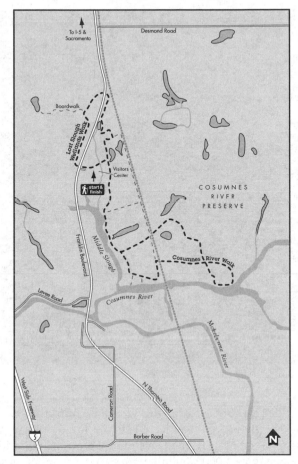

The Nature Conservancy first opened the Cosumnes River Walk to the public in 1987. As of 2011, this trail is being expanded and enhanced, so what you find when you visit may be somewhat different from what is described here. Most of the trail is located on raised levees that run alongside the river, allowing an ideal perspective for wildlife sightings. The preserve's landscape is a rich mosaic of buttonbush thickets, native grasslands, valley oak woodlands, cottonwood/willow stands, tule marsh, valley oak savannah, and a 30-acre seasonal marsh that has been lovingly restored. All this diversity invites a tremendous variety of bird and animal species.

If you visit in late fall or early winter, which is prime wildlife-viewing time, you may find that parts of the Cosumnes River Walk are closed off

A great white egret stands sentry alongside Lost Slough's wetlands.

because of flooding. But most of the year the entire trail is accessible, and the only misgiving you may have is if you forgot to bring your binoculars. This preserve is heaven on earth for migrating and resident birds, including as many as 4,000 sandhill cranes. The elegant cranes are often seen in the marshes alongside the Cosumnes River Walk's adjacent trail, the Lost Slough Wetlands Walk. These 4-foot-tall birds, known for their intricate "dancing" maneuvers, spend the winter here before flying back to their breeding grounds in Siberia, Canada, and Alaska. Their days are spent by fattening up on eelgrass, crustaceans, and invertebrates in the flooded marshes and leftover grain in the drier farming fields. The birds' numbers usually peak between November and February, but there's no guarantee how many cranes will be here on any given day, or how close up you will see them. I repeat: Don't forget your binoculars.

If you want to see the cranes "dancing," the best time of day is usually sunset or sunrise. Sunset is also the time when the cranes fly back to the marsh to bed down for the night. Seeing large numbers of these giant birds flying overhead and circling down to the wetlands is a sight you will never forget.

The preserve hosts about 100,000 migrating waterfowl as well, including mallards, wood ducks, tundra swans, and pintails. Plenty of mammals can also be seen, especially in the early mornings and at dusk. Coyotes, foxes, otters, rabbits, beavers, and raccoons make regular appearances.

The Cosumnes River Walk begins at the bridge just north of the visitor center. From there you simply walk out and back on the levee alongside the river, passing through fields of planted oaks. On the west side of the visitor center, the trail connects with the 0.5-mile Lost Slough Wetlands Walk, which is entirely wheelchair accessible. A crane-viewing platform situated amid the tule marsh provides a great place to watch the cranes from November to February.

If you are new to this type of marsh and wetland environment and want to learn more about what you are seeing, join one of the preserve's free walking tours, which are offered on Saturday mornings. Check with the visitor center for a current schedule: (916) 684 2816.

GOING FARTHER

For a longer hike, try the Rancho Seco Howard Ranch Trail, which starts at the Rancho Seco Recreational Area ($5 entrance fee per vehicle) and winds for 3.5 miles around the north end of Rancho Seco Lake. The trail travels through land that once belonged to Charles Howard, owner of the racehorse Seabiscuit. It features vernal pools, seasonal wetlands, riparian and marsh habitat, and oak woodlands, plus views of the Sierra Nevada in the distance. Bird-watching is first-rate. Again, pack along those binoculars.

In the spring, the grassy slopes of Mount Tamalpais are dotted with wildflowers.

SAN FRANCISCO BAY AREA

The San Francisco Bay Area is urban in nature. Or perhaps more accurately, it is "urban within Nature." The Bay Area is a conglomeration of cities and suburbs that are enveloped by a ring of open-space lands, parks, and preserves, which beckon us to come and explore.

It seems incongruous, but despite its six million human inhabitants, the San Francisco Bay Area is the most wild metropolitan area in the United States. Although grizzly bears no longer roam the Bay Area as they did 150 years ago, coyotes still gallop across the grasslands, herds of tule elk wander the coastal hills, and mountain lions and bobcats stalk their prey. Elephant seals still breed on the Bay Area's beaches, river otters ply the waterways, wild pigs root for acorns, and golden eagles and peregrine falcons soar overhead.

The Bay Area has all the right ingredients for hiking nirvana: a mild year-round climate, a varied landscape, and an abundance of public land crisscrossed by trails. The Bay Area's mosaic of open space includes federally designated parks such as Point Reyes National Seashore, Muir Woods National Monument, and the Golden Gate National Recreation Area, plus an incredible wealth of California state parks.

If you hike much in the Bay Area, you will be awed by the beauty and grace of centuries-old virgin redwoods. You'll wonder at the sight of rare and precious wildflowers, some of which grow here and nowhere else in the world. Your ears will be filled with the sound of crashing surf against miles of jagged coastal bluffs. You'll gaze at waterfalls coursing down basalt cliffs, pouring over sandstone precipices, and even dashing to the sea. You'll stand on summits and look down thousands of feet to the valleys below. In autumn, you'll watch black oaks and bigleaf maples turn bright gold, and in winter, you'll see a dusting of snow fall on the Bay Area's high peaks and ridges.

This much is certain: Whenever and wherever you choose to hike in the Bay Area, you'll be witness to an urban wilderness like no other.

SAN FRANCISCO BAY AREA

43. Tomales Point Trail

RATING	🚶 🚶 🚶 🚶
DISTANCE	5.0 miles round-trip
HIKING TIME	2.5 hours
ELEVATION GAIN	600 feet
HIGH POINT	800 feet
EFFORT	Moderate Workout
BEST SEASON	Spring or fall, but good year-round
PERMITS/CONTACT	Point Reyes National Seashore, (415) 464-5100, www.nps.gov/yose
MAPS	Tom Harrison Maps "Point Reyes National Seashore"
NOTES	Dogs and bikes prohibited

THE HIKE

Hike on this old ranch road along the northern tip of the Point Reyes Peninsula and you'll have a near guarantee of spotting herds of tule elk.

GETTING THERE

From Olema in western Marin County, drive north on Highway 1 for about 150 yards, then turn left on Bear Valley Road. Drive 2.2 miles on Bear Valley Road until it joins with Sir Francis Drake Highway. Bear left on Sir Francis Drake Highway and drive 5.6 miles, then take the right fork onto Pierce Point Road. Drive 9 miles to the Pierce Point Ranch parking area.

THE TRAIL

If viewing wildlife is one of the reasons you enjoy hiking, the Tomales Point Trail is sure to satisfy. You'll have a good chance at spotting big, furry animals before you even get out of your car (and not just the usual Point Reyes bovines).

The wildlife is abundant because Tomales Point Trail is located in Point Reyes National Seashore's tule elk preserve. Before 1860, thousands of native tule elk roamed Tomales Point, but in the late 19th century the animals were hunted out of existence. The National Park Service has attempted to reestablish the elk in their native habitat. Their efforts have

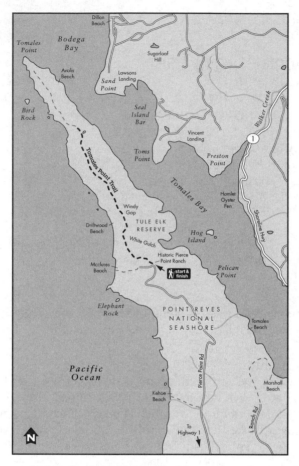

succeeded; as of 2010 the Point Reyes herd is numbered at more than 400 and going strong.

Seeing the magnificent tule elk is almost a given. Frequently they're hanging out in large numbers near the trailhead parking lot, or alongside Pierce Point Road. From July through September, when the bull elks are in their "rut" and trying to round up a harem of females, you can often hear them bugling and may even see a couple of males sparring with a magnificent clash of antlers.

It's 4.7 miles to the trail's end at the tip of Tomales Point, but you don't have to walk that far to enjoy this trip. I recommend a turnaround at a high knoll 2.5 miles out, but set your own trail distance and turn around when you please. Only a mile or two of hiking will provide splendid coastal and Tomales Bay views, plus a probable wildlife encounter. Just

Along the Tomales Point Trail, hikers are almost guaranteed the chance to see the majestic tule elk.

make sure you pick a clear day for this trip; although you can still spot tule elk in the fog, you'll miss out on the trail's blue-water vistas.

The Tomales Point Trail begins at Pierce Point Ranch, one of the oldest dairies in Point Reyes. The ranch manufactured milk and butter for San Francisco dinner tables in the 1850s. Begin hiking around the western perimeter of the ranch, or take a few minutes to inspect its buildings. Interpretive signs describe the history of Pierce Point's dairy business.

The trail curves uphill around the ranch, then heads northwest along the blufftops toward Tomales Point, the northernmost tip of Point Reyes. At 0.5 mile out, you reach the first short climb, in which you gain about 100 feet. Turn around and look behind you as you ascend: This thin peninsula of land is bracketed by the ocean on one side and Tomales Bay on the other. Look for forested Hog Island in Tomales Bay, a popular pull-up spot for kayakers.

At 1.8 miles, the path starts to descend, supplying a good view of Bird Rock jutting upward from the sea and the town and campground at Lawson's Landing across Tomales Bay. At 2.5 miles, the trail reaches its highest point, where views of Bodega Bay and the Sonoma coast to the north are a standout.

GOING FARTHER

If you choose to continue beyond the high point at 2.5 miles, you'll descend to the site of an outpost of Pierce Point Ranch, then pass by windswept Bird Rock, often covered with pelicans and cormorants. Once you pass Bird Rock, the trail becomes a bit sketchy. Amid a series of low dunes, the trail peters out, then vanishes. But the route is obvious; just keep hiking until the land runs out. You'll be rewarded with views of Bodega Head to the north, Tomales Bay to the east, and the Pacific Ocean to the west.

44. Bear Valley Trail to Arch Rock

RATING 🚶 🚶 🚶 🚶
DISTANCE 8.2 miles round-trip
HIKING TIME 4.5 hours
ELEVATION GAIN 500 feet
HIGH POINT 375 feet
EFFORT Moderate Workout
BEST SEASON Year-round
PERMITS/CONTACT Point Reyes National Seashore, (415) 464-5100, www.nps.gov/yose
MAPS Tom Harrison Maps "Point Reyes National Seashore"
NOTES Dogs prohibited; bikes allowed on the first 3.2 miles of trail

THE HIKE
Point Reyes's most popular trail follows an easy grade from lush Bear Valley to dramatic Arch Rock, a precipitous blufftop overlook.

GETTING THERE
From Olema in western Marin County, drive north on Highway 1 for about 150 yards, then turn left on Bear Valley Road. Drive 0.5 mile, then turn left at the sign for Seashore Headquarters Information. Drive 0.25 mile and park in the large lot on the left, past the visitor center. Start hiking along the park road, heading for the signed Bear Valley Trail.

THE TRAIL
The Bear Valley Trail is the most popular trail in Point Reyes National Seashore for good reasons. The trailside scenery is sublime, and the easy grade makes it suitable for any level of hiker. If you want some solitude along the route, arrive at the trailhead before 9 a.m., or plan your trip for a winter weekday. The trail is at its loveliest during the wet months of the year, when the streams are running full and the ferns are in full leafy display.

The trail begins as a wide dirt road just beyond the Bear Valley Visitor Center and Morgan Horse Ranch. Just stay on the wide main road and meander your way through a mixed bay and Douglas fir forest, following

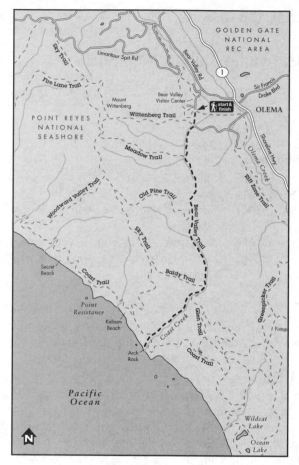

the path of Bear Valley Creek. Ferns of many kinds adorn the creek's banks, including delicate five-finger ferns. You'll notice a slight uphill grade in the first 1.0 mile, but the entire route has a very mellow grade.

At 1.5 miles from the trailhead, the trail reaches the edge of large Divide Meadow, a tranquil spot for a breather. Divide Meadow marks the divide in this valley: Bear Valley Creek, which flows north, is left behind, but soon the trail parallels Coast Creek, which flows south all the way to the sea.

Forging onward, the trail reenters dense forest, with ferns and lush streamside foliage keeping you in good company. In early spring, the trail is bordered by a profusion of blue forget-me-nots and tasty miner's lettuce, which thrive in these shady growing conditions. At 3.2 miles you reach a junction of trails and a bike rack. (Bikes are allowed only up to this point; bikers must continue on foot from here.) Glen Trail leads to the left and Baldy Trail to the right, but you simply continue straight on Bear Valley Trail to Arch Rock. After another 0.5 mile, the trail leaves this shady forest and opens out to coastal marshlands. The ocean appears straight ahead.

Nearing the sea, Bear Valley Trail splits off as it meets up with Coast Trail. Bear left to walk the last stretch to your destination, Arch Rock. These final steps are rife with drama as you traverse the top of Arch Rock's precipitous, jade green bluff jutting out into the sea. Coast Creek, the previously gentle stream you were following, now cuts a deep and eroded gorge on its way to the ocean. The top of Arch Rock provides a vista of offshore outcrops, the shoreline below, and the perpetually rolling surf.

GOING FARTHER

If it's crowded on top of Arch Rock when you arrive, backtrack a few hundred feet to Coast Trail, then follow that trail northward for 0.8 mile to Kelham Beach. The spur trail to the beach is marked by a lone eucalyptus tree.

45. Kehoe Beach

RATING	🚶 🚶 🚶 🚶
DISTANCE	2.0 miles round-trip
HIKING TIME	1 hour
ELEVATION GAIN	Negligible
HIGH POINT	50 feet
EFFORT	Easy Walk
BEST SEASON	Year-round
PERMITS/CONTACT	Point Reyes National Seashore, (415) 464-5100, www.nps.gov/yose
MAPS	Tom Harrison Maps "Point Reyes National Seashore"
NOTES	Dogs allowed, bikes prohibited

THE HIKE

This level pathway, popular with dog walkers and beach lovers, travels alongside a bird-happy freshwater marsh to the inviting sands of Kehoe Beach.

GETTING THERE

From Olema in western Marin County, drive north on Highway 1, then turn left on Bear Valley Road. Drive 2.2 miles on Bear Valley Road until it joins with Sir Francis Drake Highway. Bear left on Sir Francis Drake Highway and drive 5.6 miles, then take the right fork onto Pierce Point Road. Drive 5.5 miles to the Kehoe Beach trailhead on your left. Park along either side of the road in the pullouts.

THE TRAIL

At most beaches in California, you just drive up, park your car in the paved parking lot, walk a few feet, and plop down in the sand. Kehoe Beach beats that by a mile. Exactly a mile, in fact, because that's how far the hike is. The distance is just long enough for a pleasant, level walk, and if you want to hike farther, you can continue sauntering along Kehoe's wide strip of sandy beach.

The trail proves that the journey can be as good as the destination. The fun starts right where you park your car; in late summer you'll find a

Windswept Kehoe Beach is popular with picnickers, kite flyers, and dogs and their owners.

huge patch of blackberries near the roadside trailhead. Pick a handful to sustain you on your hike.

The pathway is gravel, almost completely level, and wide enough for holding hands with your hiking partner. It runs alongside Kehoe Marsh, a freshwater marsh that provides habitat for birds and bird-watchers. Songbirds are nearly as abundant as the nonnative ice plant that weaves thick cushions of matted foliage alongside the trail. Grasses and vines grow in profusion, encouraged by the proximity of the marshy creek and its underground spring. Colorful mustard, a nonnative but comely weed, grows waist-high during the spring wildflower season. As you near the ocean, the wet, marshy terrain transforms to sandy dunes, where you may see jackrabbits hopping among the grasses.

Before you sprint down to Kehoe's brayed, tan sands, take the spur trail that cuts off to the right (near a wooden bench) and climb up the bluffs above the beach. In springtime, these slopes are painted bright blue and gold with prolific yellow tidytips, blue lupine, and orange poppies. It's a glorious sight to behold. Once you've admired the flowers, head down to the beach to hike farther or be mesmerized by the crashing waves. You'll return on the same trail.

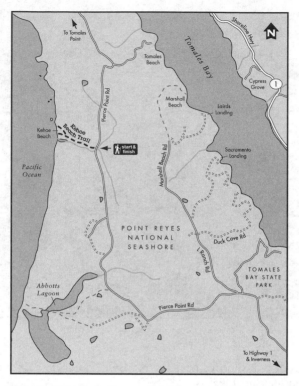

Hikers visiting with their dogs should note that although pups are welcome on the trail and on the beach north of the trail, they are not permitted on the beach south of the trail. This rule is intended to protect nesting snowy plovers.

GOING FARTHER
If you can arrange a shuttle car, you can hike from Kehoe Beach's trailhead to Abbotts Lagoon's trailhead, a 5-mile stretch that includes 2 miles on the beach.

46. North Ridge and Sunset Trail Loop

RATING	🚶 🚶 🚶 🚶
DISTANCE	4.5 miles round-trip
HIKING TIME	2.5 hours
ELEVATION GAIN	788 feet
HIGH POINT	788 feet
EFFORT	Moderate Workout
BEST SEASON	Year-round
PERMITS/CONTACT	See ferry rates below, Angel Island State Park, (415) 435-1915, www.angelisland.org
MAPS	Tom Harrison Maps "Angel Island"
NOTES	Dogs and bikes prohibited

THE HIKE
Visit the summit of Mount Livermore, the highest point on Angel Island, on this view-filled half-day hike.

GETTING THERE
Ferry service to Angel Island is available from Tiburon, San Francisco, and Oakland/Alameda. For Tiburon departures, contact Tiburon Ferry, (415) 435-2131, www.angelislandferry.com. For Oakland or Alameda departures, contact East Bay Ferry, (510) 522-3300, www.eastbayferry.com. For San Francisco departures, contact Blue and Gold Fleet, (415) 705-8200, www.blueandgoldfleet.com. Ferry rates are $15 to $20 per adult (round-trip).

THE TRAIL
There are two completely different ways to explore Angel Island on foot: One route follows the wide, paved Perimeter Trail, which circumnavigates the island. The other is the mostly single-track North Ridge and Sunset Trail Loop, which travels to the island's highest point, the summit of Mount Livermore. Both trails offer splendid views of San Francisco Bay, but the Perimeter Trail is better suited for biking. To see Angel Island on two feet, hike the North Ridge and Sunset Trail Loop.

Whether you take a ferry from Tiburon, San Francisco, or the East Bay, the boat ride is definitely part of the fun of this trip. All the ferries

The trails of Angel Island provide an unique view of the land mass of Marin County.

land near Ayala Cove, where you disembark and walk the opposite way from most of your fellow ferry riders. They're heading right toward the island's concession stands; you head slightly left to pick up North Ridge Trail just to the left of the restrooms. The trail begins with a quick, steep climb of more than 100 steps leading up to the paved Perimeter Road. This is the steepest ascent of the day.

Cross the road, pant a few times, then pick up North Ridge Trail on its far side. Now the path is gently graded and alternates through sunny, chaparral-covered slopes and a shady, fern-filled canopy of live oaks. At just over 1.0 mile up the trail, the path traverses the northern flank of Mount Livermore. Views across San Francisco Bay widen as you climb.

Where North Ridge Trail junctions with Sunset Trail and the summit trail, bear right for the summit. Ascending another 0.25 mile brings you to Mount Livermore's 788-foot summit. A few picnic tables are found at and just below the summit, as well as interpretive signs that point out the landmarks of the bay. You can pick out Berkeley, Mount Diablo, Mount Hamilton (56 miles away), Santa Clara, San Francisco's Telegraph Hill, Alcatraz Island, Montara Mountain, Twin Peaks, the Golden Gate

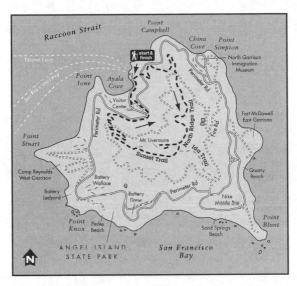

Bridge, Mount Tamalpais, Tiburon, Belvedere, San Quentin Prison, and Mount St. Helena in Napa (57 miles away).

With a view like that, it's not surprising that Mount Livermore's few picnic tables are in high demand on sunny weekend days. After you've taken it all in, head back down the summit trail. Pick up Sunset Trail at the junction with North Ridge Trail, and enjoy another 0.5 mile of bay views as you descend through the grasslands. The trail heads into a forest of oaks and bays, switchbacking gently downhill to another wide viewpoint and a crossing of Perimeter Road. Follow the paved road back downhill to Ayala Cove, or take the single-track trail just to the right of it.

GOING FARTHER

One of the best ways to explore Angel Island is by spending the night at one of its backpacking camps. Advance reservations are required; phone (800) 444-7275 or visit www.reserveamerica.com. The camping areas require a hike of only 1 to 2 miles each way, but once you've set up camp, the whole island is yours to survey.

47. Coastal, Cataract, and Old Mine Loop

RATING	🚶 🚶 🚶 🚶
DISTANCE	6.8 miles round-trip
HIKING TIME	3.5 hours
ELEVATION GAIN	700 feet
HIGH POINT	1,750 feet
EFFORT	Moderate Workout
BEST SEASON	Year-round
PERMITS/CONTACT	Mount Tamalpais State Park fee required ($8 per vehicle), (415) 388-2070, www.mttam.net
MAPS	Tom Harrison Maps "Mount Tamalpais" or download at www.parks.ca.gov
NOTES	Dogs and bikes prohibited

THE HIKE

It's all about the vistas and the wildflowers on this guaranteed-to-please day hike on Mount Tamalpais.

GETTING THERE

From U.S. 101 just north of the Golden Gate Bridge, take the Mill Valley/Stinson Beach/Highway 1 exit and continue straight for 1 mile to a stop-light at Shoreline Highway (Highway 1). Turn left on Shoreline Highway and drive 2.5 miles, then turn right on Panoramic Highway. Drive 0.9 mile to a four-way intersection. Take the middle road (straight), continuing on Panoramic Highway for 4.3 more miles to the Pantoll Ranger Station and parking lot. Turn left to park in the lot, then climb the steps on the lot's northwest side, cross Panoramic Highway, and access Matt Davis/Coastal Trail near the start of Pantoll Road, on its southwest side.

THE TRAIL

Is it a clear day in the San Francisco Bay Area? If so, then your mission is obvious: Lace up your hiking boots and head for this loop trail in Mount Tamalpais State Park. Yes, there are lots of junctions to negoti-ate, but this loop offers secluded forest groves laced with small, coursing streams, wide grasslands covered with lupine and poppies in the spring, and grand vistas of city and sea.

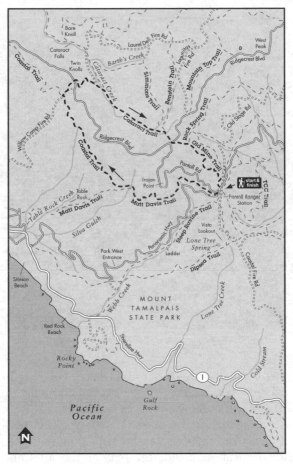

Start your trip on the Matt Davis/Coastal Trail near Pantoll Ranger Station. After an initial glimpse at the ocean near the trail's start, you'll head into a dense mixed hardwood forest and remain there for just shy of 1.0 mile. The beauty is close at hand—thick moss growing like fur on the bay laurel trees, dense ferns clustered on the banks of seasonal streams, and dappled sunlight filtering through the canopy of leaves.

Just as your eyes grow accustomed to the low light of the forest, the trail suddenly opens out to wide, sloping grasslands and bright sunshine. In spring, the mountain's wildflowers burst into colorful display, spurred on by cooling fog and plentiful sunlight. You can see far and wide down the grassy slopes of Mount Tamalpais. Mount Tam's slopes drop 1,500 feet to the ocean; the Pacific glitters in the distance. The farther you

Hikers on Mount Tamalpais' Coastal Trail enjoy wide views of the Pacific.

walk, the wider your view becomes until it finally stretches from the San Francisco skyline in the south to Stinson Beach and Bolinas in the north, then still farther north to the Point Reyes peninsula.

You'll reach a junction at 1.5 miles. Matt Davis Trail heads downhill to Stinson Beach. Head right on Coastal Trail, continuing gently uphill. Where Coastal Trail meets a wide fire road at 3.3 miles out, turn right and climb steeply uphill for a brief stretch. Look for a side trail cutting off the fire road to the left; this will deliver you to paved Ridgecrest Boulevard at its junction with Laurel Dell Fire Road. Cross the paved road (watch for cars), then take Laurel Dell Fire Road. The dirt and gravel road makes a gentle descent through a mossy, shady bay forest to the edge of Cataract Creek. Watch for a right turnoff on Cataract Trail; a footbridge will carry you across the creek.

Cataract Trail parallels its namesake stream, passing within arm's length of the mossy trunks of bays and tan oaks in a dense forest canopy. The trail opens out to a meadow near Rock Spring, then deposits you at the Rock Spring parking lot. Cross Ridgecrest Boulevard again and pick up Mountain Theater Fire Road on its far side, a few yards to the left. A brief, steep climb and a right turn on Old Mine Trail takes you to high views of San Pablo Bay, the Richmond Bridge, and San Francisco. A few large boulders on a grassy knoll make an ideal viewing platform.

Follow Old Mine Trail back downhill for 1.0 mile to paved Old Stage Road. The path drops 500 feet through a series of steep switchbacks. Finally, turn right on Old Stage Road and walk back to your car at Pantoll Ranger Station.

GOING FARTHER

Another great trail loop that starts at Pantoll Ranger Station is the 3.6-mile Dipsea and Steep Ravine Loop. Follow the paved trail from the far end of the parking lot a few hundred feet to Old Mine Trail. In 0.5 mile, go left on a fire road, then almost immediately right on Dipsea Trail. This trail is part of the famous 7-mile Dipsea Race from Mill Valley to Stinson Beach, which is held annually on the second Sunday in June. At 2 miles from the start, you'll cross a bridge and go right on Steep Ravine Trail for the climb back uphill.

48. Ocean View, Lost Trail, and Fern Creek Loop

RATING	🚶 🚶 🚶 🚶
DISTANCE	3.4 miles round-trip
HIKING TIME	1.5 hours
ELEVATION GAIN	450 feet
HIGH POINT	600 feet
EFFORT	Moderate Workout
BEST SEASON	November to April, but good year-round
PERMITS/CONTACT	Muir Woods National Monument fee required ($5 per adult), (415) 388-2595, www.nps.gov/muwo
MAPS	Download at www.nps.gov/muwo
NOTES	Dogs and bikes prohibited

THE HIKE

On this trail, Muir Woods shows off its famous coastal redwoods and coursing stream.

GETTING THERE

From U.S. 101 just north of the Golden Gate Bridge, take the Mill Valley/ Stinson Beach/Highway 1 exit and continue straight for 1 mile to a stoplight at Shoreline Highway (Highway 1). Turn left on Shoreline Highway and drive 2.5 miles, then turn right on Panoramic Highway. Drive 0.9 mile and turn left on Muir Woods Road. Drive 1.5 miles to the Muir Woods parking area.

THE TRAIL

The redwoods at Muir Woods National Monument are true beauties. The foliage growing in the big trees' understory—bays, tan oak, thimbleberry, sword ferns, and sorrel—is lush and green year-round. Redwood Creek, which cuts through the center of the park, is a pristine, coursing stream. So it's no wonder this tiny national monument, not much larger than a few city blocks, gets visited by more than one million people each year.

How do you hike in the park and see its magnificent trees without getting run over by the crowds? Summer is the busiest time, of course, so it's best to avoid May to September altogether. Winter and early spring are the least crowded and also the loveliest seasons, when Redwood

The lush greenery of Muir Woods' redwood forests inspire quiet moments of contemplation.

Creek runs full and high. Any time of year, an early morning start is a smart idea; the crowds don't usually arrive until about 10 a.m.

Start your trip from the entrance gate to Muir Woods near the small visitor center. The park's main trail is a wide, boardwalk-lined path that is mostly level and runs along the bottom of the canyon, passing the most impressive redwoods. You'll walk the entire length of this trail on your return. For now, bear right and in about 100 yards you'll reach a fork with Ocean View Trail. Follow it up the hillside to the right.

The path is completely forested, but the redwood trees are younger and smaller than in the canyon below and interspersed with many Douglas firs. Ocean View Trail climbs moderately and curves around the canyon until it reaches a junction with Lost Trail at 1.5 miles. (No, despite its name, there is no "ocean view" from this trail.) Bear right on Lost Trail,

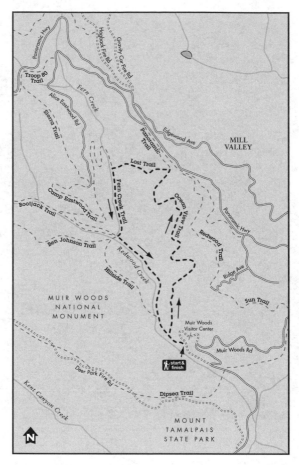

now heading downhill. Similar to Ocean View Trail, Lost Trail weaves through a young redwood, Douglas fir, and bay forest. Soon it descends more steeply on railroad-tie stair steps, and in 0.7 mile it connects with Fern Creek Trail. Fern Creek is a seasonal tributary to Redwood Creek, the main stream that flows through Muir Woods' canyon. Fern Creek Trail follows Fern Creek's delightful course for 0.5 mile, crossing it on two footbridges.

Near the end of Fern Creek Trail you pass a sign marking the border of Muir Woods National Monument. In a few more steps you're at the base of the Kent Memorial, a very large Douglas fir tree dedicated to the man who was responsible for the creation of this park. Say a few gracious words about Congressman Kent, then head back down the main trail to your starting point.

GOING FARTHER

A slightly longer hike from Muir Woods is a 4.2-mile loop that combines Ocean View, Redwood, Sun, and Dipsea Trails. Follow Ocean View Trail uphill as in the trip above, then turn right on Redwood Trail. Shortly you'll gain the ocean views you didn't get on Ocean View Trail. In 1 mile you pass the Tourist Club, a private hiking club. Near there, Redwood Trail connects to Sun Trail, which travels 0.7 mile to a junction with Dipsea Trail. Turn right on Dipsea, which crosses Muir Woods Road and drops back down to the Muir Woods parking lot in 1 mile.

49. Huckleberry Path

RATING	🚶 🚶 🚶
DISTANCE	1.7 miles round-trip
HIKING TIME	1 hour
ELEVATION GAIN	450 feet
HIGH POINT	1,265 feet
EFFORT	Moderate Workout
BEST SEASON	Year-round
PERMITS/CONTACT	East Bay Regional Park District, (888) 327-2757, www.ebparks.org
MAPS	Download at www.ebparks.org
NOTES	Dogs and bikes prohibited

THE HIKE

This peaceful trail in the East Bay Park District's Huckleberry Botanic Regional Preserve is shaded by a dense tree canopy and home to some rare native plants.

GETTING THERE

From Interstate 580 in Oakland, take the 35th Avenue exit and head north. Drive 2.4 miles (35th Avenue will become Redwood Road). Turn left on Skyline Boulevard and drive 5.2 miles to the preserve. (Skyline Boulevard makes a sharp right turn after the first 0.5 mile.)

THE TRAIL

Trailheads along Skyline Boulevard in the Berkeley hills are about as common as the million-dollar houses clinging to steep hillsides. Home to several regional parks and a large section of the 31-mile East Bay Skyline National Trail, Skyline Boulevard is a weekend recreationist's paradise. Mountain bikers, dog walkers, runners, hikers—everybody finds a trail to suit their desires.

Of many excellent choices, my favorite park on Skyline Boulevard is Huckleberry Botanic Regional Preserve. Unlike its neighboring parks, Huckleberry is designated for hikers only. No bikes, horses, or dogs are allowed; even joggers are discouraged. The park is home to a large number

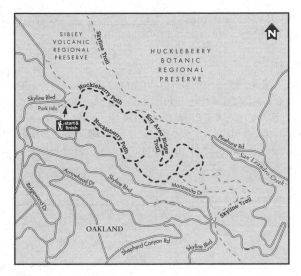

of native plants that are extremely rare in the East Bay, plus some that are extremely rare, period.

The park's main trail is called simply Huckleberry Path, and it's a narrow, snaking footpath that weaves its way through dense foliage. A self-guided trail brochure is available at the trailhead; it corresponds to numbered posts along the path. The 1.7-mile loop trail should be hiked clockwise; bear left at the first junction to do so. If you want more, you can easily tack on another 0.75 mile at the far end of the loop, where the trail connects with a trailhead at Pinehurst Road. Or, since part of the Huckleberry Path is the East Bay Skyline National Recreation Trail, you can add on a trip northward to Sibley Preserve (about 2.0 miles) or southward to Redwood Regional Park (1.0 mile).

Take your pick of the add-on trails or simply choose to linger within the boundaries of Huckleberry. Stay for a while at the sunny, manzanita-lined overlook by interpretive post 6, where the view of Mount Diablo is inspiring. Or take time to study or photograph the preserve's rare plants, such as western leatherwood (look for leathery branches and bright yellow flowers December to March), and tall pallid manzanita, with its delicate, pink, bell-like blossoms. Or perhaps best of all, time your trip so you can sample the preserve's namesake huckleberries, which fruit in late summer and early fall.

Any season is a good time to visit this preserve. The trail is completely shaded by long-limbed bay laurels, madrones, and oaks, so it remains cool even in the heat of summer. Plentiful sword and wood ferns "green up" and come to life after winter rains. Spring wildflowers are always worth a special visit; look for purple Douglas iris in the early months and orange bush monkey flower as summer approaches.

GOING FARTHER

Only a short drive north from Huckleberry Preserve is Sibley Volcanic Regional Preserve, off Skyline Boulevard. This park is the home of Mount Round Top, an ancient volcano that was the source of most of the lava rock found in the ridges of the East Bay hills. The 2-mile Round Top Loop Trail and Volcanic Trail are keyed to an interpretive brochure that explains the park's volcanic features.

50. Bay View and Red Hill Loop

RATING	🚶 🚶 🚶
DISTANCE	4.8 miles round-trip
HIKING TIME	2.5 hours
ELEVATION GAIN	350 feet
HIGH POINT	290 feet
EFFORT	Easy Walk
BEST SEASON	Year-round
PERMITS/CONTACT	East Bay Regional Park District fee required ($5 per vehicle), (888) 327-2757, www.ebparks.org
MAPS	Download at www.ebparks.org
NOTES	Dogs and bikes allowed ($2 dog fee); some trails are wheelchair accessible

THE HIKE
The home of Ohlone Indians for more than 2,000 years, today Coyote Hills Regional Park is a place to enjoy bay and marsh views and abundant bird sightings.

GETTING THERE
From Interstate 880 in Newark, take Highway 84 west for 2 miles. Take the Paseo Padre Parkway exit, turn right (north), and drive 1 mile to Patterson Ranch Road. Turn left and drive 1.5 miles to the visitor center parking lot at Coyote Hills.

THE TRAIL
A 1,000-acre patch of open space along the edge of San Francisco Bay, the grassy knolls of Coyote Hills were the homeland of Ohlone Indians for more than 2,000 years. The Indians fished bay waters for food and cut willow branches along the creeks to build their homes. Today the park is a wildlife sanctuary, both a permanent home and a temporary rest stop for thousands of resident and migratory birds.

Binoculars are a worthwhile accessory for this trail, but many of the birds are so close that you don't even need them. On one short walk at Coyote Hills, we watched a great egret stalk and catch a field mouse 20 yards from us, then fly off with it in his beak. Moments later a peregrine

At Coyote Hills Regional Park, boardwalks criss-cross the tule-lined marsh, allowing hikers opportunities for up-close bird-watching.

falcon soared overhead, shortly followed by a red-tailed hawk swooping and floating over the grasslands. In winter, great egrets and snowy egrets displaying exquisite white plumage are as common as human visitors to the park.

The park has a paved multiuse trail along its hillsides, allowing hikers, baby stroller pushers, wheelchair users, and bikers to enjoy breathtaking bay and marsh views. But hikers who prefer earthen paths to pavement won't be disappointed. Red Hill Trail climbs to the top of the park's grassy hills for panoramic views and a close-up look at some odd rock formations—outcrops of reddish gold chert that were once part of the ocean floor.

It's a park for wandering, with or without a formal plan. Start your trip at the Coyote Hills visitor center, which has some interesting displays on the natural and cultural history of the area. Then follow the gated, paved road—Bay View Trail—heading north from the visitor center parking lot.

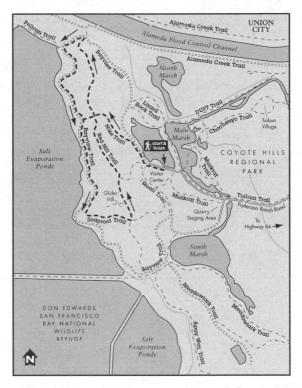

Leave the pavement in 100 yards as you turn left on wide Nike Trail, heading toward the bay. In 0.25 mile, turn right on Red Hill Trail to begin a 2.3-mile loop on Red Hill and Bay View Trails. Hike up and over a grassy hill, then drop back down to the water's edge. Rejoin paved Bay View Trail and stroll southward along the bay. Your trail is only 50 feet above the water's edge. After a full mile of nonstop views, you'll round Glider Hill and see the turnoff for Soaproot Trail. Turn left on Soaproot, then left again on Red Hill Trail to finish out your loop. As you hike to the top of Red Hill, consider the fact that when San Francisco Bay's waters were higher (before dikes were built in the late 1800s), Red Hill and its neighboring hills were islands.

After exploring Red Hill and its red-colored rock formations, return to the junction with Nike Trail and retrace your steps to the visitor center parking lot. Then head off in the opposite direction, walking 50 yards south on the road you drove in on. Watch for a wooden boardwalk crossing the tule-lined marsh on your left. Follow the boardwalk through a labyrinth of tules, cattails, and sedges. The path leads to an Ohlone Indian shell mound. The largest of four shell mounds in the park, this debris pile supplies archaeological proof that Indians inhabited this area for at least 2,200 years.

GOING FARTHER

For more bird-watching opportunities, head to neighboring Don Edwards San Francisco Bay National Wildlife Refuge, on the south side of Highway 84 off Thornton Avenue. Two of the largest egret nesting colonies in Northern California are located at the refuge. Start your trip at the large visitor center, then follow the signed boardwalk trails above the bay's tidal flats.

51. Purisima Redwoods Loop

RATING	🚶 🚶 🚶 🚶
DISTANCE	7.0 miles round-trip
HIKING TIME	3.5 hours
ELEVATION GAIN	1,000 feet
HIGH POINT	1,400 feet
EFFORT	Prepare to Perspire
BEST SEASON	Year-round
PERMITS/CONTACT	Midpeninsula Regional Open Space District, (650) 691-1200, www.openspace.org
MAPS	Download at www.openspace.org
NOTES	Dogs prohibited; bikes allowed on some trails

THE HIKE

One of the most scenic loop trails in the northern Santa Cruz Mountains travels through the dense redwoods of Purisima Canyon.

GETTING THERE

From Half Moon Bay, drive south on Highway 1 and turn left on Higgins Canyon Road (by the fire station). Drive 4.3 miles to the trailhead parking area at a hairpin turn in the road.

THE TRAIL

Purisima Creek Redwoods Open Space Preserve is a hiker's heaven. With breathtaking ocean views, towering redwood and fir trees, a year-round creek, and plentiful wildlife and wildflowers, the preserve shows off some of the best features of the Santa Cruz Mountains. Purisima delivers on its Spanish name: It's pristine.

Purisima's trails traverse the slopes between Skyline Ridge and the coast, a 1,600-foot elevation change. You can access the 3,200-acre preserve from trailheads on the ridge's Skyline Boulevard (Highway 35) or at the coast in Half Moon Bay. I prefer starting in Half Moon Bay, because that means you climb on the first leg of the loop and enjoy an easy cruise downhill on the way out.

Right from the start, wide, redwood-lined Purisima Creek Trail climbs very gently alongside Purisima Creek, gaining a mere 400 feet in 2.3

Purisima Creek gurgles and splashes alongside the canyon's old logging road.

miles. Large redwood stumps are interspersed among the young red-woods, giving you a hint of what this forest looked like before it was logged in the late 1800s. Purisima's first-growth trees were used to build Half Moon Bay and San Francisco after the Gold Rush. The trail itself is an old logging road; seven lumber mills once operated along the banks of Purisima Creek. Today the stream canyon is home to a variety of ferns and a multitude of banana slugs. Its middle reaches are lined with impressive redwood deadfall.

Purisima Creek Trail makes a long switchback 2.0 miles from its start, and heads northward to junction with Craig Britton Trail. Bear left on this hikers-only pathway, a section of the Bay Area Ridge Trail, which makes a wide curve around the steep slopes of Soda Gulch. You'll tra-verse both sides of the canyon, crossing several smaller ravines on foot-bridges. Some of the tallest redwoods found in the preserve grow in

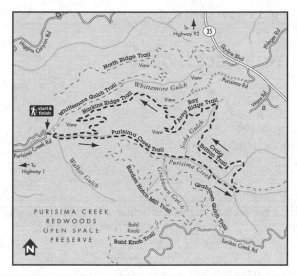

the fertile soil around Soda Gulch. Most hikers agree that this 2.6-mile stretch on Craig Britton Trail is the most enchanting part of this loop.

As the trail gains elevation, the redwood canopy gives way to mixed hardwoods and chaparral-covered slopes. Craig Britton Trail's last 1.0 mile offers occasional inspiring views of the Santa Cruz Mountains and distant Pacific Ocean. At a junction with Harkins Ridge Trail, turn left and begin the downhill leg of the loop back to the trailhead.

GOING FARTHER

You can turn this into a 10-mile loop by turning right, not left as above, on Harkins Ridge Trail and continuing uphill almost to Skyline Boulevard, where you turn left on North Ridge Trail. Follow that downhill to connect to Whittemore Gulch Trail, which will take you back to your starting point.

52. Russian Ridge Loop

RATING	🚶 🚶 🚶 🚶
DISTANCE	4.4 miles round-trip
HIKING TIME	2.5 hours
ELEVATION GAIN	550 feet
HIGH POINT	2,572 feet
EFFORT	Moderate Workout
BEST SEASON	Year-round
PERMITS/CONTACT	Midpeninsula Regional Open Space District, (650) 691-1200, www.openspace.org
MAPS	Russian Ridge Open Space (download at www.openspace.org)
NOTES	Dogs prohibited; bikes allowed

THE HIKE

Wildflowers abound in the spring and sweeping views are available year-round on this scenic trail in the hills above Palo Alto.

GETTING THERE

From Interstate 280 in Palo Alto, take the Page Mill Road exit west. Drive 8.9 winding miles to Skyline Boulevard (Highway 35). Cross Skyline Boulevard to Alpine Road. Drive 200 feet on Alpine Road and turn right into the Russian Ridge entrance.

THE TRAIL

Russian Ridge Open Space Preserve comprises more than 1,500 acres of windswept ridgetop paradise. The weather may be foggy on the coast, but the sun is usually shining brightly on top of Skyline Ridge. From the preserve's 2,300-foot elevation, you can look out and above the layer of fog blanketing the ocean.

In spring, Russian Ridge will charm you with colorful wildflowers and verdant grasslands. In summer and fall, the hillsides turn gold and the grasses sway in unison to the ridgetop winds. On a clear day in any season, you'll be wowed by the vistas from 2,572-foot Borel Hill, the highest named point in San Mateo County.

Blue-eyed grass is one of many showy spring wildflowers at Russian Ridge Open Space Preserve.

Russian Ridge has much to offer hikers, but perhaps most impressive are the spring wildflowers. Every April and May, the grasslands explode in a fireworks display of colorful mule's ears, poppies, lupine, goldfields, Johnny-jump-ups, and blue-eyed grass. Russian Ridge is considered to be one of the best places in the Bay Area to see wildflowers.

This 4.4-mile loop circles the preserve. Take the Bay Area Ridge Trail uphill from the parking lot, heading for the top of grassy Borel Hill in less than 1.0 mile. (Stay right at two junctions.) The 2,572-foot summit of Borel Hill is just high enough to serve up a 360-degree view of the South Bay, Skyline Ridge, and all the way west to the Pacific Ocean. Mount Diablo looms in the eastern horizon and Mount Tamalpais guards the north.

From the summit, descend gently for 0.5 mile to a major junction of trails near Skyline Boulevard. Bear left on Mindego Ridge Trail, then turn right on Bay Area Ridge Trail. Ridge Trail narrows, curving around grassy knolls and producing more views of the coast and the bay. To the southwest you can see Mindego Hill, an ancient volcanic formation that may be the source of this ridge's scattered rock outcrops.

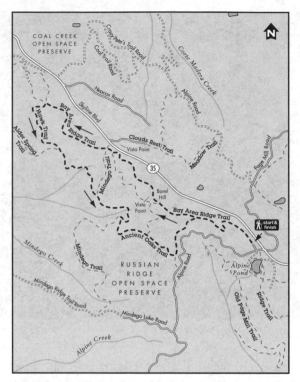

At a junction with Hawk Trail, turn left to head southeast and start your loop back. Stay straight at the next two junctions and descend to a third junction with Ancient Oaks Trail. Take Ancient Oaks Trail, which leads through a remarkable grove of gnarled, moss-covered oak trees interspersed with equally gnarled Douglas firs, plus some madrones and ferns. You may want to linger a while in this strange, enchanted woodland, at least long enough to climb a few trees. Then turn left at the next junction and cruise back out into the sunlight to rejoin Bay Area Ridge Trail and head back to your car.

GOING FARTHER

The Caltrans Vista Point on Skyline Boulevard, 1.1 mile north of the main Russian Ridge entrance at Alpine Road, is the trailhead for the 2.5-mile Clouds Rest and Meadow Loop in Coal Creek Open Space Preserve. The trail's highlight is a walk around flower-dotted Coal Creek Meadow, which provides memorable views of the Peninsula and South Bay.

53. Peters Creek and Long Ridge Loop

RATING	𝕩 𝕩 𝕩 𝕩
DISTANCE	4.6 miles round-trip
HIKING TIME	2.5 hours
ELEVATION GAIN	400 feet
HIGH POINT	2,500 feet
EFFORT	Moderate Workout
BEST SEASON	Year-round
PERMITS/CONTACT	Midpeninsula Regional Open Space District, (650) 691-1200, www.openspace.org
MAPS	Download at www.openspace.org
NOTES	Dogs prohibited; bikes allowed

THE HIKE

Easy trails follow the path of burbling Peters Creek and lace through meadows and forest on scenic Skyline Ridge.

GETTING THERE

From Interstate 280 in Palo Alto, take the Page Mill Road exit west. Drive 8.9 winding miles to Skyline Boulevard (Highway 35). Turn left on Skyline Boulevard and drive 3.1 miles to the Long Ridge/Grizzly Flat parking area on the left. The trail is located across the road.

Or, from Saratoga, take Highway 9 west to its junction with Skyline Boulevard. Turn right on Skyline Boulevard and drive 3.2 miles to the Long Ridge/Grizzly Flat parking area on the right. The trail is located across the road.

THE TRAIL

Long Ridge Open Space is a peaceful 2,000-acre preserve along Skyline Boulevard near Saratoga Gap. Its hiking, biking, and equestrian trails are perfect in all seasons—warm and windy in summer, crisp and golden in autumn, fern-laden and mossy in winter, and gilded with wildflowers in spring.

From the Grizzly Flat trailhead, only one pathway enters Long Ridge. It's the start of Peters Creek Trail, which soon connects with the Bay Area Ridge Trail. The latter makes a tight switchback and heads north; you'll

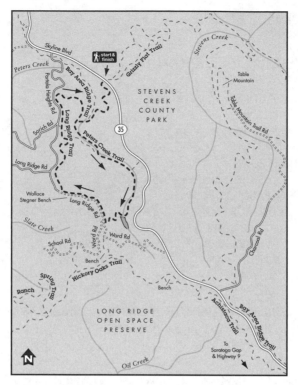

continue straight on Peters Creek Trail. Once you get moving, the sight and sound of Skyline Boulevard quickly disappears as the trail drops below the road and into a pristine canyon of grasslands and forest. Fields of wildflowers and rolling grasses in the foreground are framed by a forest of Douglas firs and oaks ahead.

At a junction with Long Ridge Trail, turn left to stay on Peters Creek Trail and begin a gentle ascent through oaks, firs, and bay laurel. Babbling Peters Creek, a major tributary of Pescadero Creek, meanders along at your side. Ferns and moss-covered boulders line the stream. Woodland wildflowers include tiny two-eyed violets (heart-shaped leaves with white and purple flowers) and purple shooting stars.

The trail wanders in and out of meadows and forest, passing an old apple orchard and ranch site. At 1.6 miles, you'll reach a small pond with huge reeds and a sea of horsetails growing around its edges. Watch for pond turtles sunning themselves. On the far side of the pond is private property belonging to the Jikoji Buddhist retreat center.

From the high point of the Long Ridge Loop, a hiker's view expands all the way to the San Mateo coast.

A few switchbacks lead you to the top of the ridge, where you meet up with Long Ridge Road. At this 2,500-foot elevation, expansive views are yours for the taking. Turn right on Long Ridge Road and traipse along, oohing and aahing at the panorama of neighboring Butano Ridge and the forests of the Pescadero Creek watershed. Be sure to pause at the bench commemorating Pulitzer prize–winning author Wallace Stegner, who lived in this area and aided in the conservation of Long Ridge.

After this sunny, view-filled stint, Long Ridge Trail heads back into the forest to finish out the loop. The path makes a wide circle to the north and then east through a dense forest of leafy oaks, then reconnects with the start of Peters Creek Trail.

GOING FARTHER

From neighboring Skyline Ridge Open Space Preserve, take the scenic Ridge Trail route to Daniels Nature Center at Alpine Pond for a natural history lesson. The 3.2-mile round-trip displays a wealth of wildflowers in the spring. The trailhead is located on the west side of Skyline Boulevard, 1 mile south of Page Mill Road.

54. Saratoga Gap and Ridge Trail Loop

RATING	🚶 🚶 🚶 🚶
DISTANCE	5.2 miles round-trip
HIKING TIME	2.5 hours
ELEVATION GAIN	1,000 feet
HIGH POINT	3,100 feet
EFFORT	Prepare to Perspire
BEST SEASON	Year-round
PERMITS/CONTACT	Castle Rock State Park fee required ($8 per vehicle), (408) 867-2952, www.parks.ca.gov
MAPS	Download at www.parks.ca.gov
NOTES	Dogs and bikes prohibited

THE HIKE

Visit Castle Rock State Park's mammoth sandstone formations and watch rock climbers strut their stuff at this deservedly popular South Bay park.

GETTING THERE

From Saratoga, take Highway 9 west to its junction with Skyline Boulevard (Highway 35). Turn left (south) on Skyline Boulevard and drive 2.5 miles to the Castle Rock State Park parking area on the right.

THE HIKE

Castle Rock is a park full of surprises. In 5.0 miles of hiking, you can visit a 50-foot waterfall in winter and spring, gaze at miles of Santa Cruz Mountains wildlands, and examine several large sandstone formations, including the local rock climbers' favorite, Goat Rock.

Take Saratoga Gap Trail from the far (west) side of Castle Rock's parking lot. The pleasure begins immediately as you travel downhill, walking along rocky, fern-lined Kings Creek through a mixed forest of Douglas firs, black oaks, and madrones. The seasonal creek begins as a trickle at the parking lot, then picks up flow and intensity as it heads downhill alongside the trail.

It's a mere 0.8 mile to Castle Rock Falls, which flows with vigor in the wet season. The trail deposits you on a large wooden viewing deck,

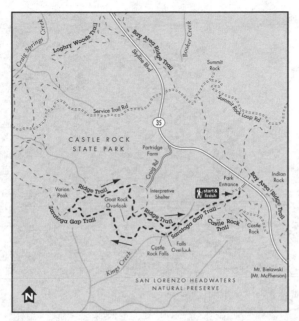

perched on top of the waterfall. Because you're at its brink, the fall is a bit difficult to see, but it's a charming spot nonetheless.

From the falls, continue on Saratoga Gap Trail for another 1.8 miles. The terrain changes quickly from a shady mixed woodland to a sunny, exposed slope with views all the way out to Monterey Bay and the Pacific Ocean. As you progress, you'll notice an ever-increasing number of sandstone outcrops that were hollowed and sculpted by wind erosion.

At 2.5 miles from its start, Saratoga Gap Trail junctions with Ridge Trail and the spur to Castle Rock Trail Camp. Turn sharply right on Ridge Trail, beginning the return leg of your loop. After a 0.5-mile uphill hike through a dense madrone forest, the trail emerges on an open ridge. (Ridge Trail roughly parallels Saratoga Gap Trail, but at a higher elevation.)

Another 0.5 mile of gentle ascent takes you past a connector trail to Saratoga Gap Trail. Just beyond is a short spur to the Emily Smith Bird Observation Point. This forested knoll is a good spot to look for raptors, although views are severely limited by the leafy black oaks.

Nearly 4.0 miles into the loop is the spur trail for Goat Rock. Turn right and follow it for 0.25 mile. (The left fork leads to a fascinating interpretive exhibit on the park's geology; you can also loop around to Goat Rock from there.) Rock climbers are usually strutting their stuff on

Castle Rock State Park's geologic attractions include weathered, Swiss cheese–like sandstone formations.

the steep south side of Goat Rock, but the north side is accessible on two feet. Signs along the path encourage hikers to visit a neighboring overlook area instead of climbing on the 100-foot-high rock, due to its steep and potentially dangerous drop-offs. Weigh the risk for yourself and take your pick. The overlook does offer a great view of the Santa Cruz Mountains parading down to the Pacific Ocean, and often more solitude than

Goat Rock. However, if you're sure-footed and cautious, the smooth back side of Goat Rock lets you examine the sandstone close-up and enjoy higher views.

Beyond Goat Rock, Ridge Trail continues eastward until it reconnects with Saratoga Gap Trail just above Castle Rock Falls. Turn left and make a short, 0.5-mile climb back up the creek canyon to the trailhead.

GOING FARTHER
In spring, the park's Summit Meadows Trail should not be missed. The trailhead is at Sempervirens Point, a drive-up overlook on the south side of Highway 9, 1.9 miles west of Skyline Boulevard. This 2-mile flower-filled walk leads out and back to Summit Meadows.

55. Año Nuevo Point Trail

RATING	🚶 🚶 🚶 🚶
DISTANCE	3.0 miles round-trip
HIKING TIME	1.5 hours
ELEVATION GAIN	Negligible
HIGH POINT	50 feet
EFFORT	Easy Walk
BEST SEASON	Year-round; guided hikes only Dec. to March
PERMITS/CONTACT	Año Nuevo State Reserve fee required ($10 per vehicle), access by guided walks only Dec. 15–Mar. 31 ($7 per person), (650) 879-0227, www.parks.ca.gov
MAPS	Download at www.parks.ca.gov
NOTES	Dogs and bikes prohibited

THE HIKE

A trip to Año Nuevo in the winter months provides a wildlife show you'll never forget.

GETTING THERE

From Half Moon Bay, drive south on Highway 1 for 27 miles to the right turnoff for Año Nuevo State Reserve. (From Santa Cruz, drive 21 miles north on Highway 1.)

THE TRAIL

Every year from December to March, Año Nuevo Island is the breeding ground for more than 3,000 elephant seals. It's a wildlife show you'll never forget.

It's not just the number of animals that's impressive; it's their immense size. Elephant seals are the kings of the pinniped family (all species of aquatic mammals with fins). The males can grow longer than 18 feet and weigh more than two tons. The females reach as long as 12 feet and weigh more than one ton.

You can show up any time of year and see pinnipeds at Año Nuevo State Reserve. The mainland beaches, as well as the shores of Año Nuevo Island, are popular with California sea lions and harbor seals year-round.

Elephant seals take over the beaches at Año Nuevo State Reserve each winter

From mid-May to mid-August, Steller sea lions breed on an isolated reef surrounding the island.

But in the winter months, the northern elephant seals steal the show. The huge males arrive in late November to claim the best spots on the beaches; the pregnant females come to shore two to three weeks later to give birth and breed. In a few months the adults and their young all disappear back into the ocean and are usually not seen again until the following winter.

Given all this, the Año Nuevo Point Trail is a basic requirement on the resume of any Bay Area nature lover. In an easy 3.0 miles, the trail leads to a viewing area for the elephant seals and a gorgeous stretch of sand at Cove Beach, where you could easily while away an entire day.

The rules at Año Nuevo are as follows: You may visit the preserve and hike on your own April to November (although you must obtain a free permit at the reserve entrance to do so). During the first two weeks of December, the reserve is completely closed to the public. Mid-December to March, entry is by guided walks only and prior reservations are recommended. Reservations can be made by phone at (800) 444-4445. Unreserved tickets are sold daily at the park on a first-come, first-served basis. January is usually the busiest month, when the baby elephant seals are born.

The trail to see the elephant seals is a pleasant walk over densely vegetated coastal bluffs. From the parking lot, you set out through the coastal scrub and soon reach a fork with Pond Loop Trail. Bear right to loop

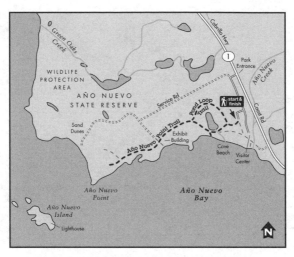

around the high side of a small pond, gaining views of its blue waters and the ocean beyond. A kiosk and staging area for the Wildlife Protection Area is located 0.75 mile from the trailhead. The kiosk features interesting displays on the pinnipeds that call Año Nuevo home. From here you continue toward Año Nuevo Point, where you gain a view of the multitudes of elephant seals on Año Nuevo Island and the mainland beaches. An abandoned lighthouse, built in 1890 to warn mariners away from the rock-strewn coastline, has been claimed by seals and sea lions.

As you near Año Nuevo Point, the cacophony of barking and snorting is tremendous. From your vantage point about 25 feet from the seals, you are close enough to see them brawling with each other and can observe their strange, jerking movements as they go from sand to sea and back.

On your return hike, be sure to walk the other leg of the loop around the pond, then take the short cutoff trail to Cove Beach. It's a great spot for a picnic or a long walk on the sand. And don't miss a visit to the terrific visitor center at Año Nuevo.

GOING FARTHER

From Año Nuevo's main entrance, drive 4.1 miles north on Highway 1 to the park's Gazos Creek Beach access. Hike south along the beach to the sand dunes at Franklin Point, where the fogbound clipper ship *Sir John Franklin* wrecked in 1865. From the top of the highest dune, the view is inspiring: Pigeon Point Lighthouse anchors the northern coast; Table Rock and Año Nuevo Island rise to the south.

Long Ridge Open Space Preserve and neighboring parks on Highway 35 invite after-work strolls and longer weekend excursions.

The seasonal miracle of snowmelt makes Cascade Falls flow with vigor every June.

LAKE TAHOE AND
THE NORTHERN SIERRA

For most visitors, the Tahoe region is clearly defined by its 22-mile-long, azure-blue lake—"a noble sheet of blue water lifted six thousand three hundred feet above the level of the sea, and walled in by a rim of snow-clad mountain peaks," in the eloquent words of Mark Twain. The 10th deepest lake in the world—1,645 feet at its deepest point—and boasting remarkable water clarity, it is among the most notable features in the landscape of North America.

Hikers with creaky knees will note two other outstanding features in the Tahoe region (besides the mammoth lake): steep hills and high elevation. There is no getting around it: this spectacular Sierra scenery can only be seen by breathing high mountain air. For lowlanders, it takes a few days to get acclimated. Even a relatively level trail can seem more challenging when its trailhead is at 7,000 feet.

But that's not to say you won't find easy hiking. This chapter describes a dozen hikes to high mountain lakes, shimmering creeks, and granite-lined waterfalls that are suitable for hikers of all abilities.

The trails detailed in this chapter also encompass a somewhat lesser traveled region north of Lake Tahoe, the outdoor recreation playground of Plumas National Forest and the Gold Lakes Basin. A sparsely inhabited land with a wealth of cabin resorts, mountain lodges, and hiking and biking trails, the Plumas area has long been known as the Tahoe vacation alternative, offering similar scenic beauty but without the crowds who flock to the world-famous lake.

The only disappointing fact about hiking in the Tahoe and Northern Sierra region is that the season is so short. Snow can fall as early as mid-October, and the spring melt can hold off till mid-June. Because of the brief season, thousands of hikers take to Tahoe's trails each year in only a few months' time. To avoid the crowds, the best time to visit is usually September and October, when the summer crowds have departed. And how fortunate, because that's when Tahoe's famous fall color show occurs. It's worth waiting for.

LAKE TAHOE AND
THE NORTHERN SIERRA

56. Grass Lake Trail

RATING	🚶 🚶 🚶 🚶
DISTANCE	3.6 miles round-trip
HIKING TIME	2 hours
ELEVATION GAIN	550 feet
HIGH POINT	5,842 feet
EFFORT	Moderate Workout
BEST SEASON	June to October
PERMITS/CONTACT	Plumas-Eureka State Park, (530) 836-2380, www.parks.ca.gov
MAPS	Plumas-Eureka State Park (download at www.parks.ca.gov)
NOTES	Dogs allowed

THE HIKE
This lake-filled basin in Plumas-Eureka State Park offers trout-fishing opportunities and the chance for a swim on warm summer days.

GETTING THERE
From Truckee, head north on Highway 89 for about 50 miles to Graeagle. At Graeagle, drive west on County Road A-14 for 4.5 miles to the Jamison Mine/Grass Lake access road on the left. Turn left and drive 1 mile to the trailhead parking area. The trailhead is on the far side of the lot, signed for Grass, Smith, Rock, Wades, and Jamison Lakes.

THE TRAIL
Grass Lake is a perfect easy-hiking destination. A trek of under an hour will get you there, and if you find you have to share the lakeshore with too many others, all you have to do is keep hiking. The trail continues to a trio of additional lovely lakes.

Pick up the Jamison Creek Trail at the old Jamison Mine buildings in Plumas-Eureka State Park. (Although the trail begins in the state park, your destination is located outside the state park border in Plumas National Forest.) The Jamison Mine was in operation from 1887 until 1919, producing gold for the Sierra Buttes Mining Company. Evidence of mining operations can be seen here and elsewhere along Jamison Creek.

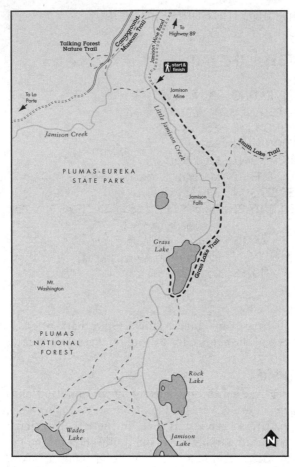

The trail is well signed and easy to follow. With a left turn at the Jamison Mine buildings, you'll climb up, up, and up on a moderately steep and rocky path until you reach a junction with a trail heading left for Smith Lake. Ignore this trail; it climbs even more steeply and then makes a mean descent to Smith Lake. Instead, continue straight to Grass Lake, now a level 0.5 mile away.

About 200 yards after you pass a sign announcing your departure from state park land, listen for the sound of running water and watch for a trail spur on your right that leads you to Little Jamison Creek's edge. Here you find a viewpoint overlooking 40-foot-high Jamison Falls. Soon after snowmelt, the cascade is quite impressive. Back on the main trail, five more minutes of level walking brings you to Grass Lake at elevation

5,842 feet. The lake is a lovely circle of blue surrounded by Jeffrey pine, lodgepole pine, and huge red firs. You'll see plenty of gnawed-off trees, a sure sign of beavers living near Grass Lake.

The trail continues along the east side of Grass Lake before heading farther to Rock, Wades, and Jamison Lakes. Circle around to the west side of Grass Lake for an awesome view of the craggy ridge that forms a backdrop on the lake's east side. A few trail camps are located here, and it's not hard to imagine how fine it would be to wake up in the morning, rub your eyes, and gaze at that view.

GOING FARTHER

Ambitious hikers can continue on the trail past Grass Lake for another 2 miles to Rock Lake, Jamison Lake, and Wades Lake.

57. Sardine Lakes Trail

RATING	🚶 🚶 🚶 🚶
DISTANCE	2.5 miles round-trip
HIKING TIME	1.25 hours
ELEVATION GAIN	400 feet
HIGH POINT	6,010 feet
EFFORT	Moderate Workout
BEST SEASON	June to October
PERMITS/CONTACT	Yuba River Ranger District, (530) 288-3231, www.fs.fed.us/r5/tahoe
MAPS	USGS Sierra City
NOTES	Dogs and bikes allowed

THE HIKE
Set in the shadow of the magnificent Sierra Buttes, the twin Sardine Lakes make a fine walking destination whether you're a guest at neighboring Sardine Lakes Lodge or just a day visitor.

GETTING THERE
From Truckee, head north on Highway 89 for about 30 miles to Highway 49 heading west at Sattley. Turn west on Highway 49 and drive about 10 miles to the town of Bassetts at the intersection of Highway 49 and Forest Service Road 24 (Gold Lake Highway). Drive 1.2 miles north on Road 24 to the turnoff for Sardine Lake and Packer Lake. Stay to the left and drive west on the Sardine Lake access road for 0.5 mile to the parking area for the Sand Pond Swim Area (before the lake and lodge). Walk up the road and past the lodge and begin hiking on the fire road that leads from the far side of the lodge parking lot.

THE TRAIL
Upper and Lower Sardine Lakes form the backdrop for Sardine Lake Lodge, a cabin resort where guests enjoy mountain and lake views from their front porches, eat gourmet meals prepared by the lodge's chef, and hike and fish to their heart's content. But you don't have to be a lodge guest to enjoy the hiking, shore-fishing, and swimming at Sardine Lakes,

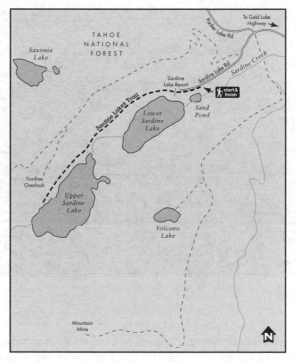

because this land is national forest—open and free to the public—even though the lodge holds a lease to operate on this piece of it.

Of all the lakes in the Lakes Basin, the Sardine Lakes are arguably the most scenic. Backed by the spectacularly jagged Sierra Buttes, a banquet of 8,500-foot peaks, the scene at the lakes is as perfect as that of any jigsaw puzzle. An easy trail leads from Lower Sardine Lake, right by the lodge, to Upper Sardine Lake, about 1.0 mile away. The path, which is actually an old logging and mining road, heads straight for the upper lake, so you march headfirst toward the Sierra Buttes. The view gets better every step of the way.

Start your walk at the lodge parking lot. Take the gravel road (it's paved for the first few yards) on the right side of the lower lake. The trail climbs gently and is completely shadeless, so carry plenty of water with you, even though the distance is short. Keep looking to your left for increasingly broad views of the lower lake as you ascend above its dam.

In short order you'll reach Upper Sardine Lake, a perfect glacier-carved lake with a jagged, rocky shoreline and deep blue water. Clamber your way over rocks and boulders to find a spot to sit, sunbathe,

In the Lakes Basin, the craggy Sierra Buttes can be seen from almost everywhere.

read a book, or drop a line in the water. On warm days, swimming is highly recommended. Some anglers pack along a float tube, although the trout fishing is only fair. But the view of the dramatic Sierra Buttes can't be beat.

GOING FARTHER

Another nearby easy trail is the Sand Pond Interpretive Trail, with its trailhead located in the same parking lot where you left your car. This 1-mile interpretive trail explores a beaver-flooded meadow and travels to Sand Pond, a popular summer swimming hole.

58. Wild Plum Loop

RATING	🚶 🚶 🚶 🚶
DISTANCE	2.8 miles round-trip
HIKING TIME	1.5 hours
ELEVATION GAIN	550 feet
HIGH POINT	4,400 feet
EFFORT	Moderate Workout
BEST SEASON	May to November
PERMITS/CONTACT	Yuba River Ranger District, (530) 288-3231, www.fs.fed.us/r5/tahoe
MAPS	USGS Haypress Valley
NOTES	Dogs and bikes allowed

THE HIKE
Explore the beauty of Plumas National Forest on this easy loop that travels part of the route of the 2,000-mile Pacific Crest Trail.

GETTING THERE
From Truckee, head north on Highway 89 for about 30 miles to Highway 49 heading west at Sattley. Turn west on Highway 49 and drive about 15 miles west toward Sierra City. Turn left on Wild Plum Road 1 mile before Sierra City. Drive 1.2 miles to the end of Wild Plum Road and the trailhead parking area. The last 0.5 mile is not paved. Begin hiking at the trail marker on the left side of the parking lot.

THE TRAIL
Plenty of rewards are found along this trail: an interesting perspective on the steep and craggy Sierra Buttes, a walk alongside the steep-walled rock gorge of Haypress Creek, and a peaceful interlude in a dense forest of cedars and firs. And for hikers eager to visit the Sierra in the early summer, the relatively low elevation guarantees that this trail will be one of the first in the region to be snow-free.

If you happen to be camping at Wild Plum Campground, you can start hiking from the upper end of the camp near site 31. If you aren't, leave

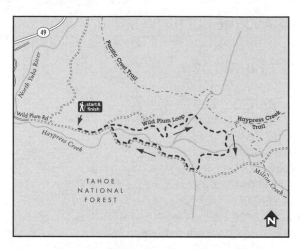

your car at the trailhead parking area, 0.25 mile before the camp. Hike the connector trail to the access road and bridge for the camp, where you'll see a sign that reads "Haypress Trail, Pacific Crest Trail, and Wild Plum Loop." Follow this mostly level path as it parallels Haypress Creek for 0.25 mile under a canopy of incense cedars, white firs, and Jeffrey pines. Near a small hydroelectric building, the trail starts to switchback up a ridge via a long series of zigzags that will get your heart rate up. Console yourself with the thought of what this hill would be like without the switchbacks.

After about 15 minutes of climbing, you'll top the ridge. Any grumbling is sure to end when you see the fine view of the towering Sierra Buttes and the Yuba River canyon. At a small clearing, you can gaze in wonder at the canyon below and the mountains above while you catch your breath. The trail continues along the top of the ridge until at 1.2 miles from the start it meets up with the Pacific Crest Trail. Turn right onto the Pacific Crest Trail here, and the remainder of the loop is either level or downhill. You'll cross a sturdy footbridge over Haypress Creek, then just beyond the bridge, turn right to leave the Pacific Crest Trail and head back to your starting point alongside Haypress Creek. This pretty, shaded stretch of trail brings you to a gravel road, where you turn right and descend to the east end of Wild Plum Campground. Finish out your walk on the connector trail to the day-use parking area and your car.

GOING FARTHER

Only a couple of miles away is a worthwhile short walk to snowmelt-fed Loves Falls. Follow Highway 49 to about 1.5 miles east of Sierra City, where there is a small gravel parking area on the north side of the road. Pick up the Pacific Crest Trail here and follow it northeast for about 0.5 mile, paralleling the highway. The falls drop below a bridge over the North Yuba River, creating a spectacular show in early summer.

59. Rubicon Point and Lighthouse Loop

RATING 🚶 🚶 🚶
DISTANCE 2.0 miles round-trip
HIKING TIME 1 hour
ELEVATION GAIN 550 feet
HIGH POINT 6,580 feet
EFFORT Moderate Workout
BEST SEASON June to October
PERMITS/CONTACT D. L. Bliss State Park fee required ($8 per vehicle), (530) 525-7277 or (530) 525-3345, www.parks.ca.gov
MAPS Tom Harrison Maps "Lake Tahoe"
NOTES Dogs and bikes prohibited

THE HIKE

The Rubicon Trail at D. L. Bliss State Park is the premier lakeside trail at Lake Tahoe, offering eye-candy views of the sparkling lake.

GETTING THERE

From Tahoe City, drive south on Highway 89 for 15 miles and turn left at the sign for D. L. Bliss State Park. Drive 0.5 mile to the entrance station. Continue straight for 0.7 mile to a sign for Camps 141–168 and Beach Area. Turn right and drive 0.7 mile to the Calawee Cove Beach parking lot. The Rubicon Trail begins on the far side of the lot.

THE TRAIL

The Rubicon Trail offers some of the best views of Lake Tahoe you'll find from any public land along the lakeshore, although it means braving the crowds. The entire 5.5-mile point-to-point trail is deservedly popular in the summer months. This shorter loop on the Rubicon gives you a taste of the trail's beauty, then steers you away from the crowds (somewhat) by looping back along the Lighthouse Trail, where you'll visit the historic Rubicon Point Lighthouse.

To have a better chance at peace and quiet, begin your trip as early in the morning as possible (and that should be easy if you are camping at D. L. Bliss State Park). Start from the trailhead at the Calawee Cove Beach parking lot. From this spot, its northern terminus, the Rubicon Trail follows

The crystal-blue waters of Lake Tahoe can be admired from every footstep on the Rubicon Trail.

a mostly level grade, but it contours along a steep slope that drops off more than 100 feet straight down to the lake's edge. The park has put up safety cables and chain-link fencing in a few spots to keep hikers safely on terra firma, but even so, some experience a spell or two of acrophobia along this path.

As you walk, you can gaze at all that blue H2O and ponder this: At 22 miles long and 12 miles wide, Lake Tahoe holds more than 37 trillion gallons of water and is the largest alpine lake in North America. It's the 10th-deepest lake in the world, boasting a greatest depth of 1,645 feet. From Rubicon Point, just 0.2 mile in on this trail, you can see several hundred feet down into the lake's depths.

If all that vastness is too overwhelming, focus on the close-up scenery, which includes plenty of chipmunks running along the path, and one

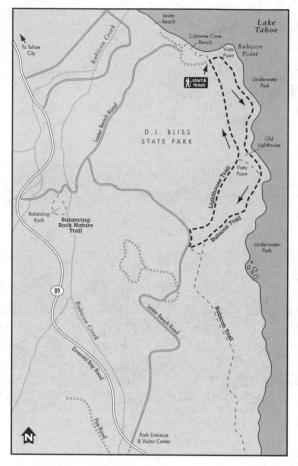

spectacular curve in the trail where you get a sudden, breathtaking view of the often snowcapped mountains ahead of you.

At 0.5 mile, you'll see a right spur trail to Lake Tahoe's diminutive, historic lighthouse. For a fascinating peek at Tahoe's navigational history, take this short spur. The Coast Guard built a gas-powered lighthouse on Rubicon Point in 1916, but keeping the light supplied with fuel proved too difficult. Even when lit, the lighthouse was situated so high above the shoreline that it only caused confusion. It was shut down in 1919 and replaced by a newer lighthouse, which still stands at Sugar Pine Point. The old lighthouse building was restored in 2001.

Return to the Rubicon Trail, then continue another 0.5 mile to the next right turn, where you will start to loop back (or if you haven't seen enough of Lake Tahoe, remain on the Rubicon Trail for another 1.0 mile or so; see "Going Farther," below). You'll exit the forest at a parking lot. Turn right and walk about 30 yards until you see a sign for the Lighthouse Trail; take it. This alternate trail is higher on the hillside than the Rubicon Trail and heads back to Calawee Cove through a dense stand of ponderosa and Jeffrey pines, firs, and cedars. A steep descent brings you back behind the old lighthouse site. Continue to the left, coasting downhill to your starting point.

GOING FARTHER

You can continue hiking on the Rubicon Trail for a total of 5.5 miles one-way. The trail ends at Emerald Bay, where you need to have a car shuttle waiting for you at the parking lot for Vikingsholm Castle. The final mile has a 500-foot elevation gain to get to that parking lot.

60. Cascade Falls Trail

RATING	🚶 🚶 🚶 🚶
DISTANCE	2.0 miles round-trip
HIKING TIME	1 hour
ELEVATION GAIN	150 feet
HIGH POINT	6,910 feet
EFFORT	Easy Walk
BEST SEASON	June to October
PERMITS/CONTACT	Lake Tahoe Basin Management Unit, (530) 543-2600, www.fs.fed.us/r5/ltbmu
MAPS	Tom Harrison Maps "Lake Tahoe"
NOTES	Dogs allowed; accessible via snowshoes in winter

THE HIKE

Billowing Cascade Falls is easily spotted from a distance while driving Highway 89 in the spring and early summer months, but this hike takes you right to its edge.

GETTING THERE

From South Lake Tahoe, drive northwest on Highway 89 for 7.5 miles to the Bayview Campground and trailhead. Turn left and drive to the far end of the campground to the trailhead parking area. If it's full, you can park across Highway 89 in the Inspiration Point parking lot.

THE TRAIL

The hike to Cascade Falls is short and level enough for almost anybody to make the trip, including young children. It has enough spectacular scenery to keep even the biggest whiners-in-the-outdoors from complaining. And the trail leads you right to the edge of a stunning 200-foot cascade that drops into the southwest end of Cascade Lake. What more could you ask for?

Cascade Falls has only one drawback: You have to see it early in the year. By August, the 100-yard-wide cataract becomes a thin, willowy stream, which greatly diminishes its dramatic effect. Plan your trip for sometime between the start of snowmelt and July, but no later.

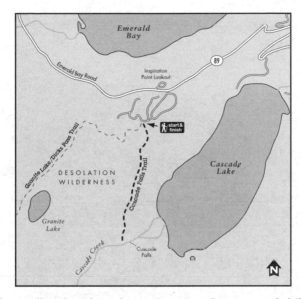

From the trailhead parking lot at Bayview Campground, hike to your left on the well-signed trail. The route meanders in and out of Jeffrey pine forest and open sunshine, alternately providing shade and views. After a mere five minutes of walking, you're rewarded with a tremendous vista of Cascade Lake, elevation 6,464 feet (about 500 feet below you). The lake looks so large you may think it's part of Lake Tahoe, but with your bird's eye view you can see that it's separated from Tahoe by a thin strip of forest and highway.

Moments later, the rumbling of the falls greets you as you break out of the forest. Shortly you have a clear view of the tumbling water. Cascade Falls was once known as White Cloud Falls. In the wind, it billows and scatters so much over its base of fractured granite that it creates a cloud of spray. From this viewpoint onward, the trail follows a narrow ledge with steep dropoffs. Watch your footing on the granite, and keep a firm handhold on small children. Watching your step is more difficult than you'd imagine, because the views of Cascade Lake and Lake Tahoe will vie for your attention.

Surprisingly, the best views of Cascade Falls are actually farther back on the trail. You lose sight of the falls in the last 0.25 mile, and when the trail peters out right next to the falls' brink, you can't see much of its 200-foot length. But upstream of the brink lie some lovely emerald-green pools and large shelves of granite perfectly situated for picnicking. In early summer, wildflowers thrive with all this water: blue lupines and

Cascade Falls tumbles down the hillside into the western edge of Cascade Lake.

pink mountain pride present a superb springtime show as they cling to crevices in the rock.

GOING FARTHER

From the same trailhead, take the trail that leads in the opposite direction to Granite Lake. Although only 1.1 mile away, this trail gains a whopping 800 feet, but there's a payoff: It offers tremendous high views of Lake Tahoe and Emerald Bay along the way.

61. Angora Lakes Trail

RATING	🚶 🚶 🚶 🚶
DISTANCE	1.0 mile round-trip
HIKING TIME	30 minutes
ELEVATION GAIN	270 feet
HIGH POINT	7,380 feet
EFFORT	Easy Walk
BEST SEASON	June to October
PERMITS/CONTACT	Lake Tahoe Basin Management Unit parking fee required ($5 per vehicle), (530) 543-2600, www.fs.fed.us/r5/ltbmu
MAPS	Tom Harrison Maps "Lake Tahoe"
NOTES	Dogs and bikes allowed

THE HIKE

Two glacially carved lakes and a historic cabin resort, complete with its own lemonade stand, are visited on this trail.

GETTING THERE

From Lake Tahoe's Emerald Bay, drive south on Highway 89 for 5 miles to Fallen Leaf Lake Road and turn right. At 0.8 mile the road splits; stay to the left (do not head toward Fallen Leaf Lake) and continue 0.4 mile. At the junction, turn right on Forest Service Road 12N14, which alternates as paved and unpaved. Drive 2.3 miles, passing the Angora Fire Lookout, to the parking lot at the road's end. The trailhead is on the left side of the upper parking lot.

THE TRAIL

The adventure of visiting Angora Lakes begins with a scenic 5.0-mile drive off Highway 89 near Fallen Leaf Lake. Some of the road is unpaved, but it's easily navigated by passenger cars. Along the way, be sure to stop along Angora Ridge and check out the far-and-away view from the Angora Fire Lookout: To your right and far below is Fallen Leaf Lake, to your left is a wide valley that was burned in the 2007 Angora Fire, and straight ahead is Angora Peak, elevation 8,588 feet. The lookout tower was in operation until the late 1970s, when it was made obsolete by

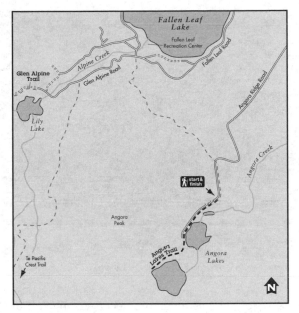

improvements in aerial and satellite technology. The first lookout tower was built here in 1924; the structure you see now was built in 1935.

When you finally reach the Angora Lakes trailhead, you may be amazed (and dismayed) by all the cars parked here. Yes, this is a popular summer hike, and the only way to avoid the crowds is to time your visit for late September or October. Avoid summer weekends if you possibly can, but even on the busiest days, this is a fun trip. Whenever you visit, don't forget to pay the $5 parking fee and leave the receipt on your dashboard, or you'll likely get a ticket.

Start hiking on the dirt road that climbs uphill from the upper parking lot's left side. In 0.3 mile, the wide road reaches the first lake, Lower Angora. A few private homes are perched on the lake's far side, so most hikers just cruise by. The trail levels out, and in another few minutes you reach Upper Angora Lake, home of Angora Lakes Resort. Since 1917 the resort has been renting out its picturesque little cabins. Not surprisingly, it is almost impossible to get a reservation to stay here. But day visitors are welcome, and a small store sells snacks and the resort's famous lemonade.

Upper Angora Lake, at 7,380 feet in elevation, is a perfectly bowl-shaped, glacial cirque lake. The granite wall on its far side is snow-covered most of the year, and in early summer a waterfall of snowmelt flows down its face. Some people paddle around the lake in rubber rafts, and by mid- to late summer, swimmers find the water warm enough to

A busy place all summer long, Upper Angora Lake is popular with swimmers, kayakers, and anglers.

take a dip. Brave (or perhaps foolhardy) teenagers dive off of the granite cliffs. Day visitors can take advantage of the lake's small beach or rent rowboats, kayaks, or paddleboards for a few bucks an hour.

GOING FARTHER
On your drive back down from Angora Lakes, pull in to Fallen Leaf Campground at Fallen Leaf Lake and park in the day-use area. Walk the 1-mile Moraine Trail to the edge of the beautiful lake, then wander along its southern and western shores as far as you please.

62. Glen Alpine Trail to Susie Lake

RATING   🚶 🚶 🚶 🚶 🚶
DISTANCE   8.4 miles round-trip
HIKING TIME   5.0 hours
ELEVATION GAIN   750 feet
HIGH POINT   7,240 feet
EFFORT   Prepare to Perspire
BEST SEASON   June to October
PERMITS/CONTACT   Fill out a free self-serve permit form at the trailhead;
Lake Tahoe Basin Management Unit, (530) 543-2600,
www.fs.fed.us/r5/ltbmu
MAPS   Tom Harrison Maps "Lake Tahoe"
NOTES   Dogs allowed; wear good boots for this rocky trail

THE HIKE

Get a taste of the wonders of the Desolation Wilderness on this rocky but gradually ascending trail to Susie Lake, which makes a fine day-hiking or backpacking destination.

GETTING THERE

From the Y-junction of Highway 50 and Highway 89 in South Lake Tahoe, drive 3 miles northwest on Highway 89 to Fallen Leaf Lake Road on the left (1 mile past Camp Richardson). Turn left and drive 5.4 miles to the end of the road and the Glen Alpine trailhead. Day hikers are required to fill out a self-serve wilderness permit at the trailhead.

THE TRAIL

The Glen Alpine Trail leads into a lake-filled basin in the Desolation Wilderness, with dozens of great destinations accessible, depending on how far you want to hike. First-time visitors looking for a good introduction to this area would do well to choose Susie Lake as their target. The mileage may seem long (4.2 miles each way), but the trail's grade is so gentle that the hike is easier than you'd expect.

The trailhead is found at the end of narrow, winding Fallen Leaf Lake Road. Be sure to drive very slowly along this road, which in some spots has barely enough room for bikers and walkers, let alone cars. From the

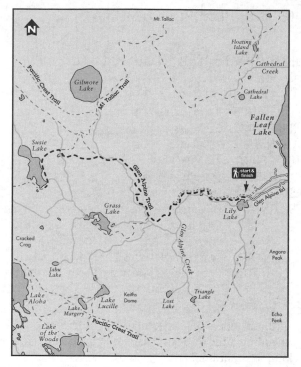

trailhead, an easy walk up the gravel and rock road/trail leads 1.0 mile to the site of the historic Glen Alpine Springs Resort. A "curative" mineral spring made this remote spot a popular getaway from the late 1800s until the 1930s. A few interpretive signs are in place here among the old resort buildings, and docents are often on site on summer weekends. The resort's social hall, designed by famed architect Bernard Maybeck, is worth a look.

Beyond the historic resort, the path narrows to a single-track trail and climbs gently but steadily for 0.8 mile to the Desolation Wilderness boundary and a left fork for Grass Lake. Keep this short, easy hike in mind for your next visit—from here, it's only 1.0 mile to the edge of lovely Grass Lake, where swimming is a popular pastime. But for now, skip the Grass Lake turnoff and continue straight ahead for another 1.6 miles. A switchbacking ascent is made easier by the trail's occasional retreat into forest cover. At the next junction, bear left for Susie Lake, passing by a series of small ponds, then left again 0.5 mile later at a junction with the Pacific Crest Trail.

Finally at 4.2 miles you'll reach Susie Lake's southeast shoreline. An abundance of established backpacking sites are tucked amid groves of

Susie Lake's tree-dotted island is framed by the high peaks of Desolation Wilderness.

whitebark pines and hemlocks. Large, island-dotted Susie Lake would be ideal for an introductory backpacking trip, but it's also a great place to spend an afternoon, with ample opportunities for swimming, fishing, and napping on the granite boulders that line its shore. Those who prefer to stay out of the high-altitude sun will find plenty of tree-shaded spots.

GOING FARTHER
Once you've made it to Susie Lake, it's a pity not to continue 1 mile farther to even more dramatic Heather Lake, a treeless, granite-bound beauty. The additional ascent is minimal and much of the walk is a lovely stroll around Susie's southwestern shore. Where the trail reaches Heather Lake, it skirts along its northern edge on a steep, rocky slope.

63. Dardanelles and Round Lakes

RATING	🚶 🚶 🚶 🚶
DISTANCE	7.8 miles round-trip
HIKING TIME	4.5 hours
ELEVATION GAIN	1,000 feet
HIGH POINT	8,070 feet
EFFORT	Prepare to Perspire
BEST SEASON	June to October
PERMITS/CONTACT	Lake Tahoe Basin Management Unit, (530) 543-2600, www.fs.fed.us/r5/ltbmu
MAPS	Tom Harrison Maps "Lake Tahoe"
NOTES	Dogs and bikes allowed

THE HIKE

The Big Meadow trailhead for the 165-mile Tahoe Rim Trail is the starting point for this trek to volcanic Round Lake and glacially carved Dardanelles Lake.

GETTING THERE

From the T-junction of Highway 50 and Highway 89 in Meyers, drive 5.3 miles south on Highway 89 to the Big Meadow parking area on the left (west) side of the highway. Park near the restrooms.

THE TRAIL

Nowhere is it more obvious that the land around Lake Tahoe was shaped by diametrically opposed forces—fire (volcanic action) and ice (glacial action)—than on this pleasant day hike to Dardanelles and Round Lakes. The trip begins at the large Tahoe Rim Trail parking lot at Big Meadow. Pick up the trail from the south side of the parking lot loop and follow it to a crossing of Highway 89 in about 200 yards. Employ an extra dose of caution when you cross.

On the far side of the highway, the trail ascends moderately through red fir and lodgepole pine forest for 0.5 mile until it reaches a three-way junction. Veer right and your surroundings soon open up at expansive Big Meadow. The meadow is filled with wildflowers in early summer, but unfortunately with the flowers come the mosquitoes. If you are visiting

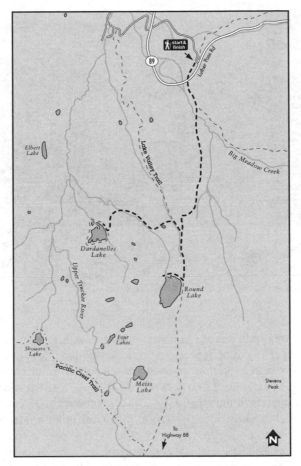

in late June or July, you might want to lather up with bug spray before setting foot in this beautiful but buggy place.

After a level stroll through the grasses, you head back into the trees for another 1.0 mile of climbing—this is the most difficult stretch of trail—then reach a saddle and make a short, steep descent. At the bottom, you're at a junction; turn sharply right on the Meiss Meadow Trail toward Christmas Valley, leaving the Tahoe Rim Trail behind. You'll return to this junction to continue to Round Lake later. In about 200 yards, turn left at the next junction, boulder-hop across two creeks, and walk the final 1.2 miles to the west shore of Dardanelles Lake. This last level stretch is pure eye candy, as it is lined with aspen and alder trees, which put on a colorful display in autumn, and punctuated by

Beautiful Dardanelles Lake can be reached via a mellow hike through forest and meadows.

small ponds and odd-shaped volcanic outcrops. A highlight is a massive western juniper tree that appears to be the granddaddy of them all.

At 7,760 feet in elevation and with a bold granite backdrop, Dardanelles Lake is enchanting. It offers plenty of spots for picnicking, swimming, camping, or simply whiling away the hours. Linger as long as you wish, then backtrack to the Tahoe Rim Trail junction, turn right for Round Lake, and follow the trail 0.75 mile to its shores. A stark contrast to Dardanelles Lake, Round Lake is brownish green in color and surrounded by dark volcanic rock, not granite. Although perhaps not as picturesque as Dardanelles Lake, this lake, too, provides a chance for a swim, plus good fishing for cutthroat trout.

GOING FARTHER

It's possible to turn this into a 10.5-mile shuttle hike by having a car waiting for you at the Meiss Meadow trailhead across from Carson Pass summit on Highway 88. A one-way hike from trailhead to trailhead will pass through both Big and Meiss meadows and along the shoreline of Round Lake. If you want to see Dardanelles Lake as well, you'll need to add on a side trip of 1.3 miles each way.

64. Emigrant Lake

RATING 🚶 🚶 🚶 🚶
DISTANCE 8.4 miles round-trip
HIKING TIME 4.5 hours
ELEVATION GAIN 800 feet
HIGH POINT 8,600 feet
EFFORT Prepare to Perspire
BEST SEASON June to October
PERMITS/CONTACT Amador Ranger District, (209) 295-4251,
www.fs.fed.us/r5/eldorado
MAPS USGS Caples Lake
NOTES Dogs allowed; bikes prohibited

THE HIKE
A surprisingly level trail follows the shoreline of Caples Lake and sections of an old emigrant route to the granite-lined shores of Emigrant Lake.

GETTING THERE
From the junction of Highway 89 and Highway 88 in Hope Valley, drive west on Highway 88 for 13.5 miles to the west side of Caples Lake and the trailhead parking area by the dam (5 miles west of Carson Pass).

THE TRAIL
Although the mileage is substantial along the trail to Emigrant Lake, the grade is so gentle you may find yourself wondering if you are still in the Sierra Nevada. In fact, the trail is basically level for the first 2.4 miles as it edges the southwest shore of Caples Lake, traveling under a shady conifer canopy. A mixed forest of white firs and lodgepole pines frames this large man-made lake, where fishermen ply the waters daily for trophy trout—even in winter when the lake is ice-covered.

At 1.3 miles from the start, you'll reach a junction with the Historic Emigrant Trail, used by thousands of late-1800s emigrants who were trying to make their way to the Nevada silver mines. Stay straight at this junction and continue along the lakeshore, slowly moving farther away from its edge.

Rockbound Emigrant Lake is set in a classic glacial cirque and surrounded by snowfields long into summer.

Just when you've settled into easy-cruising mode, it's time to get to work. Almost all of the elevation gain on this trail takes place in the last 1.8 miles, starting soon after the trail passes by the south end of Caples Lake. You'll ascend moderately alongside Emigrant Creek, crossing it once, then march up a final few switchbacks to the lake at 8,600 feet.

The payoff? In the final stretch to the lake's east shore, the hike returns to the mode of a level stroll. Emigrant Lake is a spectacular sight, set in a classic glacial cirque with steep granite walls rising up to Covered Wagon Peak and Thimble Peak, both higher than 9,500 feet. Snowfields can linger along these granite walls until very late in

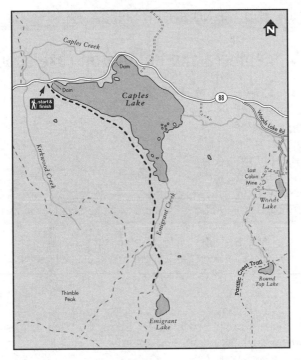

summer. Swimming in the frigid water, sunbathing, and scenery-admiring are the preferred activities here, although some anglers may be tempted to throw a line in the water.

GOING FARTHER

If you'd like to learn more about the Historic Emigrant Trail, stop in at the Carson Pass Information Station and ask the docents to direct you to the dirt road just west of the summit, where you can hike through the forest and look for boulders on which the emigrants etched their names.

65. Winnemucca and Round Top Lake Loop

RATING	🚶 🚶 🚶 🚶 🚶
DISTANCE	5.0 miles round-trip
HIKING TIME	3.0 hours
ELEVATION GAIN	1,100 feet
HIGH POINT	9,347 feet
EFFORT	Prepare to Perspire
BEST SEASON	June to October
PERMITS/CONTACT	Amador Ranger District parking fee required ($5 per vehicle), (209) 295-4251, www.fs.fed.us/r5/eldorado
MAPS	USGS Caples Lake and Carson Pass
NOTES	Dogs allowed, but they must be leashed; bikes prohibited

THE HIKE

One of the Sierra's premier wildflower hikes, this loop trip is especially popular during the peak bloom time in July.

GETTING THERE

From the junction of Highway 89 and Highway 88 in Hope Valley, drive west on Highway 88 for 10.5 miles to the Woods Lake Campground turnoff on the left (south) side of the highway, 1.5 miles west of Carson Pass. Turn left and drive 1 mile to the trailhead parking area, which is 0.5 mile before the campground, or continue to the day-use parking area at Woods Lake. You can pick up the trail from either parking area.

THE TRAIL

As with most hikes in the Carson Pass area, this trail is incredibly popular all summer long, but especially so during the height of the wildflower bloom in July. As many as 300 people per day hike to Winnemucca Lake on summer weekends. Although most simply walk out and back to this beautiful lake, you might as well pack in the maximum amount of scenery by trekking the full loop past Winnemucca and Round Top Lakes.

Although you can also access these lakes by starting from the Carson Pass trailhead, the best wildflower viewing can be had by starting from the trailhead at Woods Lake Campground. This car campground also

Round Top Peak towers over the volcanic landscape and vast flower fields of Carson Pass.

happens to be one of the loveliest in the Northern Sierra, with about 20 spacious, private sites spread out among the Sierra junipers and red firs. If you are camping, you can simply walk from your tent, but if you're just visiting for the day you must park in the day-use area at Woods Lake or the backpacking trailhead 0.5 mile from camp. (The mileage shown above reflects parking at Woods Lake.)

The path wanders through the forest for a bit, then breaks out onto open slopes with a straight-on view of 10,381-foot Round Top Peak, an ancient volcanic vent that is the highest peak in the Carson Pass area. Its slopes typically hold on to some snow even in late summer. The outlet creek from Winnemucca Lake flows merrily on your right; the hillsides to your left are completely covered with flowers during the peak of the season. In a mere 1.9 miles, the trail reaches the shore of Winnemucca Lake, a gorgeous blue-green gem that is set directly below Round Top Peak and surrounded by mule's ears, scarlet gilia, Indian paintbrush, and a host of other colorful flowers. At the lake, you'll probably meet up with

233

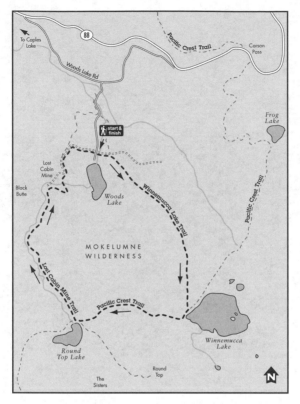

plenty of other hikers who have arrived on the other trail from Carson Pass to the northeast.

Your loop continues to the west for another 1.0 mile of moderate ascent to Round Top Lake. Heading in this direction, you'll leave most of the crowds behind. Beautiful Round Top Lake is considerably smaller than Winnemucca, but its deeply carved bowl is quite dramatic. A few stands of whitebark pines provide shade for picnickers.

At Round Top Lake, you've gained almost 1,100 feet from your start at Woods Lake, but now it's mostly downhill for your loop's final leg (unless you opt for the butt-kicking climb to Round Top Peak; see "Going Farther," below). From the junction right by the lake, finish out your trip with a descent on the Lost Cabin Mine Trail alongside Round Top Lake's outlet creek, skirting through more wildflower gardens and past the structures of an old mine site. You'll wind up back at the west end of Woods Lake Campground. Walk to your right through the camp and down the access road back to your car.

GOING FARTHER

To turn this trip into a butt-kicker, climb to the summit of 10,381-foot Round Top Peak, which towers 1,000 feet above Round Top Lake. To do so, follow the obvious use trail from the lake's east end. The path struggles up, up, and up over the gritty volcanic slope. As you near the top, you may need to use your hands as well as your feet; most hikers are satisfied with attaining a false summit a few yards below the actual summit, as the last stretch is a bit hairy. Truthfully, it doesn't matter how high you go; the views are dazzling from just about everywhere along Round Top's knife-thin ridge.

66. Pyramid Creek Loop

RATING	🥾 🥾 🥾 🥾
DISTANCE	2.0 miles round-trip
HIKING TIME	1.0 hour
ELEVATION GAIN	600 feet
HIGH POINT	6,700 feet
EFFORT	Moderate Workout
BEST SEASON	May to October
PERMITS/CONTACT	Pacific Ranger District parking fee required ($5 per vehicle), (530) 644-2349, www.fs.fed.us/r5/eldorado
MAPS	USGS Echo Lake
NOTES	Dogs allowed

THE HIKE
Drivers weary of the mountain roads leading into and out of Lake Tahoe can pull off at the Twin Bridges trailhead for this leg-stretching walk in beautiful granite country.

GETTING THERE
From South Lake Tahoe, drive south on Highway 89 to Highway 50. Drive west on Highway 50 for about 15 miles to Twin Bridges, where there is a huge parking area on the north side of the highway just before the bridge. (It's 0.5 mile west of the turnoff for Camp Sacramento.) The trailhead is marked by a large signboard.

THE TRAIL
You'll know why they call it Horsetail Falls the minute you see it. Most people get their first look while cruising west or east on Highway 50, heading into or out of the Tahoe basin. Straight and narrow at the top and fanning out to a wide inverted V at the bottom, Horsetail Falls swishes hundreds of feet down Pyramid Creek's glacier-carved canyon. Its powerful stream is reinforced by four lakes: Toem, Ropi, Pitt, and Avalanche.

Don't be put off by the crammed parking lot at this trailhead, known as Twin Bridges. Many of the cars belong to backpackers who are far off in the Desolation Wilderness on multiday trips, and many more belong

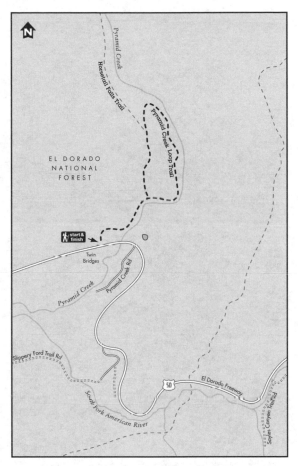

to people just milling around the trailhead, picnicking and admiring Horsetail Falls from afar. An estimated 15,000 people visit this trailhead and hike at least a portion of the trail each summer, and yet it's not hard to find your own special spot somewhere along the pools of Pyramid Creek.

From the parking area at the highway bridge, pick up the Pyramid Creek Trail at the large signboard. Hike east and then north through a dense cedar and pine forest, which smells like Grandma's cedar chest in the attic. You leave most of your trail companions behind in the first 0.5 mile as people wander off the route and choose their spots along Pyramid Creek.

Horsetail Falls can be seen from many vantage points along the Pyramid Creek Loop.

About 0.5 mile in, you reach a junction where you can continue straight toward Horsetail Falls and the Desolation Wilderness boundary, or veer off to the right and follow the 1.5-mile Pyramid Creek Loop Trail. You want the latter; save the Desolation Wilderness for a multi-day backpacking trip. A right turn (head toward the sign for "Cascade Vista") brings you in close for views of the torrential flow of Pyramid Creek rushing down-valley. As it follows the creek, the trail opens out to an exposed, rocky area. Much of the Pyramid Creek Loop traverses huge slabs of granite, the handiwork of glaciers. The trees and plants that thrive in this stark granite environment deserve admiration. There are ancient, twisted junipers, sturdy Jeffrey pines, and brightly colored lichens that coat the granite boulders. Small brown hiker signs nailed on trees make it easy to stay on the path, and the open landscape provides excellent long-distance views of the falls, the American River Canyon, and the granite formation known as Lover's Leap, across the highway (you'll know it when you see it).

The trail heads roughly north and then loops back heading south across the granite slabs. Probably the most scenic spot on the loop is a lacy cataract on a stretch of Pyramid Creek known as The Cascades. Hopefully you brought a picnic with you, but even if not you should still find a spot along this granite lined waterway where you can relax and relish the scenery.

GOING FARTHER
Experienced hikers can choose to leave the Pyramid Creek Loop and enter the Desolation Wilderness boundary (to do so, you must fill out a self-serve wilderness permit). It is possible to make your way to the lower cascade of Horsetail Falls, although there is no maintained trail to get you there. It's more of a path made by use, not design. If you attempt this trip, use extra caution. Accidents happen near Horsetail Falls every year because of the slick rock and fast-moving water.

67. Twin and Island Lakes

RATING 🚶 🚶 🚶 🚶 🚶
DISTANCE 6.6 miles round-trip
HIKING TIME 4.0 hours
ELEVATION GAIN 1,200 feet
HIGH POINT 8,150 feet
EFFORT Prepare to Perspire
BEST SEASON June to October
PERMITS/CONTACT Day hikers must fill out a free self-serve permit at the trailhead, Pacific Ranger District, (530) 644-2349, www.fs.fed.us/r5/eldorado
MAPS USGS Pyramid Peak
NOTES Dogs allowed

THE HIKE

This classic Sierra hike leads to a series of glacially sculpted lakes in the heart of the Crystal Range, the western section of Desolation Wilderness.

GETTING THERE

From the Y-junction of Highway 50 and Highway 89 in South Lake Tahoe, drive 17 miles southwest on Highway 50 to the signed Wrights Lake turnoff on the right (4.5 miles east of Kyburz). Drive 8 miles north on Wrights Lake Road to Wrights Lake Campground. Bear right at the information center and continue 1.2 miles to the road's end at the Twin Lakes trailhead. Day hikers are required to fill out a self-serve wilderness permit at the trailhead.

THE TRAIL

Sculpted by glacial ice more than 1,000 feet deep during the last ice age, the granitic Crystal Range is one of the gems of the Tahoe Sierra's Desolation Wilderness. The Crystal Basin Recreation Area provides convenient access to this rugged landscape of glaciated basins and sawtoothed peaks. Of a host of trail choices, the 3.3-mile day hike to Twin and Island Lakes offers the best payoffs in the least mileage: spectacular wildflower displays, swimming opportunities in four rockbound lakes, and miles of solid granite beneath your feet as you walk. Not surprisingly, this is the

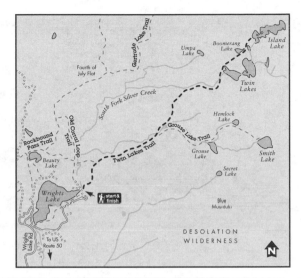

most popular day-hiking trail in the Crystal Basin, so don't expect much solitude on summer weekends.

The path's first stretch meanders past a lush, flower-filled meadow, overflowing with lupine and tiger lilies in early summer. A gentle climb through a red fir and lodgepole pine forest leads to a major junction just beyond the wilderness boundary, 1.3 miles out, where the trail to Grouse, Hemlock, and Smith Lakes cuts off to the right. Bear left and ascend more vigorously for 0.75 mile on exposed granite slabs. At the top of the ridge, another wildflower garden awaits, this one bursting with fireweed, paintbrush, and ranger buttons. Vistas of the Crystal Range's stark, jagged peaks to the northeast produce an inspiring backdrop as you start to descend.

At 2.4 miles you enter Twin Lakes' dramatic granite basin, where the receding glaciers polished each rock to a glowing sheen. The outlet stream from Upper Twin Lake cascades into the shimmering depths of Lower Twin Lake, forming a boisterous waterfall. If you can tear yourself away from the lake's inviting picnic spots, cross its old stone dam and continue along the northwest shore to well-named Boomerang Lake, shaped like an L, at 3.0 miles. Its tantalizing waters tempt you to swim, but be prepared for chilly temperatures. Near the lakeshore you'll find the tiny, white, bell-shaped cassiope, one of John Muir's favorite flowers.

Another 0.25 mile of climbing leads you to the shallow glacial valley that contains enchanting Island Lake, dotted with a multitude of rocky

Stark granite and azure blue water is the signature "look" of the Crystal Basin's lake-filled landscape.

islands. From this high point, views of the Crystal Basin's granite-ringed cirque are the best of the trip.

GOING FARTHER

Many other trails begin at Wrights Lake Campground, and every single one is worth lacing up your boots for. The path to Grouse, Hemlock, and Smith Lakes follows the same trail described above for the first 1.3 miles, then bears right. It's a steeper climb than the trail to Twin and Island Lakes, but the mileage is about the same. Smith Lake, the highest of the three lakes, is perched near tree line at 8,700 feet, and it's stark and staggeringly beautiful.

Yosemite's high peaks tower over the granite domes of Tuolumne Meadows.

YOSEMITE AND MAMMOTH LAKES

Plunging waterfalls, stark granite, alpine lakes, pristine meadows, giant sequoias, and raging rivers—you'll find them all in the Yosemite and Mammoth Lakes region, which encompasses not only world famous Yosemite National Park but also the popular recreation areas of Mammoth Lakes and the eastern Sierra.

The centerpiece of this region, of course, is Yosemite National Park, a must-see on every hiker's itinerary. From Yosemite Valley's famous waterfalls—three of which are among the tallest in the world—to the towering granite domes and glistening meadows of Tioga Pass, Yosemite is a place that can only be described in superlatives.

Equally as scenic as the national park itself are the resort areas on the east side of the Sierra, particularly Mammoth Lakes and June Lake on the U.S. 395 corridor. The alpine lakes of this region are a major draw for day hikers, but equally as compelling are the alpine meadows, fir and pine forests, and sagebrush-covered plains. This is a region known for its geologic oddities, including volcanic craters, hot springs, lava flows, and the strange beauty of Mono Lake, an ancient and majestic body of salt water covering 60 square miles.

More uncommon geologic features are found nearby at Devils Postpile National Monument. This 800-acre national park preserves the Devils Postpile—a "pile" of 60-foot-high basalt columns that are remnants of an ancient lava flow—plus breathtaking 101-foot Rainbow Falls.

Key to enjoying your experience in the Yosemite and Mammoth Lakes region is planning your visit for the least crowded months of the year. Summer weekends are the busiest time and best avoided, especially in Yosemite (although the trails described in this chapter avoid crowd-packed Yosemite Valley altogether). After school starts in September, the crowds lessen substantially. Likewise, if there is a perfect time to visit the Mammoth Lakes area, it's in the transition between summer and winter. Autumn transforms the region into a wave of blazing color as aspens, willows, and cottonwoods don showy coats of orange, yellow, and red. Peak viewing time is usually late September and early October, and it's a show not to be missed.

YOSEMITE AND MAMMOTH LAKES

68. Merced Grove of Giant Sequoias

RATING	🚶 🚶 🚶 🚶
DISTANCE	3.0 miles round-trip
HIKING TIME	1.5 hours
ELEVATION GAIN	520 feet
HIGH POINT	5,840 feet
EFFORT	Moderate Workout
BEST SEASON	May to November
PERMITS/CONTACT	Yosemite National Park fee required ($20 per vehicle, valid for seven days), (209) 372-0200, www.nps.gov/yose
MAPS	Yosemite National Park (download at www.nps.gov/yose/planyourvisit/brochures.htm)
NOTES	Dogs and bikes prohibited; accessible in winter with snowshoes

THE HIKE

This lovely forested hike follows an old wagon road to the smallest and least visited of Yosemite's three giant sequoia groves.

GETTING THERE

From Yosemite's Big Oak Flat entrance station on Highway 120, drive southeast 4.3 miles to the Merced Grove trailhead on your right. Or, traveling from Yosemite Valley through Crane Flat, drive west 3.7 miles on the Big Oak Flat Road to the trailhead on your left.

THE TRAIL

Measured by volume—sheer bulk—giant sequoia trees are the largest living trees on earth. Coastal redwoods may be taller, but sequoias are much broader at the base. To gain a perspective on our diminutive stature as humans, there's nothing quite like standing next to a massive sequoia.

Of the three giant sequoia groves in Yosemite National Park—Merced, Tuolumne, and Mariposa—the Merced Grove is the smallest, the least visited, and generally the most peaceful. It's a fine place to go for a stroll through a lovely mixed forest, and then be awed by the sight of the giant

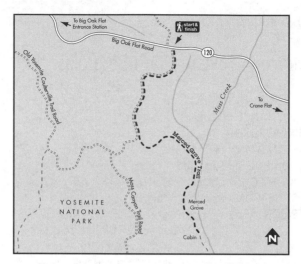

sequoias dwarfing all the other trees. This hike is a winner on any day, in any season (although you'll need snowshoes to make the trip in winter).

The hiking trail is a closed-off dirt road that was Yosemite's first carriage road. It runs level for the first 0.5 mile until it reaches a junction. Take the left fork and head downhill through a forest of white firs, incense cedars, ponderosa pines, and sugar pines. Azaleas bloom in early summer beneath the conifers' branches.

You'll spot the first sequoias at 1.5 miles—a cluster of six along the trail to your right. These are not of record-breaking size, but they're certainly impressive. A few yards farther down the trail and you spot two more big trees on the left and one on the right. A total of only 20 sequoias are found in this grove, but because they grow so close together, they make a big impact.

The sequoias in the Merced Grove were "discovered" in 1833 by the Walker party, a group of explorers headed by Joseph Walker who were looking for the best route through the Sierra Nevada. Most likely local Indian tribes had long known about the location of the big trees.

The largest sequoias of this grove are found directly across the road/trail from a handsome log cabin. The cabin was originally built as a retreat for the park superintendent. Have a seat near the largest trees, pull a sandwich from your pack, and stay a while. For your return, simply retrace your steps from the cabin, hiking back uphill.

The Merced Grove's giant sequoias are less visited, but no less impressive, than those of Yosemite's other groves.

GOING FARTHER

The trail continues beyond the cabin and the giant sequoias for another mile to a spot known as Twin Bridges, following the path of the Old Coulterville wagon route to Yosemite. Despite the name, you'll find no bridges here, only two streams sized just right for rock-hopping across.

69. Lukens Lake Trail

RATING	🚶 🚶 🚶 🚶
DISTANCE	1.5 miles round-trip
HIKING TIME	1 hour
ELEVATION GAIN	200 feet
HIGH POINT	8,250 feet
EFFORT	Easy Walk
BEST SEASON	June to October
PERMITS/CONTACT	Yosemite National Park fee required ($20 per vehicle, valid for seven days), (209) 372-0200, www.nps.gov/yose
MAPS	Yosemite National Park (download at www.nps.gov/yose/planyourvisit/brochures.htm)
NOTES	Dogs and bikes prohibited

THE HIKE

This peaceful subalpine lake is often bypassed by Yosemite hikers, but it's an excellent destination for summer wildflowers and a tranquil spot for a picnic.

GETTING THERE

From Yosemite's Big Oak Flat entrance station on Highway 120, drive southeast 7.7 miles to Crane Flat, then turn left to stay on Highway 120. Drive 16.2 miles to the Lukens Lake trailhead parking area on the south side of the road. The trail begins across the road.

THE TRAIL

The Lukens Lake Trail is the perfect lake hike for hikers seeking to take it easy in Yosemite National Park. It has all the best features of a long backpacking trip to a remote subalpine area, without the long miles, steep hills, and heavy weight to carry.

As you drive out of Yosemite Valley and up Tioga Pass Road, the trail-head for Lukens Lake is one of the first you'll reach. If you've been hiking around the Valley, your body has become accustomed to its 4,000-foot elevation, but Lukens Lake is at 8,250 feet. This may take some getting

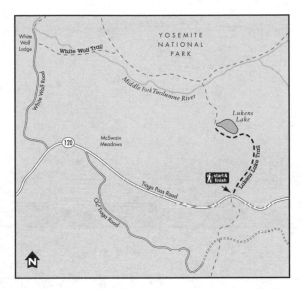

used to—don't be surprised if you're huffing and puffing a little more than you'd expect.

After parking at the Lukens Lake pullout, cross the highway to reach the trailhead. The wide trail climbs gently through a magnificent red fir forest for 0.5 mile. The red firs, with their red-brown, deeply engrained bark, prefer areas of heavy winter snowfall, usually between 7,000 and 8,000 feet in elevation, where the soil is well drained. They grow to be very large (more than 150 feet tall) and cluster in thick stands, making it nearly impossible for other trees or plants to grow near or around them.

After a brief climb, the trail descends to Lukens Lake in another 0.25 mile. The trail winds around the lake's south side, skirting a verdant meadow on its east end. Pink shooting stars are the most prevalent flower here, and if you time your trip for mid- to late July, you may catch the peak of the bloom. Earlier in the summer, patches of snow linger along the trail and in the shady forest. Tioga Pass Road usually opens for travel in early June, but that doesn't mean that all the snow has vanished from the trails. Soon after snowmelt, huge emerald green corn lilies grow in the standing water of the flooded meadow.

The best picnic spots are found on the lake's far (west) end. In late summer, many hikers are tempted to swim. Because spring-fed Lukens Lake is quite shallow, the water is surprisingly warm, but don't let your feet expect a smooth granite bottom. Lukens Lake is grassy and muddy underneath its blue waters.

Tranquil Lukens Lake is a great spot for wildlife watching or picnicking.

GOING FARTHER

The trail continues from the west side of Lukens Lake to White Wolf Campground (an additional 2.3 miles) and then all the way to Ten Lakes and the Grand Canyon of the Tuolumne River. You can hike as far as you please.

70. Lembert Dome Trail

RATING	🚶 🚶 🚶 🚶 🚶
DISTANCE	2.4 miles round-trip
HIKING TIME	1.5 hours
ELEVATION GAIN	900 feet
HIGH POINT	9,450 feet
EFFORT	Moderate Workout
BEST SEASON	June to October
PERMITS/CONTACT	Yosemite National Park fee required ($20 per vehicle, valid for seven days), (209) 372-0200, www.nps.gov/yose
MAPS	Yosemite National Park (download at www.nps.gov/yose/planyourvisit/brochures.htm)
NOTES	Dogs and bikes prohibited

THE HIKE
The mileage may be short on this hike, but the steep climb up the bald face of this granite dome will make you feel like a real mountaineer.

GETTING THERE
From Yosemite's Big Oak Flat entrance station on Highway 120, drive southeast 7.7 miles to Crane Flat, then turn left to stay on Highway 120. Drive 39 miles to the Lembert Dome/Dog Lake/Glen Aulin trailhead on the left, in the heart of Tuolumne Meadows. The trail begins near the restrooms.

THE TRAIL
When you see 800-foot-high Lembert Dome from the trailhead and parking area, you'll never think you can make it to the top. It just seems too big and imposing to be scaled without ropes and carabiners. But although the west side of Lembert Dome is an intimidating sheer face—the playground of technical climbers—the northeast side is gently sloped, and achievable by an easy walk up.

Granite domes, a common geological feature in the Sierra, are essentially large rounded rocks formed by the creation of slowly expanding granite. As the granite expands, cracks form, creating individual layers

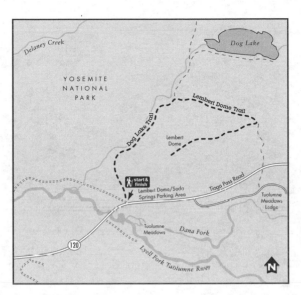

of rock near the surface. Over time, a process called exfoliation occurs, in which these outer layers of rock break apart and fall off, removing all sharp corners and angles from the rock and leaving a smooth round dome. Lembert Dome is a special kind of dome called a *roche moutonée*, a French geologic term that designates a dome with one sheer side and one sloping side.

To hike to its summit, take the trail by the restrooms that is signed for Dog Lake and Lembert Dome. In about 300 yards, your trail splits off from the path to Dog Lake. Take the right fork for Lembert Dome and prepare to climb steeply through a lodgepole pine forest. This trail will get your heart pumping as it picks its way up the steep and rocky slope. As you pass underneath Lembert Dome's west side, you'll hear the shouts of rock climbers dangling from the granite high above you.

The trail curves around the back (north) side of the dome, then disappears completely on the dome's hard granite. Simply pick your own route to Lembert Dome's exposed summit. Some hikers make a beeline for the top; others zigzag their way.

No matter how you get there, the rewards are great. The outstanding view from the top of Lembert Dome, elevation 9,450 feet, takes in all of Tuolumne Meadows and its surrounding peaks. The steep slope of the dome can be downright dizzying, so if you're afraid of heights, hold on to your hiking partner. The wind often howls on top, adding to the excitement.

Lembert Dome looks imposing from the trailhead, but attaining its summit is a fairly easy climb for most hikers.

On your return from Lembert Dome, make sure you pay close attention at all trail junctions and follow the signs for "Lembert Dome Parking." Otherwise, you could wind up back at the Tuolumne Meadows horse stables or Tuolumne Lodge instead of at your car. The multiple trail junctions are simple to follow on the way up, but easier to miss on the way down.

GOING FARTHER

After descending to the base of Lembert Dome, continue on the trail to Dog Lake. This will add 0.8 mile to your round-trip.

71. McGurk Meadow and Dewey Point

RATING	🚶 🚶 🚶 🚶
DISTANCE	7.8 miles round-trip
HIKING TIME	3.5 hours
ELEVATION GAIN	500 feet
HIGH POINT	7,200 feet
EFFORT	Moderate Workout
BEST SEASON	June to October
PERMITS/CONTACT	Yosemite National Park fee required ($20 per vehicle, valid for seven days), (209) 372-0200, www.nps.gov/yose
MAPS	Yosemite National Park (download at www.nps.gov/yose/planyourvisit/brochures.htm)
NOTES	Dogs and bikes prohibited

THE HIKE
Slightly off the beaten path, McGurk Meadow and Dewey Point are two spectacular destinations along Yosemite's Glacier Point Road. The panorama of Yosemite Valley from the promontory at Dewey Point is one you will long remember.

GETTING THERE
From Highway 41 in Yosemite National Park, turn east on Glacier Point Road and drive 7.5 miles to the signed McGurk Meadow trailhead on the left. Park in the pullout about 50 yards farther up the road, then walk back to the trailhead.

THE TRAIL
The McGurk Meadow Trail leads through a fir and pine forest to a pristine, mile-long meadow with a stream meandering through its center. The trail travels right past an old pioneer cabin still standing in half-decent repair, a remnant of bygone days when sheep and cattle ranchers grazed their stock in Yosemite. Less than 3.0 miles beyond the meadow lies Dewey Point, one of the most spectacular overlooks in all of Yosemite.

After parking at the pullout, walk west along the road for about 50 yards to the McGurk Meadow trailhead sign. Fifteen minutes of gentle

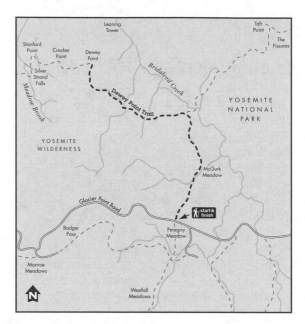

descent on the forested trail will bring you to the cabin of rancher John McGurk, only 0.8 mile from the trailhead. Built with logs and nails, the cabin was obviously used only in the summer. Its front door is so low that it would be snow-covered in winter.

Beyond the old cabin, a few more footsteps take you to the edge of verdant McGurk Meadow, where a trail sign directs you to Dewey Point in 3.0 miles and Glacier Point in 7.0 miles. A footbridge carries you over a small stream, which cuts long, narrow "S" marks through the tall grass. For a too-brief period, usually in July, McGurk Meadow abounds with wildflowers. If your timing is good, you may catch a stunning display of purple alpine shooting stars with tiny rings of white and yellow, their stigma tips pointing to the ground like bowed heads. Corn lilies may also be in bloom, along with patches of penstemon, Indian paintbrush, gentian, lupine, and yampah.

The trail crosses the meadow and skirts its southern edge before entering a dense lodgepole pine forest, punctuated by a handful of much tinier meadows. After hiking north for about 2.0 miles, you'll merge with the Pohono Trail. Turn left to go to Dewey Point. The path meanders gently through the trees before popping out at the southern rim of Yosemite Valley. It's a breathtaking moment when you emerge from the trees and see so much granite laid out before you. If you dare, climb out to the highest rock and take in all you survey, from the tiny cars

Rancher John McGurk built this ramshackle cabin on the edge of Yosemite's McGurk Meadow.

traveling along the Valley floor 4,000 feet below to the imposing granite monolith of Half Dome, guarding the east end of the Valley.

GOING FARTHER
To see more, from Dewey Point continue hiking west on the Pohono Trail along Yosemite Valley's southern rim. You'll have more (and different) views from Crocker Point, 0.75 mile farther.

72. Sentinel Dome

RATING	🚶 🚶 🚶 🚶
DISTANCE	2.2 miles round-trip
HIKING TIME	1.0 hour
ELEVATION GAIN	400 feet
HIGH POINT	8,122 feet
EFFORT	Easy Walk
BEST SEASON	June to October
PERMITS/CONTACT	Yosemite National Park fee required ($20 per vehicle, valid for seven days), (209) 372-0200, www.nps.gov/yose
MAPS	Yosemite National Park (download at www.nps.gov/yose/planyourvisit/brochures.htm)
NOTES	Dogs and bikes prohibited

THE HIKE

This granite dome is climbed by hundreds of Yosemite hikers every summer day. For the best experience, visit early in the morning or just before sunset, when you have the best chance of claiming the summit for your own.

GETTING THERE

From Highway 41 in Yosemite National Park, turn east on Glacier Point Road and drive 13.2 miles to the Taft Point/Sentinel Dome trailhead on the left.

THE TRAIL

It's hard to believe you can get so much for so little, but on the Sentinel Dome Trail, you can. The summit of this bald granite dome is perched about 1.0 mile west and 1,000 feet higher than Glacier Point—which means that world-class views are yours for the taking. Make sure you bring your camera on this trip, because few places in the park offer such panoramic views. In all of Yosemite Valley, only Half Dome is a higher summit, and reaching it is a heck of a lot more work.

A nearly level 1.0-mile walk leads you to the base of Sentinel Dome. From the Taft Point/Sentinel Dome trailhead, take the path leading right,

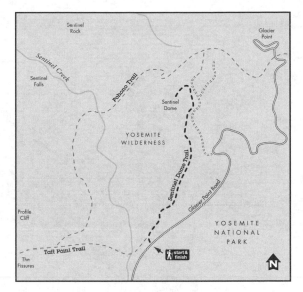

which heads very gently uphill. The terrain is mostly exposed granite except for some Jeffrey pines and white firs. In summer, tiny purple and white mountain phlox add a splash of color to the sandy soil.

You'll enter a grove of old-growth fir trees and then approach Sentinel Dome from the southeast side. Your trail meets up with an old, paved road, which leads around the east side of the dome to its northern flank. Stay left at two junctions and you'll be deposited at the base of Sentinel Dome. There's no trail on the exposed granite, but the route is obvious and the top is in sight. With only a few minutes of climbing, you're on top.

The view can only be described as breathtaking. You can see both Lower and Upper Yosemite Falls and the Middle Cascades between them. Half Dome is easy to spot, and just to its left are two twin domes, Basket Dome and North Dome. Behind Half Dome is Quarter Dome, situated at the head of deep, forested Tenaya Canyon. In front of Half Dome is Liberty Cap and Nevada Falls, and farther to the right is Bunnell Cascade, which slides straight down to Bunnell Point.

There's almost no soil structure on Sentinel Dome, but a few hardy plants manage to dig their roots into the granite and survive. Sentinel Dome was once famous for a very photogenic, wind-tortured Jeffrey pine perched at its summit, but the tree finally gave way to the forces of nature. Still, plenty other photo opportunities abound.

The twisted remains of wind-sculpted Jeffrey pines are found on top of Sentinel Dome.

GOING FARTHER

You can easily combine this hike with the trail to Taft Point (hike #73 in this guide), which begins at the same trailhead but travels in the opposite direction. If you hike out and back on both trails, you'll complete 4.4 miles.

73. Taft Point Trail

RATING	🚶 🚶 🚶 🚶 🚶
DISTANCE	2.2 miles round-trip
HIKING TIME	1.0 hour
ELEVATION GAIN	240 feet
HIGH POINT	7,500 feet
EFFORT	Easy Walk
BEST SEASON	June to October
PERMITS/CONTACT	Yosemite National Park fee required ($20 per vehicle, valid for seven days), (209) 372-0200, www.nps.gov/yose
MAPS	Yosemite National Park (download at www.nps.gov/yose/planyourvisit/brochures.htm)
NOTES	Dogs and bikes prohibited

THE HIKE

From Taft Point's high promontory, you stand at the edge of a 3,500-foot dropoff and marvel at the geologic drama of Yosemite Valley.

GETTING THERE

From Highway 41 in Yosemite National Park, turn east on Glacier Point Road and drive 13.2 miles to the Taft Point/Sentinel Dome trailhead on the left.

THE TRAIL

It's not so much the sweeping vista from Taft Point that you remember, although certainly the point's vistas of Yosemite Valley and its north rim are stunning. Instead, what sticks in your mind is the incredible sense of awe, perhaps mixed with a little fear and a lot of respect, that you felt as you peeked over the edge of Taft Point's 3,500-foot cliff.

The Taft Point Trail starts off innocently enough from the same trailhead as the Sentinel Dome Trail (hike #72 in this guide). Take the path to the left through a dense forest of Jeffrey pine, lodgepole pine, and white fir. In the first 0.25 mile, you pass a large pile of white quartz, its orange and gray veins visible upon closer inspection.

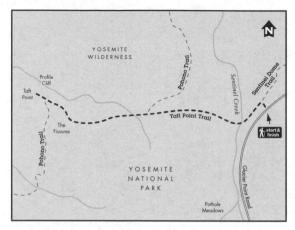

Continue through the forest and cross a couple of small creeks, including one that is surrounded by dense corn lilies and grasses. At nearly 1.0 mile out, the trees disappear and you begin to descend along a rocky slope. The trail vanishes on the granite; just head toward Yosemite Valley. In a few hundred feet, you reach the edge of the cliff. You expect to be able to see some distance down, but nothing can prepare you for how far "down" it is.

Walk a few hundred feet farther, contouring along the edge of the cliff. Head for the metal railing you see at the high point on top of Profile Cliff. Keep an eye out for The Fissures, wide-open cracks in the granite that plunge straight down to the valley below. One of The Fissures has a couple of large granite boulders captured in its cleft; they're stuck there waiting for the next big earthquake or ice age to set them free.

Profile Cliff's overlook caps off the trip. Its railing, a meager piece of metal, performs an important psychological job by removing some of the fear of peering 3,000 feet straight down. Clutch it tightly while you gawk at the view. If you have kids with you, be sure to keep a firm hand on them.

At 7,503 feet in elevation, Profile Cliff is approximately the same height as 7,569-foot El Capitan, which is directly across from you. If you happen to be at Taft Point at sunset, you may notice flashes of light on El Cap's vertical face; those are the headlamps of rock climbers preparing to bed down for the night on tiny rock ledges.

Also in view is Upper Yosemite Fall across the valley, the Merced River cutting in front of El Capitan, and tiny cars parked near the meadow by its side.

A metal railing keeps hikers safely back from the dramatic edge of Taft Point's Profile Cliff.

Another 100 yards west is Taft Point proper, which has even better views of El Capitan. There is no railing here, but the clifftop is broad enough that you can locate a safe, and view-filled, picnic spot.

GOING FARTHER

To make a longer day out of your trip to Taft Point, you can easily combine this hike with the trail to Sentinel Dome (hike #72 in this guide). Choose from either hiking out and back on both trails (4.4 miles), or making a 5.6-mile loop. To make the loop, hike back on the Taft Point Trail for 0.5 mile, then bear left at a trail junction. Follow the Pohono Trail for 1.5 miles to the Sentinel Dome cutoff, then turn right and follow the trail uphill to the dome. To finish out your loop, circle back to the parking lot on the Sentinel Dome Trail.

74. Panorama Trail to Illilouette Fall

RATING 🚶 🚶 🚶 🚶
DISTANCE 4.0 miles round-trip
HIKING TIME 2.0 hours
ELEVATION GAIN 1,200 feet
HIGH POINT 7,240 feet
EFFORT Prepare to Perspire
BEST SEASON June to October
PERMITS/CONTACT Yosemite National Park fee required
($20 per vehicle, valid for seven days),
(209) 372-0200, www.nps.gov/yose
MAPS Yosemite National Park (download at www.nps.gov/
yose/planyourvisit/brochures.htm)
NOTES Dogs and bikes prohibited

THE HIKE
Postcard-perfect views of Yosemite are delivered on this "upside-down" hike from the top of Glacier Point.

GETTING THERE
From Highway 41 in Yosemite National Park, turn east on Glacier Point Road and drive 15.7 miles to Glacier Point. Park and walk toward the main viewing area across from the snack and gift shop. Look for the Panorama Trail sign about 150 feet southeast of the shop (to your right).

THE TRAIL
In Yosemite, we gaze at one world-class natural wonder after another—Bridalveil Falls, Cathedral Rock, Half Dome, Yosemite Falls, El Capitan, Vernal and Nevada Falls, and more. Every one of these features is worthy of its very own park.

Many park visitors make the trip to Glacier Point to see all this splendor from up high. But for an even better look, take a walk on Glacier Point's Panorama Trail. The trail begins just to the right (south) of the main viewing area. Head downhill on the trail, switchbacking through a fire-scarred pine forest in the direction of Illilouette Fall, a rushing cascade on Illilouette Creek. That's pronounced "ill-ILL-ew-et."

The High Sierra view from Yosemite's Glacier Point is only surpassed by the continual series of views from Glacier Point's Panorama Trail.

The sparse forest provides an open vista, which includes spectacular Vernal and Nevada Falls. Vernal Falls (the lower one) is a wide, block-shaped waterfall that drops more than 300 feet into a gorge. Nevada Falls, narrower and taller at 594 feet, is shaped like an inverted V. You can also admire the gleaming granite of Half Dome, Quarter Dome, and Liberty Cap—a banquet of domes.

After a series of switchbacks, the Panorama Trail junctions with a trail leading to Mono Meadow, but continue left for Illilouette Fall. In a few more footsteps you reach an overlook directly across from the waterfall. Illilouette doesn't pour from the back of a canyon; it rushes over a lateral cliff, where the creek drops 370 feet over a granite lip. "Illilouette" sounds like a French name, but it's not; it's actually an awkward English translation of a Yosemite Indian word. To the Indians, the word was the name for the place where they gathered to hunt for deer.

After you've admired the waterfall, follow the trail as it descends farther and then crosses a bridge over Illilouette Creek, just above the falls. Posted signs warn hikers not to swim here. Instead, enjoy the granite and

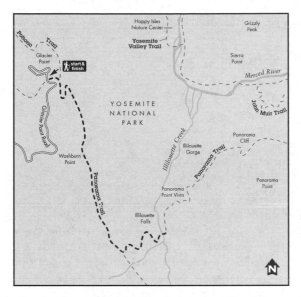

whitewater scenery by the bridge and rest up: You have a 1,200-foot climb back to Glacier Point.

GOING FARTHER

Ambitious hikers can follow the Panorama Trail all the way downhill to Yosemite Valley, but it's a strenuous 8.5 miles with 3,200 feet of elevation loss and a serious workout for your knee joints. At Yosemite Valley, you will need to have a car shuttle to take you back to Glacier Point. Or you can take the tour bus to Glacier Point from Yosemite Lodge at the Falls in the morning, and then hike back down to your car in the Valley in the afternoon. Phone (209) 372-1240 for bus fees and pickup times.

75. Mariposa Grove

RATING	🚶 🚶 🚶 🚶
DISTANCE	6.4 miles round-trip
HIKING TIME	3.5 hours
ELEVATION GAIN	1,200 feet
HIGH POINT	6,800 feet
EFFORT	Prepare to Perspire
BEST SEASON	May to November
PERMITS/CONTACT	Yosemite National Park fee required ($20 per vehicle, valid for seven days), (209) 372-0200, www.nps.gov/yose
MAPS	Yosemite National Park (download at www.nps.gov/yose/planyourvisit/brochures.htm)
NOTES	Dogs and bikes prohibited; accessible in winter with snowshoes

THE HIKE

Get away from the notorious crowds at the Mariposa Grove of Big Trees by hiking uphill to its less visited upper reaches. Here, you'll find peace and quiet among magnificent giant sequoias.

GETTING THERE

From Yosemite's south entrance station on Highway 41, turn east on the Mariposa Grove access road and drive 2 miles to the Mariposa Grove parking area. This access road may be closed in winter, and on summer weekends and holidays, visitors are often required to ride a free shuttle bus to the Mariposa Grove parking lot. If the shuttle bus is in service, you will be directed to continue driving north on Highway 41 for about 4 miles to the Wawona store, where you board the bus.

THE TRAIL

Giant sequoias are the largest living things on earth in terms of volume. That, quite simply, is the single most important reason that hundreds of people each day tour the Mariposa Grove in Yosemite National Park. Sure, the trees are also old—as much as 2,700 years—but they're not the

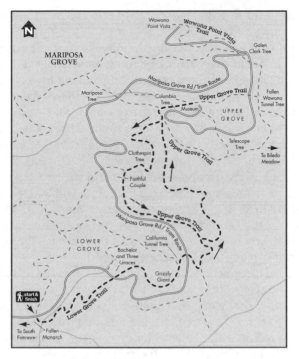

oldest trees on earth. They're the biggest, with basal diameters that will blow your mind.

The Mariposa Grove is the largest of Yosemite's three sequoia groves with about 500 mature trees, and it's also the most developed, with a big parking lot, restrooms, and a museum. Motorized trams run through the grove. But why ride a tram when you can walk among these majestic giants?

To get the most out of your trip, you must visit the Mariposa Grove either very early in the morning or late in the day, when the crowds have lessened. Your goal is to see more playful chipmunks than tourists with video cameras, but on summer days this can be achieved only with strategic timing. Weekends are best avoided. The trail described here visits the uber-popular lower grove, but then moves away from the crowds by heading uphill to the upper grove.

Begin your hike at the trailhead by the parking lot. You'll head toward the Fallen Monarch, a big sequoia that fell more than 300 years ago. It was made famous by an 1899 photograph of the U.S. Cavalry and their horses standing on top of it. Even though it has been on the ground all these centuries, its root ball and trunk are still huge and intact, a testament to how long it takes for sequoias to decay. Sequoia wood has a surfeit of tannic acid.

Continue hiking gently uphill on the obvious trail. The sequoias are mixed in with lots of other trees, including white firs, sugar pines, and incense cedars; the giants appear sporadically among them, like treasures in a treasure hunt. Your next sequoia "find" is the Bachelor and Three Graces (one big tree with three smaller trees at its side). At the next junction, turn right and start a steeper ascent to the Grizzly Giant. This is the largest tree in the Mariposa Grove, with a circumference of more than 100 feet, and also one of the oldest at approximately 2,700 years old. The Grizzly has one particularly impressive branch that is almost 7 feet in diameter.

Now the trail starts to descend to the California Tunnel Tree, which was tunneled in 1895 so stagecoaches could drive through it. Just beyond, you'll see a trail marker that points you to the Upper Grove and Museum. This is your ticket for moving away from the crowds. The path climbs moderately past many more wonderful tree specimens, until finally it tops out at a small sequoia museum set inside a 1930s log cabin. Exhibits showcase the ecology of the giant sequoias.

After visiting the museum, simply retrace your steps to the junction by the California Tunnel Tree, then take the fork that leads past the Bachelor and Three Graces and the Fallen Monarch again, or stay straight and make a slightly wider loop back to the parking lot.

76. Bennettville Mine and Mine Creek

RATING	🚶 🚶 🚶 🚶 🚶
DISTANCE	3.6 miles round-trip
HIKING TIME	2.0 hours
ELEVATION GAIN	300 feet
HIGH POINT	9,900 feet
EFFORT	Easy Walk
BEST SEASON	July to October
PERMITS/CONTACT	Mono Basin Scenic Area Visitor Center, (760) 647-3044, www.fs.fed.us/r5/inyo
MAPS	USGS Tioga Pass or Tom Harrison Maps "Yosemite High Country"
NOTES	Dogs allowed

THE HIKE
Get a fascinating look at the history of Yosemite's Tioga Pass Road and the miners who braved the elements at 10,000 feet in elevation in search of silver.

GETTING THERE
From the Tioga Pass entrance to Yosemite National Park, drive east on Highway 120 for 2 miles to the left turnoff for Saddlebag Lake. Turn left and then left again immediately to enter Junction Campground. The trail begins at the campground entrance; park in the small day-use parking area about 50 yards before the trailhead.

THE TRAIL
This first-class high-country hike is suitable for even the creakiest of knees and is sure to spark your imagination. Remote Bennettville, just a mile outside of Yosemite's park boundary, was the site of a 19th-century silver mining community. Although the town thrived only from 1882 to 1884, it was the primary reason for the construction of the Tioga Pass Road from the west. This road, which today provides access to thousands of Yosemite visitors every summer, was built out of highly ambitious dreams. The Great Sierra Consolidated Silver Company constructed the

Two of Bennettville's mining town buildings still stand at 10,000 feet in the High Sierra.

original wagon road in anticipation of the vast riches it would make from the mines at Bennettville.

Despite herculean efforts, no minerals were ever extracted and the company went broke in record time, leaving Bennettville another of California's ghost towns.

The trail starts near the entrance to Junction Campground, then makes a gentle ascent through classic High Sierra scenery—red rock, lodgepole and whitebark pines, and sparkling streams. At just under 1.0 mile it reaches two restored buildings remaining from Bennettville's heyday: the mine's assay office and bunkhouse, each posed against the dramatic backdrop of 13,000-foot Mount Dana.

Follow the trail from these buildings across Mine Creek on a footbridge to the colorful cliffs 100 yards to the west. Here, an open mine tunnel lined with railcar tracks can be seen, as well as some rusting mining equipment. Much of the machinery and supplies for this mine were hauled here in 1882 from the equally remote May Lundy Mine, 9.0 miles away. Utilizing block and tackles and 1,000 feet of rope, twelve men and

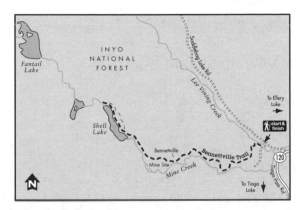

a few mules carried tons of equipment on bobsleds and their backs, often through driving snowstorms in the middle of winter.

After pondering the tenacity of the miners who worked and dreamed here, follow the trail uphill from the mine tunnel. You'll need to cross back over the footbridge at Mine Creek, then head left and uphill, away from the mine buildings. Only 0.5 mile farther lies shallow and lovely Shell Lake, followed by two more high-alpine lakes in the next mile: Fantail and Spuller. The high-country landscape here is a mix of open meadows, delicate high-alpine wildflowers, and wind-sculpted whitebark pines. The scenery is as lovely as you'll find anywhere, and you'll want to return to this area again and again.

GOING FARTHER

This trail continues beyond Fantail and Spuller Lakes, heading into the Hall Natural Area. Hike for as long as you wish in this beautiful high-alpine landscape.

77. Mark Twain Scenic Tufa Trail

RATING	🚶 🚶 🚶 🚶 🚶
DISTANCE	1.0 mile round-trip
HIKING TIME	30 minutes
ELEVATION GAIN	Negligible
HIGH POINT	6,400 feet
EFFORT	Stroll in the Park
BEST SEASON	Year-round (snow may be present in winter)
PERMITS/CONTACT	Mono Lake Tufa State Reserve, (760) 647-6331 or (707) 647-3044, www.parks.ca.gov
MAPS	Mono Lake Tufa State Reserve (download at www.parks.ca.gov)
NOTES	Dogs and bikes prohibited; bring binoculars for bird-watching

THE HIKE

A hike along the shoreline of Mono Lake will leave you with a great appreciation for what Mark Twain called "one of the strangest freaks of nature to be found in any land."

GETTING THERE

From Lee Vining, drive south on U.S. 395 for 5 miles to the Mono Lake South Tufa exit. Turn east and drive 4.6 miles to a dirt road on your left signed for South Tufa Area parking. Turn left and drive 1 mile to the parking area and trailhead.

THE TRAIL

At first look, the most impressive feature of Mono Lake is its immense size. Gazing at it from the highway, the lake appears like a glorious inland sea, punctuated by two large, bald islands. Its geographical setting—framed by the snowcapped mountains of the Sierra on one side and the sagebrush plains of the desert on the other—is unsurpassed.

Read a few interpretive signs and you'll find more that's unusual about Mono Lake, like the fact that it's 3 times as salty as the ocean and 80 times as alkaline. Not only that, the lake is remarkably old. Its age is estimated at 700,000 years, one of the oldest lakes in North America.

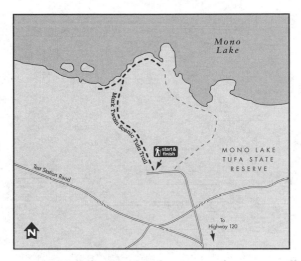

But your appreciation for Mono Lake grows when you walk the Mark Twain Scenic Tufa Trail in Mono Lake Tufa State Reserve. Why Mark Twain? The great writer visited Mono Lake in 1863 and described it in his book *Roughing It*. Like most visitors today, Twain was fascinated by the tufa structures found near the lake's edges. These off-white, coral-like formations are created when underwater springs containing calcium are released from the lake bottom and combine with the lake's water. This forms calcium carbonate, the chemical expression for tufa. The tufa formations grow upright, swelling into odd vertical shapes as springwater pushes upward inside them. Along the lakeshore many are 6 feet high.

The Mark Twain Scenic Tufa Trail takes you on a level 1.0-mile walk around the tufa formations and the southern edge of Mono Lake. You'll pass some high-and-dry inland tufas on your way to the lakeshore, where you'll find smaller tufa islands in the water. You can touch the tufa, which feels surprisingly hard, like concrete, although it appears brittle to the eye. Some hikers wade into the lake or take a swim. Most people just walk around feeling a bit dazed, amazed at this strange place they've just discovered.

Among the birding community, Mono Lake is Mecca. Mono Lake's islands are important nesting grounds for California gulls; 90 percent of the state's population of gulls are born here. Endangered snowy plovers nest on the lake's eastern shore. But it's the migratory birds that make the bird-watchers flock here. Many come specifically to see the congregation of Wilson's and red-necked phalaropes that arrive in July and August. In some years, as many as 100,000 phalaropes will spend a few weeks at Mono Lake before heading to South America for the winter. But those

The saline waters of Mono Lake are a geologic wonder and a birdwatcher's mecca.

numbers don't hold a candle to those of the eared grebe. An estimated 1.5 million grebes stop at Mono Lake during their autumn migration.

The main controversy surrounding Mono Lake regards the regulation of its water level. In 1941, four streams that fed Mono Lake were diverted into the California Aqueduct to provide water for Los Angeles. The lake started to shrink rapidly, losing an average of 18 inches per year. As the water level dropped, a land bridge to the islands was formed. Coyotes and other predators could now access the gulls' nesting area, which was bad news for the birds. Elevation markers along the trail show the lake level in different years. In 1941, the lake's elevation was 6,417 feet. In 1993, it was down to 6,376 feet. Today, it's the job of the Water Resources Board to regulate the level of Mono Lake so that its resources remain protected.

GOING FARTHER
You can add on a 3-mile round-trip hike to Panum Crater, a volcanic crater in the state reserve, by driving your car back (west) along Highway 120 for 2 miles to the turnoff for the Panum Crater trailhead.

78. Parker Lake Trail

RATING	🚶 🚶 🚶 🚶
DISTANCE	3.6 miles round-trip
HIKING TIME	2 hours
ELEVATION GAIN	500 feet
HIGH POINT	8,400 feet
EFFORT	Moderate Workout
BEST SEASON	June to October
PERMITS/CONTACT	Mono Basin Scenic Area Visitor Center, (760) 647-3044, www.fs.fed.us/r5/inyo
MAPS	USGS Mount Dana and Koip Peak
NOTES	Dogs allowed

THE HIKE

While most trails in the Eastern Sierra ascend mercilessly, this hike to 8,400-foot Parker Lake provides access to the steep escarpment of the mountain range via a mellow, well-graded pathway.

GETTING THERE

From Lee Vining, drive 5 miles south on U.S. 395 to the Highway 158 turnoff for the June Lake Loop (make sure you take the northern end of the loop, not the southern end, which is farther south at June Lake Junction). Turn right and drive 1.3 miles on Highway 158, then turn right on a dirt road signed for Parker and Walker Lakes. Drive 2.4 miles to the Parker Lake trailhead at the end of the road (stay straight at all junctions).

THE TRAIL

The Parker Lake Trail in the Ansel Adams Wilderness is a study in contrasts. The first part of the trip traverses open sagebrush plains, the second part winds through a shady streamside aspen forest, and the third part travels to a glacial lake where the mountain wind ricochets off the lake surface. You get a little bit of everything on this trail.

Most of the trail's 500-foot elevation gain occurs right at the beginning, allowing no opportunity for a warm-up. You'll climb hard for 15 to 20 minutes, but the remainder of the hike is much more gentle. As

One of the many gems of the Eastern Sierra, dramatic Parker Lake is easily reached by a short hike.

you ascend, be sure to stop, turn around, and catch your breath while you gaze at the far-off views of Mono Lake. On these slopes, the air is pungent with the smell of sage, which grows in profusion at your feet. In early summer, the sage is joined by flowering yellow mule's ears. As you walk, you may get buzzed by a cicada, a large insect that makes its home in the sagebrush.

Soon the trail levels out and your surroundings begin to change. You have been paralleling Parker Creek but now you move much closer to it. The trail enters a grove of quaking aspens, which have white bark and small, round leaves that quake in the wind. Early summer wildflowers thrive in this wetter stretch of trail. Making an appearance are yellow alpine butterweed, lavender hooker's onion, dark blue irises, orange paintbrush, dark blue brewer's lupine, and white mariposa lilies.

Continue walking and the forest changes again. The trail enters a grove of immense Jeffrey pines mixed in with tall and narrow lodgepole pines. Pass a trail spur on your left that leads to Silver Lake, then head into a

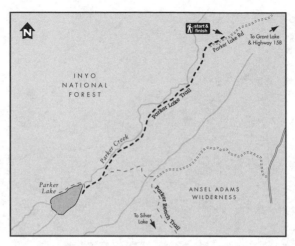

peaceful, shady dell alongside Parker Creek. The raging stream you saw at the beginning of your hike is now tamed and quieted into small riffles and clear pools. Aspens, pines, and wildflowers abound.

The trail levels out completely for the last 0.25 mile to Parker Lake, a picturesque glacial water set in a basin below 12,861-foot-high Parker Peak. With an aspen grove at the far end of the lake completing the picture, the scene is like a postcard, too beautiful to be believed. A fisherman's trail leads all the way around the lake, so you can circle its perimeter, if you like.

GOING FARTHER

A short drive farther on the same dirt road is the trailhead for much larger Walker Lake. Although the lake is only 0.5 mile from the trailhead, the hike is nearly straight down on the way in and straight up on the way back. If you don't object to the return climb, Walker Lake is worth a visit for summer fishing and autumn aspen-viewing.

79. Devils Postpile and Rainbow Falls

RATING	🚶 🚶 🚶 🚶 🚶
DISTANCE	5.0 miles round-trip
HIKING TIME	2.5 hours
ELEVATION GAIN	600 feet
HIGH POINT	7,700 feet
EFFORT	Moderate Workout
BEST SEASON	June to October
PERMITS/CONTACT	Shuttle bus ticket purchase required (see details below), Devils Postpile National Monument, (760) 934-2289, www.nps.gov/depo
MAPS	Devils Postpile National Monument (download at www.nps.gov/depo)
NOTES	Dogs and bikes prohibited

THE HIKE

Containing one of the finest examples of columnar basalt in the world, Devils Postpile National Monument is also home to 101-foot Rainbow Falls and one of the most famous fly-fishing stretches of the San Joaquin River. This hike visits them all.

GETTING THERE

From the town of Mammoth Lakes near U.S. 395, take Highway 203 west for 4 miles, then turn right on Minaret Road (which is still Highway 203). Drive 4.5 miles to the Devils Postpile bus stop across from Mammoth Mountain Ski Area. Purchase an access pass at the Mammoth Mountain Adventure Center ($7 per adult or $4 per child) and board the bus; disembark at the Devils Postpile Ranger Station. If you arrive before 7 a.m. or after 7 p.m. you may drive your own car into the monument.

THE TRAIL

What the heck is the Devils Postpile? Finding the answer requires taking a wonderful walk in Devils Postpile National Monument.

But don't plan to drive your car to the trailhead. The road into the monument is narrow, steep, and winding, and because of that, all daytime visitors must ride a shuttle bus. You leave your car by Mammoth ski

At Devils Postpile National Monument in early summer, Rainbow Falls drops with astounding vigor.

area, purchase an access pass, and board the bus. If you have a reservation to camp in the monument, you will be allowed to drive your own car, but you still must purchase an access pass for your vehicle.

And there's one more catch: Solitude lovers should plan on a weekday visit, or a very early morning visit (there's a loophole that allows hikers to drive their own cars before 7 a.m.). The trail to Devils Postpile and Rainbow Falls is incredibly popular; summer weekends bring a continual parade of hikers.

The trailhead is at the ranger station, where the bus drops you off. The Devils Postpile Trail begins in a verdant meadow alongside the headwaters of the San Joaquin River. If you time your trip right, you will be wowed

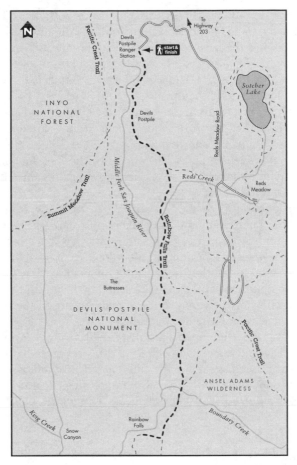

by the meadow wildflowers, especially the masses of shooting stars and Indian paintbrush. In a mere 0.4 mile on a level, easy trail, your curiosity will be sated as you reach the base of the Devils Postpile. What is it? It's a pile of volcanic rock posts or columns made from lava that was forced up from the earth's core. At the base of the standing columns is a huge pile of rubble—the crumbled remains of columns that collapsed. Notice the shapes of the various lava columns; some are almost perfectly straight, while others curve like tall candles that have been left out in the sun.

The Mammoth Lakes area is volcano country. Less than 100,000 years ago, lava filled this river valley more than 400 feet deep. As the lava began to cool from the airflow on top, it simultaneously cooled from the hard granite bedrock below. This caused the lava to harden and crack into tall, narrow pieces, forming nearly perfect columns or posts. The Devils Post-pile is considered to be the finest example of lava columns in the world.

After examining the base of the Postpile, take the trail on either side of it to its top. Under your feet, the tops of the columns look like honey-comb, or tiles that have been laid side by side. A bonus is the view of the rushing San Joaquin River below.

When you're ready, return to the base of the Postpile and continue past it on the well-marked trail to Rainbow Falls. You'll skirt in and out of the monument boundary and Inyo National Forest as the trail descends gently through lodgepole pines. The sound of the San Joaquin River is always apparent, although you won't see the stream again until you get close to the waterfall.

At a trail junction directing you straight to Rainbow Falls or left to Reds Meadows (many Rainbow Falls hikers start here for a shorter trip), continue straight. After a stream crossing on a two-log bridge, the path begins its final descent to Rainbow Falls. You'll hear its roar before you see it. If you're hiking in the late morning on a sunny day, you may get lucky and see Rainbow Falls' namesake—two big, beautiful rainbows arc-ing over the falls' mist. The angle of the midday sun on the water drop-lets creates the perfect recipe for a rainbow.

Keep walking past the lip of the falls. You'll see that Rainbow Falls' drop makes a grand statement, plunging 101 feet over hard rock. The trail has two viewing areas for the falls, about 30 yards apart. A path from the second viewpoint descends granite steps to the base of the falls—definitely worth the steep descent (and climb back up).

GOING FARTHER

Devils Postpile National Monument offers a wealth of trails leading into the Ansel Adams Wilderness. For a longer trip, hike the 7.6-mile Shadow Lake Trail, a serious workout with about 2,000 feet of elevation gain, but offering eye-popping Sierra scenery. For something easier, try the Sotcher Lake Nature Trail, a nearly level 1.2-mile loop around a pictur-esque, trout-filled lake. Hikers visiting in the evening or early morning may see the lake's resident beavers at work.

80. Heart Lake and Mammoth Consolidated Gold Mine

RATING	🚶 🚶 🚶 🚶
DISTANCE	3.0 miles round-trip
HIKING TIME	1.5 hours
ELEVATION GAIN	400 feet
HIGH POINT	9,600 feet
EFFORT	Moderate Workout
BEST SEASON	June to October
PERMITS/CONTACT	Mammoth Ranger Station, (760) 924-5500, www.fs.fed.us/r5/inyo
MAPS	Tom Harrison Maps "Mammoth High Country"
NOTES	Dogs allowed

THE HIKE
Take a walk into history at the old mine buildings of the Mammoth Consolidated Gold Mine, then hike to heart-shaped Heart Lake and its wide-open vistas of the Minaret Range.

GETTING THERE
From the Mammoth Lakes junction on U.S. 395, turn west on Highway 203 and drive 4 miles through the town of Mammoth Lakes to the junction of Minaret Road/Highway 203 and Lake Mary Road. Continue straight on Lake Mary Road and drive 3.5 miles to a fork just before Lake Mary. Turn left and drive 0.6 mile to the Coldwater Campground turnoff on the left. Turn left and drive 0.9 mile through the camp to the Mammoth Consolidated Gold Mine trailhead at the farthest parking lot.

THE TRAIL
There are so many day-hiking trails to choose from in the Mammoth Lakes Basin, you could easily visit for two weeks, hike a different trail every day, and not even scratch the surface. With Sierra scenery this lovely and accessible, it's hard to pick a starting point, so you might as well start from the door of your tent at the popular Coldwater Campground, across the road from Lake Mary.

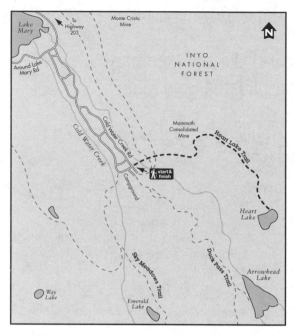

Not camping? No problem. Noncampers are welcome here too, with plenty of free parking for day visitors at the trailhead. Just make sure you get the "right" trailhead; three different trails lead from Coldwater Campground. You want the one that starts at the sign for the Mammoth Consolidated Gold Mine, 0.2 mile past the Duck Pass trailhead (it's also signed for Heart Lake).

Both the gold mine and Heart Lake are perched on the slopes of colorful Red Mountain, which was originally called "Gold Mountain" during Mammoth's first mining boom, which occurred around 1880. Despite the hardships of cold temperatures, deep snow, and frequent avalanches, many miners made and lost their fortunes on Gold Mountain/Red Mountain in the last 130 years.

One of the first Mammoth trails to become snow-free each spring, the Heart Lake Trail is a lovely walk through aspen groves and sagebrush plains to the aptly named heart-shaped lake, but a visit to the fascinating mine structures at the trailhead make this hike into a guaranteed crowd-pleaser. The buildings and mine tunnels of the Mammoth Consolidated Gold Mine aren't terribly old; most date between 1927 and 1933. The miners' bunkhouses, cookhouse, assayer's office, and manager's office are still standing, as well as the ore-processing mill and parts of the ore-transportation system. The mine was reported to have produced

The trail to pretty Heart Lake is one of the first in the Mammoth Lakes area to be snow-free for hiking.

about $100,000 worth of gold, but it is unlikely that was enough to pay the owners' expenses.

After a self-guided tour of the mine site, head uphill on the signed Heart Lake Trail, gradually ascending the slope of Red Mountain to the basin where Heart Lake is cradled. As you ascend, turn around to enjoy panoramic views of Mammoth Mountain and the jagged Minaret Range. Once you arrive at the small lake, determine the best spot to discern its heart-like shape, then pull a sandwich out of your pack and savor this beautiful place. Some hikers bring along their fishing rods for this trip, and if you do, you might catch a trout or two.

GOING FARTHER
Several other trails lead from Coldwater Campground. During wildflower season (usually late July), the 3.6-mile round-trip to Emerald Lake and Sky Meadows is highly recommended. The trailhead is found on the opposite side of the campground loop.

Index

About the Author

Ann Marie Brown is the author of many guidebooks on California recreation—ranging from the best waterfalls to the most outstanding biking routes—and her writing has been featured in *Sunset*, *VIA*, and *Smithsonian* magazines. She lives in South Lake Tahoe, California.

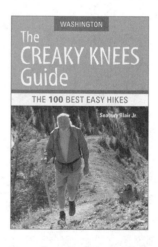
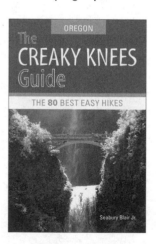